Stan Brakhage

Marco Lori would like to dedicate this book to his family and friends.
Formando di desio nova persona (Guido Cavalcanti)

Published with support from University for the Creative Arts.

Stan Brakhage
the realm buster

Edited by Marco Lori and Esther Leslie

British Library Cataloguing in Publication Data

Stan Brakhage. The Realm Buster

A catalogue entry for this book is available from the British Library

ISBN: 9780 86196 728 5 (Paperback)

ISBN: 9780 86196 940 1; 9780 86196 946 3; 9780 86196 947 0 (Ebook editions)

Cover: Stan Brakhage, *Roman Numeral VI* (1980).
[Courtesy of The Estate of Stan Brakhage and LUX]

Published by
John Libbey Publishing Ltd, 205 Crescent Road, East Barnet, Herts EN4 8SB,
United Kingdom
e-mail: john.libbey@orange.fr; web site: www.johnlibbey.com

Distributed Worldwide by **Indiana University Press**,
Herman B Wells Library – 350, 1320 E. 10th St., Bloomington, IN 47405, USA.
www.iupress.indiana.edu

Printed and bound in China by 1010 Printing.

Contents

Colour plates

Plate 20: Marks on the filmstrip resemble muscae volitantes in Stan Brakhage, *Dog Star Man* (1961–1964). Screen grab from digital reproduction of a 16 mm film. [Courtesy of the Estate of Stan Brakhage and The Criterion Collection.]

Plate 21: Purkinje trees in Stan Brakhage, *Dog Star Man* (1961–1964). Screen grab from digital reproduction of a 16 mm film. [Courtesy of the Estate of Stan Brakhage and The Criterion Collection.]

Plate 22: Phosphenes in Stan Brakhage, *The Dante Quartet* (1987). Screen grab from digital reproduction of a 16 mm film. [Courtesy of the Estate of Stan Brakhage and The Criterion Collection.]

Plate 23: 'Bad' camerawork in Stan Brakhage, *Dog Star Man* (1961–1964). Screen grab from digital reproduction of a 16 mm film. [Courtesy of the Estate of Stan Brakhage and The Criterion Collection.]

Plate 24: Stan Brakhage, *Dog Star Man: Prelude* (1961). [Courtesy of the Estate of Stan Brakhage and Fred Camper (www.fredcamper.com).]

Plate 25: Stan Brakhage, *Lovesong* (2001). [Courtesy of the Estate of Stan Brakhage and Fred Camper (www.fredcamper.com).]

Plate 26: Stan Brakhage, *Chinese Series* (2003). [Courtesy of the Estate of Stan Brakhage and Fred Camper (www.fredcamper.com).]

Plate 27: Stan Brakhage, *Mothlight* (1963). [Courtesy of the Estate of Stan Brakhage and Fred Camper (www.fredcamper.com).]

Plate 28: Stan Brakhage, *Two: Creeley/McClure* (1965). [Courtesy of the Estate of Stan Brakhage and Fred Camper (www.fredcamper.com).]

Plate 29: Stan Brakhage, *23rd Psalm Branch* (1966–67). [Courtesy of the Estate of Stan Brakhage and Fred Camper (www.fredcamper.com).]

Plate 30: Stan Brakhage, *Yggdrasill: Whose Roots Are Stars in the Human Mind* (1997). [Courtesy of the Estate of Stan Brakhage and Fred Camper (www.fredcamper.com).]

Plate 31: Stan Brakhage, *Yggdrasill: Whose Roots Are Stars in the Human Mind* (1997). [Courtesy of the Estate of Stan Brakhage and Fred Camper (www.fredcamper.com).]

Plate 32: Stan Brakhage, *Anticipation of the Night* (1958). [Courtesy of the Estate of Stan Brakhage and Fred Camper (www.fredcamper.com).]

Plate 33: Stan Brakhage, *23rd Psalm Branch* (1966–67). [Courtesy of the Estate of Stan Brakhage and Fred Camper (www.fredcamper.com).]

Plate 34: Stan Brakhage, *The Dante Quartet* (1987). [Courtesy of the Estate of Stan Brakhage and Fred Camper (www.fredcamper.com).]

Plate 35: Stan Brakhage, *The Dante Quartet* (1987). [Courtesy of the Estate of Stan Brakhage and Fred Camper (www.fredcamper.com).]

Plate 36: Stan Brakhage, *The Dante Quartet* (1987). [Courtesy of the Estate of Stan Brakhage and Fred Camper (www.fredcamper.com).]

Plate 37: Stan Brakhage, *The Riddle of Lumen* (1972). [Courtesy of the Estate of Stan Brakhage and Fred Camper (www.fredcamper.com).]

Plate 38: Stan Brakhage, *Boulder Blues and Pearls and...* (1992). [Courtesy of the Estate of Stan Brakhage and Fred Camper (www.fredcamper.com).]

Plate 39: Stan Brakhage, *Loving* (1957). [Courtesy of the Estate of Stan Brakhage and Fred Camper (www.fredcamper.com).]

Plate 40: Stan Brakhage, *Stellar* (1993). [Courtesy of the Estate of Stan Brakhage and Fred Camper (www.fredcamper.com).]

Plate 41: Stan Brakhage, *Ellipses Reel 5* (1998). [Courtesy of the Estate of Stan Brakhage and Fred Camper (www.fredcamper.com).]

Plate 42: Stan Brakhage, *Yggdrasill: Whose Roots Are Stars in the Human Mind* (1997). [Courtesy of the Estate of Stan Brakhage and Fred Camper (www.fredcamper.com).]

Acknowledgements

For permissions to reproduce stills and digital grabs from Stan Brakhage's films, the editors wish to thank the following: The Estate of Stan Brakhage, Fred Camper, LUX, The Criterion Collection.

For permission to reprint the essay *Bottom-Up Processing, Entoptic Vision and the Innocent Eye in Stan Brakhage's Work* by Paul Taberham, the editors wish to thank Berghahn Journals.

For permission to reprint the essay *Stan Brakhage, Ludwig Wittgenstein and the Renewed Encounter With the Everyday* by Rebecca A. Sheehan, the editors wish to thank Oxford University Press.

For permission to use the title words of the conversation between Michael McClure and Steve Anker *Realm Buster: Stan Brakhage* as part of the title of this volume, the editors wish to thank Chicago Review.

For permission to reproduce pages from her book *How To Do Things With Words*, the editors wish to thank Joan Retallack.

For permission to reproduce pages from *Shrieks and Hisses* by Bob Cobbing, the editors wish to thank Etruscan Books.

Introductory Notes

If the character of a given problem is its insolubility, then we solve the problem by representing its insolubility.[1]

In approaching the figure of Stan Brakhage, the critic is often impelled to undertake the task of defining his cinema rather loosely, in an effort to divine its artistic, historical, political, or other, coordinates. This may represent some kind of standard and reasonable approach, but in Brakhage's specific case, it is necessitated by a reaction to the *fluid* nature of his films, and to the ambiguous and uncertain situation in which they put the viewer. The controversial, sometimes enigmatic, frequently paradoxical, and contradictory nature of his art has been often noticed – most explicit on this is Fred Camper, whose phrase might be directed at any and all of the film-maker's oeuvre: 'For almost any generalizing statement one might make about a major Brakhage film, some form of its opposite is also true'.[2] The crucial point is that often such opposites do not invalidate each other, especially when they were willingly sought after by Brakhage, who was either looking for a balance or for an utopian harmony between contraries. Thus the paradox which Camper underlines is that the law of non-contradiction does not apply to Brakhage's art:

> … his greatest films … have a synoptic, almost "oceanic" quality. This results in part from the fact that Brakhage doesn't arrange the oppositions as pieces of some intellectual puzzle; rather, they are presented as signposts of extremes which allow the filmmaker to articulate the gap between them by including a variety of expressions situated at various intermediate points.[3]

Camper went on to argue that Brakhage's films 'undermine any answers the viewer might obtain from the film with a barrage of new questions'.[4] Brakhage himself confirmed his positive stance towards the contradictory and the paradoxical when, in a lecture on Gertrude Stein, in 1990, he argued that a too simple truth 'is bound to be a lie, considering the complex nature of Being', and that '[t]he Paradoxical' is 'a way to get at Complex Truth'.[5] This idea of multiplicity as a distinctive and ultimate character of reality, though, did not originate in Stein, but was one of the cornerstones of Romantic philosophy, a movement of which Brakhage declared himself a lifelong advocate. In Romanticism, an ultimate definition of reality is deemed impossible, but at the same time this impossibility is regarded as rich with new possibilities. Brakhage, in order to intellectually resolve reality's multiplicities and keep together or harmonise fragmented, discontinuous, and often contradictory states, embraced John Keats's negative capability. In a 1992 interview, Brakhage responded to the question 'What would you expect of your audience?' by saying

> ... I would hope, if I had a wand, I would touch them with Keats's negative capability, "to live in appreciation of mystery without any irritable reaching after fact or logic ... ". I'm paraphrasing here.[6]

But Camper's paradigm can also be useful for the critical investigation of Brakhage's art. Just as Camper further articulates that 'extremes which should logically exclude each other are felt to be "true" at every moment', and that his image, 'viewed in context, tends to include oppositions, resulting in a kind of "having it all" vision that doesn't exclude the validity of seeing only a single aspect';[7] similarly, this volume aspires to elevate the variety and inescapable contradictoriness of a collection of essays about such a multifaceted subject and his outputs, to a paradigm and a specific quality, representing a core feature of the subject itself.

Brakhage's career coincided almost exactly with the second half of the last century, from 1952, the year of his first film, until 2003, the year of his death. Born in 1933 he had a troubled childhood, often moving from one place to another with his adoptive parents, who eventually divorced. He then settled in Denver, Colorado, with his mother. His childhood was troubled with a number of health issues, but soon he discovered a propensity for art, being talented in singing, and later in literature, especially poetry, and drama. But his artistic interests soon extended also to painting, music, and then of course cinema. His eclectic attitude manifested, in particular, at the end of the 1950s and throughout the 1960s, when, already affirmed as a young film-maker, he started to develop an interest in science. The diversity of his interests always converged in his cinema.

The 1950s constituted a period of apprenticeship. Originally intending to become a poet, he subsequently dropped the idea when his interest in cinema seemed to him more suited to his sensibilities and abilities. During this decade he started to travel once more from town to town, from West to East coast. During these trips he met and befriended figures such as Robert Duncan, Kenneth Rexroth, John Cage, Edgard Varèse, Kenneth Anger, Bruce Conner, Marie Menken, Maya Deren, Jonas Mekas, Joseph Cornell and others. At the end of the decade he married his first wife Jane, with whom he retired to a log cabin close to Boulder, Colorado. There he cultivated the dream of merging artistic activity and family life far away from society.

His oeuvre can be characterised by thematic 'trends', raising, intensifying, then declining until they disappear, or resurface elsewhere. While the 1960s were characterised by the remoteness from society and the biographical, lyrical depiction of his family life in the wilderness, he traversed the 1970s with a more distanced documenting approach to the things filmed, in search of objectivity but, at the same time, developing his reflections on representation and the perception of inside and outside. The 1980s brought many dark biographical works, motivated by his marital crisis, but the engagement with the possibilities and limits of representation and perception in film continued to grow, until it became a central theme from the end of that decade, when his second marriage brought simultaneously emotional peace and a ban on photographing the family. This freed him definitely from seeing the family as a central and constant source of material for his films, and allowed new, fresh energies to pour into his art, veering decisively to what might appear as abstraction in both the photographed and hand-painted films. The 1990s were certainly marked by such 'abstraction', as well as by a more meditative and calmer mood, possibly due also to the serious health problems he experienced in that decade. In general terms, it seems that with time his work became progressively more complex and refined, as he included and tried to articulate more 'fleeting' issues, working within the interstices of contraries.

His financial situation was never secure, and alongside personal events and intellectual interests, this factor should be borne in mind in assessing the trajectory of his career. One of the most famous instances of its effect was the theft of his 16mm equipment in 1964, which forced him to employ 8mm equipment for several years. This hindrance turned out to be a new aesthetic resource, and in this period he completed what is now one of his most famous and important series, the *Songs* (1964–1969). Another instance is the low cost of hand-painted films, which he exclusively produced from 1993 to 1996 (though the use of this technique intensified from the end of the 1980s). While the case of the 8mm format was unexpected but turned out to be fruitful, the second constituted a precise aesthetic choice, even if it also understood to be necessitated by a difficult financial situation.

Brakhage's approach to cinema was idiosyncratic, radical and visceral. It is impossible to describe in a synthetic and exhaustive way an oeuvre of around 350 titles, with its unprecedented diversity of themes and techniques. What David James has described as 'the most radical intervention by a single individual in the medium's history',[8] has been a lifelong and total dedication to, and struggle with, this artform, in an effort to avoid not only the accepted forms of the medium, but most of all the audience's way of perceiving. For the variety of techniques employed, experimented with, or invented, and the means through which he managed to do that, only the term artisan suffices to communicate a sense of the craftmanship he deployed and the dedication he displayed.

As for the themes of his films, they are rarely specific enough to be characterised any differently from how he himself described them in 1963: 'birth, sex, death, and the search for God'.[9] To this remark one may add a pronounced tendency to biographical situations and occasions, first centred around his family, then around himself, but then significantly dropped from the late 1980s onwards. The additional themes of perception and representation, always outside of accepted conventions, constitute the frame within which such instances are articulated. For this reason, he often referred to his cinema as a documentation of the act of seeing, a quest so tangible that the audience joined in and this protected his films from the lack of interest otherwise caused by purely solipsistic and self-referential artforms. His cinema may be described as visceral, somatic, apparently visionary although never decorative, problematic in posing more questions than attempting answers, paratactical in its negation of narrative forms, documentarist, if we accept that not only objective things can be documented, and non-capitalist if we consider the conditions of its production.

Brakhage's oeuvre is too vast and diverse to be inscribed within even the category of personal cinema. When in 1963 he said that his films, once finished, were to go out in the world, with the confusing metaphor of being like children, he was not totally mistaken.[10] His art certainly exceeds the limits of his intentions, whereas and in any case, when it comes to avant-garde cinema in particular, it is very difficult to control or force the audience's response and understanding.[11] To prove this point, it would be sufficient to watch one of his films imagining knowing nothing about him. In watching one of his works, we often learn more about ourselves, than about the film, which would continue to exist, as he would have said, 'in mystery'.[12]

The argument that Brakhage was only ever an inventor of fantasies, and thus a purely visionary film-maker, is dismissed by Brakhage himself.[13] It is now clear that the ways his films relentlessly challenge our assumptions about perception, representation, and cinema itself (just to name few 'macro-issues') are far beyond the simple discharging of such imagery as 'fantasy'. In addition, his radical technical experimentations and mastery rarely leave the audience lost within the illusion of a self-sufficient solipsism, forgetful of the cinematic apparatus. The argument that Brakhage's art is apolitical is also easily refuted. His cinema bears in its form(s) the same political potential that adheres in any other aesthetics. It may be noticed though, that sometimes his specific 'anarchic' and unpredictable form rebels so much against visual social conventions, that it transcends the intentions of the author (especially in some of his early themes such as the celebration of the nuclear family).

The contributors to this volume have been selected for their perspectives are as independent as possible from previous critical work. Yet it will be evident that many issues, especially those that revolve around paradoxical situations in Brakhage's art, resurface and echo one another across the essays. There is no ideal reading order or privileged point of entry for this book, but each piece constitutes an enrichment to the next one and vice versa.

Nicky Hamlyn discusses the use and value of black in Brakhage's cinema through some particularly meaningful examples. This 'virtual' colour is discussed from its intrinsic paradox of being both an absence and a presence, in technical and semantic terms. In Brakhage's films this hybrid status is intertwined with the film-maker's struggle against the dichotomy of representation and abstraction. From the creative and semantic use of such colour in Brakhage's early films, through the 'restless and mutable' blacks of the late 1970s and early 1980s series that absorb all apparatus and pro-filmic antinomies, to the monolithic darkness of a unique 1990 work, Brakhage usage of black can tell us much about the film-maker's artistic quest.

Peter Mudie investigates a quest Brakhage pursued throughout his career against mimetic representation. The aim of such a quest was to demystify the arbitrariness of the processes by which we connect (understand) what we see (perceive) with something we already know in our mind. In Mudie's terms, the film-maker attempted to unify the 'it' of the image seen, with the image itself as physical object presented through the process of projection. All his effort was directed to this paradoxical tension of the image (in his case the cinematographic image). Mudie concentrates his analysis around two kinds of Brakhage's films in which this effort was most explicit: the collage films, and the hand-painted ones. He shows how in such 'pure' films Brakhage played with the expectations of the viewer (always looking for something recognisable), and never fully deprived his works of some kind of reference to actual things, or to other art forms. Mudie concludes that at the end of his life, after having reached significant results, such as a spiritualisation of light through a subject, Brakhage solved this conundrum by grounding 'filmic light with the material'.

Paul Taberham employs the lens of cognitive theories to investigate Brakhage's claims about renewing human visual perception. There is just one previous attempt at this, but in that case it took the direction of fitting Brakhage's aesthetics within cognitive theories' categories.[14] Taberham, on the contrary, investigates Brakhage's imagery *through* the tool of cognitive theories. While viewers are often compelled to attend to their visual perceptions in a unique way when engaging with his films, this does not mean the achievement of a totally untutored or innocent eye, but a sort of retutoring of our eye by either paying special attention to entoptic phenomena, or by employing techniques that compel us to process visual information on the screen not on the base of semantic salience but in relation to surface details. In the end Taberham reveals how the film-maker might be considered a sort of practical psychologist.

While Brakhage spoke of cinema only in relation to sight, his career can be seen as a relentless critique to the Western hegemony of that sense over the others. Finding visual perception deeply mingled with other senses and proprioception, he continued a tradition that finds important precursors in Romantic poets and philosophers. Gareth Evans investigates Brakhage's critique of ocularcentrism in the relationship between vision and touch, through the work of Gilles Deleuze on the painter Francis Bacon, establishing four ways in which eye and hand are connected in the production and 'consumption' of the work of art. Brakhage's hand-held camera, the manual application of chemicals upon the film strip, and his attempts at documenting entoptic phenomena and giving the sense of an innocent eye, are all taken into consideration in examining three groups of films (from the 1950s, the 1960s and 1970s, and the end of his career) that demonstrate how the alteration of the accepted hierarchy between vision and touch was a continuous concern of his artistic life.

Rebecca A. Sheehan considers Brakhage's lyrical films through the philosophy of the late Ludwig Wittgenstein, in whom Brakhage was long fascinated. Wittgenstein's ideas have been involved in a debate about the future of film theory,[15] and Sheehan brings Brakhage to the centre of such a debate by taking him as a crucial example of how films can actually 'philosophise', and offer a model for thought by questioning our previous assumptions about perception. Through engagement with the ordinary and the common, the employment of the fragment, and the subsequent immediacy of the present, Brakhage's films foreground a model of meaning characterised by the provisional and the fluid that Sheehan terms 'nomadic'.

Christina Chalmers' essay considers the politics of aesthetic form in *23rd Psalm Branch* (1966–67), a film Brakhage made in response to war, or specifically to being bombarded by TV imagery of the Vietnam war. Chalmers' essay contrasts Brakhage's work to the revolutionary film-making tradition of Eisenstein, with its technique of montage and its epic sense of historical change through proletarian agency. It also considers the debates on Epic and Lyric forms amongst contemporaneous poets, notably Charles Olson and J. H. Prynne, and the theorist T. W. Adorno. Brakhage's 'dance' with the horrors of war lacks Eisenstein's 'cosmic alignment with a glyph of the people', but through its fragmentation and disruption, it gestures at the missing place of the universal subject. Chalmers probes the boundaries between the Epic and the Lyric, and considers the ways in which Brakhage achieves a 'disfiguration' in relation to perspective, whereby epic and lyric, history and individual, outside and inside pose questions of each other, and 'History' in the grand sense is disassembled, dissolved, and confronted by subjective presence.

Stephen Mooney relates the temporality of Brakhage's films to that of *innovative poetry* of the late twentieth and early twenty-first centuries (with authors such as Jackson Mac Low, Joan Retallack, Bruce Andrews, Gilbert Adair, Bob Cobbing, and others). He argues that a similar reconfiguration (or dis-configuration) of time was carried on, in each specific medium (technically, thematically, and structurally), turning the artwork towards variability, flexibility, disjunction, disruption, dissociation, and unfixity. The works display their making processes. These processes are released from notions of strict determination, structure, and causality. This in turn leaves the audience's subjective temporality free to interact with the open temporality of the works, while at the same time a further level of reflexivity takes place inasmuch as the works emancipate themselves from author, audience, their compositional process, and a deterministic reading. Through such reflexivity, as well as the avoidance of codification, and the loosening of interpretative and structural parameters, a phenomenological awareness of temporal experience and perception is reached, and Gilles Deleuze's image-time is realised. Brakhage's cinema is revealed then as very close to innovative poetry in proposing a reflexive, disjunctive, and phenomenological temporality.

Marco Lori investigates the origin of Brakhage's ideas about art as a primarily spiritual activity, and the subsequent spiritual quest undertaken in his artistic endeavour. He proposes that their source lies in the complex of occult-derived notions about art and spirituality articulated by Ezra Pound. Lori further identifies such a complex of ideas as having its roots in a mix of medieval doctrines synthesised by the love poets of Provence and Tuscany, among whom Dante was one of the major figures. Working through the echoes of such a tradition, which Giorgio Agamben terms pneumophantasmology, in Brakhage's career allows the identification of an underground spiritual quest which came to affirm itself more markedly during the last part of his life. Issues such as the Muse, the trance state,

7

being an instrument of alien forces, the artwork as vector of spiritual revelation, the definition of the divine, are all points to which Brakhage insistently returned. In this essay an attempt is made to align such concepts with an historical perspective, drawing in particular on *The Dante Quartet* as a privileged example of Brakhage's direct inspiration by such a tradition.

The result of collecting diverse and new approaches in a single volume should point beyond the sum of the single essays and give back to the reader a prismatic and fluid impression of their subject. Each of these trajectories, with their precise drives, their exclusions, their coherence, implicitly points to what is *beyond* them, partially explored by the other essays. So the ostensible 'limits' of Brakhage's art become signals of what lies beyond, in unexpected territories and possibilities that Brakhage himself did not foresee. Thus the hope is that, apart from being accomplished essays, these works can stimulate new reflections and investigations in the many issues still arising from Brakhage's figure and art.

Notes

1. Novalis quoted in Andrew Bowie, *From Romanticism to Critical Theory* (London/New York: Routledge, 1997): 78.

2. Camper, 2001/2002: 72. This condition sometimes had absurd consequences, such in the case of *eyes*, a 1971 documentary about police work, which was projected by the Black Panthers to show the brutality of the police, and by police officers to demonstrate how correct and kind they were (see Brakhage in MacDonald, 2005: 93).

3. Camper, 2001/2002: 74.

4. Ibid., 74–75.

5. See Brakhage, 2001: 194.

6. Brakhage in Higgins, Lopes, and Connick, 1992: 62. Keats originally defined negative capability as 'when man is capable of being in uncertainties, Mysteries, doubts, without any irritable reaching after fact and reason'. See John Keats, *Selected Letters of John Keats: Revised Edition*, Grant F. Scott, ed. (Cambridge, MA/London: Harvard University Press, 2002): 60.

7. See Camper, 2001/2002: 75.

8. James, 2005: 3.

9. Brakhage, 1963: not paginated.

10. '... when a man and a woman ... give birth to a child, that child is not a thing enclosed between them. He's something that's given out; and that child is free to live his own life, to have his own form and his own growth. ... In that sense the work of art arising from such a process out of the total needs Jane and I share is like a child arising out of that kind of love and is then free of each of us'. Brakhage, 1963: not paginated.

11. '... my compulsion to make films, to be an instrument for all these messages, many of which I do not understand at first, any more than anyone else in the audience does'. Brakhage in MacDonald, 2005: 61.

12. 'The arts traditionally exist in mystery'. Brakhage in Higgins, Lopes, and Connick, 1992: 60.

13. See Brakhage, 1982: 188; and Brakhage in MacDonald, 2005: 93.

14. See James Peterson, *Dreams of Chaos, Visions of Order: Understanding the American Avant-Garde Cinema* (Detroit, Michigan: Wayne State University Press, 1994): mainly chapters 3 and 4.

15. See Turvey and Allen, 2001; and Rodowick, 2007.

1 Brakhage's Blacks

Nicky Hamlyn

The *speed of fade* and the *time length* of the black reminds us that movies aren't moving *pictures* only: structurally, they're time-based *graphics* (like a black screen), some of which aren't pictures at all.[1]

Black has the specific quality of being only ever virtual. Natural luster, imperfect pigments, ambient light, and neighboring colours all inflect surfaces we perceive as black: achieving solid, lasting blacks takes considerable effort, the more so the more we deal with screen media that either reflect or emit light as the basis of their working.[2]

There is metaphysical pressure to keep the contribution of shadows 'off the books'. Philosophers and physicists alike have a strong conviction that reality is positive. They think a negative statement such as "There is a permanent absence of light in the Shackleton crater" is really about where light is rather than where it is not … [they] are uncomfortable with absences and so gerrymander discussion to disenfranchise black shadows, black space and the black sky of the lunar day.[3]

The ideas for this essay have their origins in an earlier piece on Brakhage's *Roman Numeral* series,[4] which touched briefly on the various ways Brakhage used black in those films. Subsequently the work was developed, rather haphazardly, for a presentation at a conference, of which this essay is a refinement. In a lot of thinking on the topic, black is conceived as negative, as an impure absence, but my aim here is to show how the blacks in Brakhage's films, while they are literally areas of apparent absence of light, or at least relatively reduced absences i.e., they can be construed as 'negative' in this strict sense, they are also, or also function, positively, in imagistic, graphic and structural terms. For painters, black is conceived of as a colour, something that is evident in its availability in a variety of shades with exotic names: Lamp, Ivory, Mars etc. These pigments reflect varying quantities of light, and each has a colour-cast, i.e., is impure. A truly black black, one that would absorb almost all of the light cast upon it, exists: Vantablack absorbs 99.96% of light.[5] Unlike the paints and the film blacks described by Sean Cubitt above, which are subject to the influence of ambient light among other things, Vantablack absorbs everything, and this puts it strangely out of balance with other elements when it is combined to make a painting or other kind of images, because it falls so far outside the typical contrast ratios of a painting or a photographic image.

Black, and the shadows with which it is often associated, have a curious status in film. Notably in the film noir genre, shadows are often completely solid, which is almost never the case in perceptions of the real world, where the eye can peer into relatively solid blacks and adjust to differentiate detail and variety of density. Shadows in film noir have a quasi-autonomous compositional function and thus become a structural part of the image, imparting a degree of abstraction to what is otherwise a representation. But this is rare in cinema generally.

Whereas black in a painting is a reflective coloured surface, and is what it is in its literal material sense, in the celluloid filmstrip has a curious double status. At the point of image formation, 'black' is simply the area of the film where light registers strongly on the film's light-sensitive surface. Materially it is an area of density (silver halide crystals that have been blackened by light) that holds back that light in projection, so in a sense it is a refusal or interruption thereof; while at the level of the image it is, paradoxically, a representation of the (relative) absence of light, i.e., shadow or darkness. More precisely, it defines an area where there would be visible things had there been enough light when the image was made. Yet insofar as this absence impinges upon other areas of the frame contents, it becomes part of the image's form: it takes up space in the frame. Furthermore its density means that it is often stronger (denser) than other parts of the image that in its pro-filmic would be materially more substantial: the image of a shadow cast by a tree may be stronger than that of the tree itself.

The question of whether black is an image is also dependent on the specificities of a film and how it is conceived. Films like Peter Kubelka's *Arnulf Rainer* (1960) and especially Tony Conrad's *The Flicker* (1966), which are composed of wholly black or white frames, are conceived as imageless, because the intention is to create patterns of light interruptions, structured from the presence and absence of light on the screen. In the case of *The Flicker* this was achieved by exposing the film to light with a lens-less camera, and by taking frames with the lens cover on for the white and black frames respectively. The film-maker Bruce McClure creates his black and white loops simply by bleaching selected frames on a strip of black leader to create the white frames, while leaving the black frames untouched. In these examples there is no intention to create an image and thus no image in the usual sense, even though the flicker stimulates hallucinatory colour patterns when the films are viewed. A selection of Brakhage's films can be made that demon-

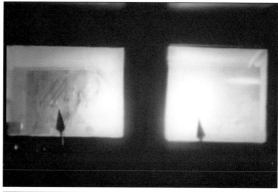

Figure 1. Stan Brakhage, The Way to Shadow Garden *(1954). Screen grabs from digital reproduction of a 16 mm film. [Courtesy of the Estate of Stan Brakhage].*

Figure 2. Stan Brakhage, The Way to Shadow Garden *(1954). Screen grabs from digital reproduction of a 16 mm film. [Courtesy of the Estate of Stan Brakhage].*

strates all of the above, including the last category of imageless blackness, which is a specific feature of *Passage Through: A Ritual* (1990), as discussed below.

The creative use of black has been a feature of Brakhage's oeuvre, starting right from the beginning with the noirish psycho-drama *The Way to Shadow Garden* (1954), a high contrast black and white film that turns to negative in the second part, after its protagonist has blinded himself and becomes a seer. At the end of the opening shot the camera pans to settle for five seconds on the exterior of the house in which the film will unfold. Dazzling light pours from two square windows, which are framed by an entirely solid area of black, creating a simple abstract composition, something which establishes a pattern for the rest of the film, as well as, in a wider sense, Brakhage's working against the simplistic dichotomy between representation and abstraction.

A single bare bulb is established as the film's only apparent light source, giving us to suppose that this precarious illumination is all that's keeping the film alive, warding off the total darkness that would otherwise ensue. At one point the camera lingers on the bulb in close up, seemingly in an effort to break with the positive meanings usually associated with light. The oppressive light momentarily threatens to obliterate the image.

Figure 3. Stan Brakhage, The Way to Shadow Garden *(1954). Screen grabs from digital reproduction of a 16 mm film. [Courtesy of the Estate of Stan Brakhage].*

Figure 4. Stan Brakhage, The Way to Shadow Garden *(1954). Screen grabs from digital reproduction of a 16 mm film. [Courtesy of the Estate of Stan Brakhage].*

Figure 5. Stan Brakhage, The Way to Shadow Garden *(1954). Screen grabs from digital reproduction of a 16 mm film. [Courtesy of the Estate of Stan Brakhage].*

The young protagonist lurches around inside the house and we see, inter alia, a framing with a black wine bottle on a table on the left side of the frame, his shadowed face on the other, thus a graphic presentation of two strongly contrasting forms of black. At the point where, having blinded himself, he staggers towards a French window and opens the doors, the composition is divided into three roughly equal vertical bands. The man is framed centrally in silhouette, bordered on either side by black. At this point the exact same shot cuts to negative and in what were solid black borders we suddenly see previously invisible details,

Figure 6. Stan Brakhage, The Way to Shadow Garden *(1954). Screen grabs from digital reproduction of a 16 mm film. [Courtesy of the Estate of Stan Brakhage].*

Figure 7. Stan Brakhage, The Way to Shadow Garden *(1954). Screen grabs from digital reproduction of a 16 mm film. [Courtesy of the Estate of Stan Brakhage].*

Figure 8. Stan Brakhage, The Way to Shadow Garden *(1954). Screen grabs from digital reproduction of a 16 mm film. [Courtesy of the Estate of Stan Brakhage].*

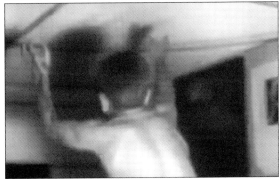

though what we are looking at is all but impossible to decipher in negative. The anomaly is explained by the fact that negative images are low in contrast and rich in detail, whereas the positive print made from that negative is higher contrast and is furthermore printed darker to strengthen the silhouetted form of the man, so that a level of detail is sacrificed in favour of stronger blacks and highlights.

This framing is pre-figured earlier in the film when the camera settles momentarily on the same pair of doors, between which is a rectangle of solid black, thus a reversal of the disposition of black and white in the two shots, a move which also prefigures the later transformation into negative. A similar reversal also occurs

13

when the windows seen from the outside in the opening shot are seen from the inside, before the protagonist desperately lowers the blinds on them.

After he has blinded himself he picks up the lamp and waves it around, causing shadows to play on the walls. He then puts down the lamp and writhes around between the lamp and a white wall, continuing the shadow play by other means.

Anticipation of the Night (1958) is the film that marks Brakhage's transition from human-centred psychodrama to a corresponding form in which the camera replaces the figure as protagonist. It opens with the same motif as the transitional shot in *Shadow Garden*, but framed very differently: an illuminated threshold, bordered by black, across which the shadow of a figure passes, momentarily darkening the screen. As if to mark the transition from rectilinear framing to the more oblique angles that will figure in subsequent films, the borders of the threshold fall diagonally across the screen, fanning out in a manner that strongly evokes the conical shape of a projector's light beam or indeed the cone of human vision.

This was the point at which Brakhage rebelled against the conservatism of conventional optics and stable points of view modelled on traditional perspective, in favour of a subjectivised vision achieved by hand-holding the camera. In this sense the sequence may indicate a kind of farewell to conventional framing. The shot is repeated several times in the opening minutes, first from one angle and then from the opposite (but not the reverse, as in narrative shot-reverse-shot grammar), and laterally inverted (mirrored, probably by flipping the negative over during the printing stages). The shot becomes a mobile movement of black within a light frame, from representation to abstraction, breaking down the distinction (which Brakhage disliked) between the two. This figure in a doorway is interspersed with compositions that contrast strongly in a formal sense, but which are made of similar stuff: sparkling points of white light on a dark ground. In both though, there is a flattening of the image through the silhouetting process, and this continues in twilight shots, filmed contre-jour from a moving car, of trees, which obliterate the slivers of evening sky. There is also a repeating pan around an object, which in effect functions as a horizontal wipe, from light to black. These shots also prefigure or *anticipate* the onset of night and thus black performs a precise semantic-thematic function.

As the film moves from day to night there is a form of double reversal from negative to positive and vice versa. In the first sense the trees' obliterating the night sky is a negation through interruption (a rhythmic process that also figures the way the projector's shutter interrupts the light at the moment when the next frame of film is pulled into the gate to be flashed onto the screen) of the illuminated scenery. These early scenes can be seen as light fields interrupted by dark movements. In the second sense there is a reversal of this field, from light to dark, against which spots of artificial light, and sometimes the moon, assert themselves uninterruptedly against the blackness of night. In their assertiveness they present as positive in a way that was not the case in the twilight part of the film.

Insofar as the subsequent *Wedlock House: An Intercourse* (1959) features figures (Brakhage and his then new wife, Jane Collum) it returns in part to the early psychodramas. At the same time it is one of his blackest films, with long sections where the screen is entirely dark apart from a small point of light or a curved shape arcing through the frame, though the arcing effect is as much that of the lamp's movement as it is the movement of any object. Brakhage makes much use of this device. As in *Shadow Garden*, the illumination is precarious and highly unstable: raw lights such as a hand-held lamp with a naked bulb and occasionally candles being the only apparent sources. The lamp is rhythmically waved to create flashes of bleached highlights and enveloping shadows on and of doorways, often reflected in mirrors, creating a double framing. Cigarette smoke, both frontally lit (white) and silhouetted (black) and an alarm clock, interspersed with repeated sexually explicit shots in negative, are rhythmically permutated. The film is notable for the way in which what is thematically an explicit film about young love is rendered in so highly an abstract way. The blacks are dense and solid and the fragmentary scenes emerge sporadically out of this dark. Black consistently dominates the image, immediately enveloping the momentary light flashes, so that rather than functioning as part of a differentiated pattern made from a range of grey tones, as it would in a negative of a conventional image, black and white are in battle.

As Brakhage's career developed one can detect a gradual move towards a concentration of colour and crystalline forms, which were often expressed as highly saturated colours, both primary and prismatic, as if the more broadly distributed colour of many of the films made in the 1960s and 1970s condensed into small intense areas. In these works, notably films like *Arabic Numeral 12* (1981), black becomes more like the colour described by Cubitt above, inflected and tinted by adjacent light spilling into the dark areas through refraction, reflection and lens flare (see plate 1).

The blacks in *Arabic 12* are less dense and often very grainy, sometimes because the prints are blown up from Super 8 originals. Often the black grain briefly freezes to form a greyish textured surface, upon which, or seemingly within which, new colour movements develop. Although, then, the film has been reworked in an optical printer, it has the quality of an improvisation. The hand-held camera is pointed at the sun through indiscernible obstructions, through and around which light leaks into the camera in the form of prismatic flashes, lens flare, including isolated arcs, lines of intense, star-shaped colours, and curvy, deformed geometric shapes; rhomboids, rectangles and triangles, as well as less defined patches and hues, including a bluish cast that overlays the whole image at times, modifying the contrast unpredictably.

The film-maker juggles with these elements, shifting the balance by increasing or decreasing the amount of light/colour in relation to black and by pointing the camera directly and indirectly at the light source. The object causing the blackness isn't itself black, but a blue something that most of the time is held too close to the lens for light to reach it. However it more often than not appears black. It has a kind of double status: any object will appear black when it is under-lit, as is the case here, but it also generates blackness by blocking the light to the camera, thereby depriving itself of light. The moving colour shapes also have movement occurring within them in the form of animated texture, and this texture impinges on the notional black surface too, so that its own colour changes. There's a gesture to Goethe's colour phenomenology, in which the prismatic colours arise in the interaction between white and black, which is appropriate because black here does appear to contain and juggle many colours. It is chromatically mutable, assuming surrounding colour-shapes, squeezing and dispersing, intensifying and darkening them, catalysing an endless succession of transitory phenomena. Throughout the film there are freezes, at which point the black becomes a static, textured grey field. Almost immediately small movements begin within this field, but the freezes remind us that underpinning the image is a volatile ground of grain movement, which becomes most visible when it is seen in greyish mid-tones (grain is imperceptible in areas of pure white and black). For instance in Paul Sharits' *Axiomatic Granularity* (1973), grain is re-filmed and magnified to the point where the solidity of a plain colour field fragments into dancing crystals of grain, illuminated by the light that strikes through and around them. Thus the solidity of any given colour on a film strip, including, black, is dependent in part on the density of grain and the magnification at which it is observed.

Arabic Numeral 12 is one of Brakhage's most restless and probing films. It is the product of an interactive interplay between hand, eye, camera body, lens, film, light and objects. The lens's limitations and weaknesses are harnessed to generate an extensive range of optical events that also echo Goethe's interest not only in 'subjectively produced colors (after images, light and dark adaptation, irradiation, colored shadows, and pressure phosphenes), but also in physical phenomena detectable qualitatively by observation of color (absorption, scattering, refraction, diffraction, polarization, and interference)'.[6] Refraction was crucial to Goethe's account of colour phenomena, and *Arabic 12* is replete with both refractions and diffraction in the form of prismatic fan-shapes that arise seemingly out of nothing.

At the same time as making the *Arabic Numeral* series, Brakhage also worked on a smaller but similar series of seven films, the *Roman Numeral* series (1978–81). Like the *Arabics*, they eschew the distinction between representation and abstraction. The films are ineffable; hard to write about, appropriately, given Brakhage's concept of film as 'moving visual thinking', and hence antithetical or at least resistant to exegesis. As in *Arabic 12*, Brakhage often appears to be working with a set of elements, if not a formal system, in which parameters like focus, brightness and depth of field, and occlusions, like the unidentifiable black object of *Arabic 12*, are interplayed through camera movement and aperture manipulation during shooting, though in a manner more restrained and less rhetorical than in *Arabic 12*. Most of the films in the series are blown-up from Super 8, hence the heavy grain structure generates pointillist quasi-separated colours, which are an integral part of how the films work: they are colour films in the same way that there are colour paintings (Derain, Matisse, Newman, etc).

The first film, *Roman Numeral I* (1979), has a predominant scheme of off-white through salmon pink to deepish mid-red. A camera circles over a knot of fuzzy, reddish lines. Underneath (or beyond?) these light, caressing moves, presumably lies an unidentifiable object, but it is just as easy to see this knot as a spatial array, since it is neither enclosed by a contrasting border which would locate it in a putative space, nor does it appear to be cropped by the camera's framing. As such it has no perceptible depth but neither does it obviously lie on the picture plane. The familiar octagonal refracted image of the lens diaphragm, formed when light enters the camera directly, are rendered circular by the lack of focus, and form an integral part of the image. Could this be because the object is a light-cluster (incident light) and not an object, which would help it to harmonise with the light/lens refractions? Or is it simply that defocusing blurs, literally, the distinctions between objects and light, or rather between reflected and incident light? Here are the first of the many cinematic antinomies that are dissolved in the film, between the pro-filmic and the apparatus, between conventionally wanted and unwanted optical phenomena (see plate 2).

Periodically, we see what appears to be a zoom, but into what? The idea of zooming supposes a final target detail in a predefined field, but when that field is already undefined (defocused) there is little against which to measure the zoom's progress, and thus the distinction between wide and close loses its purchase. What we have in effect is a kind of reframing, or better still, a pure cinematic movement, one that is not dependent on a pre-established pro-filmic which retains itself as a function of the apparatus, but a new kind of abstract movement which progresses, or evolves, the image.

Like *Arabic 12*, many of the *Roman Numeral* films consist of prolonged shots, in which Brakhage gives himself time to establish and develop a similar juggling of elements, though the films are generally more enigmatic, less concretely and discernibly of something, and, by contrast, more luminous. Single black frames perform a variety of functions in the films. They punctuate these longer shots, and dynamise the relationship between longer and shorter ones. Because the longer shots are often very similar to each other, the black frame serves to indicate the end of one shot and the start of the next by a clear and emphatic, albeit momentary, pause. The black frames also generate rhythm, or in some cases augment an existing one. They have a mildly disruptive effect, without creating pauses, as longer sections of black would. This disruptive effect can also be seen as an anti-montage device: once shots are separated, even if only by a blink of black, montage is frustrated, the clash of the cut which generates Vertov's essential interval, is disabled. It is also worth mentioning that a single frame of white would be much more disruptive than black because it is an intrusive, dazzling flash, as opposed to a moment of darkness. Therefore, the black functions in part as a discrete but powerful punctuation mark, which inflects meaning and rhythm in the same way a comma does in a text. These punctuations energise flowing passages of what are often closely similar shots.

There is another way that black frames work, which contrasts with the examples given in the foregoing paragraph. It is quite often the case that the black frame is next to the over-exposed first frame of a shot (see plate 3). This happens because the first frame to be exposed receives more light than those that follow, because the camera is not yet running at full speed – it takes one or two frames to accelerate to 24fps, hence the first and to a much lesser extent the second are exposed for longer than subsequent frames, when the exposure time is stabilised at 1/50th of a second. This technical fact results in a visible flash when the film is viewed at normal speed, but the insertion of a black frame increases the contrast between the light and adjacent frames. By the same token this contrast also increases when the frames adjacent to the black frame are lighter.

There is one more thing to say about the insertion of single black frames between shots. If two pieces of negative are joined together using a cement join, the splice is highly visible when it is printed, as the edges of the film overlap each other within the frame area. A simple and economical way to avoid this is to insert a frame of clear film between the two shots, which becomes black when the negative is printed. It is also cheaper to do this than to use the special methods required to create invisible cuts, because laboratories charge less for printing from a single roll of negative. It is quite possible that this was Brakhage's reason for using this technique, but in any case it is a good example of an economic necessity generating aesthetic effects, in the same way that financial constraints often prompted production of the many films he made by working directly onto the film strip without a camera.

Roman Numeral V (1980) has a roughly symmetrical structure, beginning and ending with greenish dark forms (see plate 4), with a long stretch of black in the middle, which is spotted with warm-toned flashes of colour (see plate 6). We also see for the first time shapes that are apparently generated from pro-filmic objects, in other words things which do not look only like light effects, although, as always, one cannot be entirely sure. These too are dominated by black, so that the light parts of the image are strictly isolated. The main image is a kind of eclipse-like semicircular line, which partially encloses a roundish shape in centre-frame, before dissolving away (see plate 5). Black is articulated by colour rather than the opposite, as might be imagined, with many shots that are almost entirely black. Whereas in *Arabic 12* a black object is used to generate and control colour phenomena, here the colours frame and hence define the areas of black as something, by implication.

The colours in *Roman Numeral VI* (1980) are green, orange and pale red: not pink, but a de-saturated red. Immediately one is set to think about the relationship between hue, brightness and saturation, factors that are in turn complicated by the brightness of the projector bulb and variations in the colour temperature of white. Pinkness is a function of white being added to the mix, and which, therefore, given that white is opaque, is an opaque colour itself. But the whiteness in a film pink comes from the projector lamp shining through a certain density of redness, so how is a colour like pink even possible in film? Furthermore, opaque colours tend to look flat, that is, non-shiny and so relatively homogeneous (think of Vantablack, which is absolutely homogeneous because wholly non-reflective). Yet in films there is always an impurity of colour, and a certain depth at the grain level, since the image is a composite of coloured layers in grain, as seen in *Axiomatic Granularity*.

Roman Numeral VI opens with a brilliant pulsating soft form, a warm-toned and glowing shape that hovers over a field of dense black (see plate 8). There are long black pauses whose colour flare-ends fall within the frame. Thus each black stretch is announced with a momentary flash of brilliant red/yellow fringes and ends with the same, creating a kind of overhang into the next shot. The sections of black spacing announce themselves as shots, not just pacing devices, through these colour flashes. They imply that the black has some kind of meaning beyond its rhythmic/pacing function. This may be nothing more than the intention to dramatise the contrast between black (colourless and lightless) and red-yellow (coloured and light). In this respect it relates to the single black frames in the first film. The sense of high contrast is continued within images, as opposed to between them, and the colour end fringes of the black sections are echoed in the colour fringing of actual images.

The colour fringes also generate their own optical effect, in a film of optical effects, and remind us that buried in black celluloid are colour layers which may only become visible if the emulsion is scratched into, or if the shot is fogged at its very end. Thus it is implied that black contains other colours, even if they are not visible. They are latent, waiting to be revealed, and once we understand this we can no longer think of the black as simply the absence of light or colour.

The film is almost didactic in the way it works through a series of colour and graphic possibilities, starting with cuts between loosely complementary coloured, contrasting forms (see plates 9 and 10). These are followed by a series of shots in which the interaction between different kinds of graphic forms and the constant tonality in the film, black, are rehearsed; slashes, a circle in lower right corner, diagonal divisions of the frame (see plates 11, 12 and 13). These different forms all imply different kinds of black and all function in a slightly different way, even though the black itself does not change. It does not move, but it punctuates, articulates and dramatises, as well as unifying in a thematic sense, in that all the *Roman Numeral* films are unified by a dominant colour. Black forms a background in that the lighter shapes imply it as such, but insofar as there is no depth to the black it is more like the ground in a painting than a background in the photographic sense. One wants to read it illusionistically as deep space, but the urge to do this is based on assumptions, which are themselves based on conventions, not on strict observation and reflection thereon. *Roman Numeral VI* can be seen as a condensed, abstract echo of *Anticipation of the Night*, as the balance between light and black forms shifts towards the latter as the film progresses.

Roman Numeral VII (1980) begins with what appears at first to be a TV roll bar, but it soon becomes apparent it is not: its movements are too discontinuous. It is actually a black bar on a white ground whose position shifts arbitrarily. And yet there is surely a comment on TV here (see plate 14). Brakhage's dislike of both broadcast TV and video as media have nevertheless inspired some of his best films, including *23rd Psalm Branch* (1966–67) and *Delicacies of Molten Horror*

Synapse (1991), with its extraordinary ghostly grey textures and images in negative, overlaid with looped, hand painted material. In *Roman Numeral VII* the comment seems to be more on the violence of the electronic process by which the interlaced TV image is constructed and disseminated, a disturbing, a-rhythmic electronic emission.

Diminishing the size of a camera lens's aperture extends the depth of field (the spatial axis between the lens and infinity) so that 'stopping down' brings things into focus that were out when the aperture was wide open. Stopping down concomitantly darkens the image as progressively less light reaches the film. Brakhage made repeated use of these principles in the film, creating fades to near black from out of focus beginnings, so that shots come tantalisingly into focus just as they fade away. One says 'fades to black', but in fact the device as used here is not really a way of fading, more a strategy for shifting emphasis within the image, in effect altering the hierarchy of elements within the scene, or 'leading the eye around', to borrow a phrase from painting. Darker areas, of course, are the first to go, and highlights the last, so that at a certain point in a given shot, the image will shift from being a variegated, multi-coloured field, to a dark, modulated one with a constellation of soft highlights. Here it seems black is the product of a technical procedure, conjured into being as the lens aperture is closed. An image is formed at the same time as it is destroyed, at the point that most of the frame goes dark. The last fifty seconds of the film comprise a gradual darkening of a blue ground, so that one is again led to understand that what becomes black is not really. It is also yet another example of the application of Goethe's idea about blue being next to black.

In *Roman Numeral IX* (1980), the final film in the series, black spacing comes to dominate even more. The film begins with 17 seconds of black, which are interrupted by two half-second bursts of white. There is a similar vignetting process to *Arabic 12* with star-like forms emerging and receding and the image of the setting sun emerging repeatedly out of a black field. The film has a 'hot spot' at its centre, as if it has been re-filmed using a crude back projection system. Focus-pulls are deployed extensively, notably to change the shape of clusters of star-like highlights, which morph into horizontal bar shapes and back again, hence motion and mutation are achieved through focus pulling. An alternative approach to such cinematically created movement, that is, movement as the product of camera strategies, not pro-filmic movement, is for instance rigorously elaborated in Wilhelm and Birgit Hein's film *Structural Studies* (1970). Where the Brakhage films are restless and animated, the Hein's is cool and methodical. It may be compared, in its taxonomical rigour, to the photographic work of Bernd and Hilla Becher, who photograph industrial buildings in a meticulously uniform manner. This is not to say that their work is not also about the apparatus in important ways, but there is a settled equilibrium in their pictures between the apparatus and its subject which in Brakhage's films is always precarious and unstable.

In complete contrast to the restless and mutable black of *Arabic 12* and the *Roman Numeral* series is the bold and unvarying density of the fifty-minute-long *Passage Through: A Ritual* (1990), less than a minute of which has any imagery. It is one of Brakhage's most uncompromising and experimental films. It falls far outside the terrain of the family romances, landscape studies and light plays that make up so much of his oeuvre. By contrast, *Passage Through* is surely the most austere and unusual film to be made by Brakhage, or indeed anyone else. It arose after he received a sound work by the composer Philip Corner, titled *Through the Mysterious Barricades Lumen 1 (After F. Couperin)*, a long, minimal solo piano improvisation based on one of François Couperin's most celebrated keyboard works, the rondo *Les Barricades Mystérieuses*, the fifth piece in the sixth suite (*Ordre*) from Book Two of his *Pièces de Clavecin* (1717). The piece is pitched relatively low on the keyboard, mostly in the lower register, i.e., below middle C, and this is reflected in the score, in that both hands are written for the bass clef, instead of the standard arrangement of bass clef for left hand and treble for right. This gives the work a 'dark' tonality compared to pieces that are more equally balanced between bass and treble. When played on the harpsichord the piece has a rich clangorous quality, which Corner's composition replicates in pianistic terms through long sustained accumulations of notes. Couperin's short composition (two minutes to Corner's 40 plus) is mesmerizing in its use of rotating figures in both left and right hands, among which repeated single notes ring out insistently, and Corner's extended version is structured around repetitions derived from Couperin, specifically the minor second that comes at the end of the first section of the rondo and which is repeated in the final. The minor second recalls some of Morton Feldman's later piano works, notably *Palais de Mari* (1986), one of his very last compositions. Corner's composition features rolling, repeated notes in the treble, which are periodically joined by noisy clusters in the bass. The sustain pedal is held down throughout (a device also used by Feldman in his longest work for solo piano *Triadic Memories* (1981), which lasts at least 90 minutes). After about 33 minutes of what is often nothing more than a single note played repeatedly, we hear the whole of Couperin's original, played at about half speed, including the last two notes that form the minor second, from which Corner's piece then directly resumes, making explicit its derivation from its source, and accelerating for the last few minutes of the film.[7]

Brakhage's film challenges what a film is, or needs to be, or to have, to qualify as such and in this sense is almost *paracinematic*,[8] in that it raises the typical question of whether a roll of imageless black leader running through a projector is a film. What do we see when we experience such a work? There is, on the other hand, just enough visual material to secure its being as a film, assured by the presence of the very few, tantalisingly short shots dispersed throughout. The first of these, a light source partially occluded by foliage and/or some kind of mesh, filmed through an out of focus window frame, appears after several minutes and lasts just over one second. Subsequent shots of similar length flash up every few minutes until after 25 minutes we see a relatively slow and lengthy shot of a cloudy sky that fades in and out in around five seconds, followed in short succession by shots of a similar length, before returning to longer periods of black.

Insofar as there is nothing on screen for most of the time, we have the space to listen to the continuous and rhythmic soundtrack, whose repeated notes are connected by sustained drone-like tones. The inevitable division of attention occasioned by the simultaneity of sound and image in most movies, something Brakhage objected to, and which is reflected in the fact that all but about 25 of his almost 400 films are silent, is avoided by the same logic in this case. The situation of, in effect, listening to a piece of music in place of watching a film is arguably the most conducive possible situation for so doing, more than at a concert, where there are plenty of visual distractions. Black is the ideal colour for the film: non-symbolic, non-associative, tonally neutral, devoid of any inherent modulating or irrelevant aspects (notwithstanding, of course, the variations due to different screening venues, levels of ambient light in the space, etc.). Equally, black maximises the impact of the images when they do appear, by virtue of its contrast. The images are sufficiently infrequent so that one becomes immersed in the music. When an image does appear it is always by surprise and it disappears before one has had time to take stock. Only at the halfway point, where the aforementioned cluster of slightly longer shots appear in quick succession, does one begin to get the measure of things, anticipating the next shots after two or three of about six have appeared. However, this is a film, not a static image (a projected slide, for example) and so one is inevitably also always in a state of anticipation, however much this is etiolated by the scarcity and infrequency of images: something, anything, could happen. On the other hand, the black is consistently solid and unvarying, so that the question of what we are looking at and why, inevitably arises. The state of anticipation gives way to absorption in the music, or perhaps the mind, and indeed the eye, wanders. One might not look at the screen yet still be absorbed in the music, which is, after all, part of the film. A film without sound is unambiguously a film and no less so for being silent.

On the other hand a film with sound but no images is a much more dubious object. What is it really? One is reminded of Clement Greenberg's statement about the minimal requirements for something to be a painting, based on his idea that flatness and its delimitation were fundamental to painting:

> thus a stretched or tacked-up canvas already exists as a picture – though not necessarily as a successful one. (The paradoxical outcome of this reduction has been not to contract, but actually to expand the possibilities of the pictorial … .[8]

Thus, like the unpainted surface of the canvas, the black of *A Passage Through* is intended, bears intentionality and functionality, and this is true of almost all of Brakhage's uses of black. Black is never simply or only a pause. It always has some other function, disruptive or rhythmic, or to serve a specific graphic purpose by contrasting with or emphasising the character of adjacent shots or frames.

Brakhage stated that *Passage Through* 'required the most exacting editing process ever'.[10] It is hard to work out what this might mean, at least in considering it at the level of sound-image relations in terms of synchronisation. The main cluster of shots, a pivotal point in effect, occurs halfway through the film, but several minutes before the recital of Couperin's rondo, which is a corresponding point in the music, however the relationship between the sound and the images (fleeting close ups of foliage, human gestures and skies) is impossible to pin down, and surely this was intentional, since anything that even hinted at some form of synchronicity would nudge the viewer to recuperate the work as a kind of quasi-generic music video or simply a conventional 'film', albeit of an extreme and unusual variety.

The brevity, semi-abstraction and tentative character of the images are wholly contrasted to the transparency and literalness of the music. Like Feldman's later works, the structure is on the surface, lucid, legible and almost didactic in its workings-out, unlike a lot of complex C20 serial compositions, for example Pierre Boulez's *Structures* (1951), where recondite analytical procedures are required to uncover the organising principles of a work, work that furthermore made a virtue of avoiding repetition, thereby frustrating the memory functions that commonly help the listener to orientate themselves. For most of the time *Passage Through* does not require memory function, since there is almost nothing to remember, on account of the limited and repetitive nature of the material. However, it makes acute demands at the point where images do appear and overall on reflection, at the end: what were those images and how are they related? Is there a cumulative effect, or are they deliberately spaced far apart so as to frustrate efforts to concatenate meaning?

The inflected blacks described by Sean Cubitt in the opening quotation are ubiquitous in Brakhage's oeuvre, but there are a few films where they are explicitly explored. For instance in *The Cat of the Worm's Green Realm* (1997), a black cat is filmed washing itself, the camera zooming in until the frame is filled with iridescent, animated fur. These shots are contrasted with close ups of saturated greenery, behind and among which lies a density of blackness. Texture has migrated from the black of the cat's fur to that of the leaves, concomitantly shifting the kinds and effects of black from one to another and so on. Almost uniquely, Brakhage's films, in the process of getting us to attend to the complexities of our seeing the world, as inflected by the interplay between the myriad of perceptual phenomena the films both record and stimulate and the peculiarities of the apparatus, lead to a reflection on the possibilities of black. There is a negation of the negative, so that although black is always in some way the absence of light, this absence is never absolute, invariable or reduced, even in *Passage Through*, where its reduced function serves a specific purpose and is in any case crucially rescued by the few short shots it contains. Rather, Brakhage was constantly working black in different ways (formal, semantic, phenomenal, metaphorical) to diversify and expand its possibilities. Black is an equal partner in so many of these films which are more usually described in terms of their light qualities.[11]

Notes

1. Durgnat, 2003: 53. Author's italics.

2. Cubitt, 2014: 22.

3. Sorensen, 2008: 16 and 201.

4. See Hamlyn, 2005.

5. See https://www.surreynanosystems.com/vantablack (accessed 13 September 2016).

6. Judd, 1970: xi.

7. *Les Barricades Mystérieuses* has been a major resource for Corner in his improvisations. He has recorded improvisations based on it several times using a variety of similar titles, in solo and collaborative versions of differing lengths.

8. *Paracinema*, a term coined by film-maker Ken Jacobs, applies to films made without film technology (cameras, etc.) or to works that are called 'films' but which are not in any normative sense, for example Anthony McCall's *Long Film for Ambient Light* (1975), which was simply an empty room illuminated by daylight during the day and light bulbs at night. For an evolving theorisation of *paracinema* see Walley, 2003.

9. Greenberg, 1993: 131–132.

10. See Canyon Cinema catalogue: http://canyoncinema.com/catalog/film/?i=411 (accessed 13 September 2016).

11. Thanks to Emilie Vergé and Fred Camper for suggesting some of the films that I would not otherwise have known about, and to LUX, London, for kindly making their collection available for me to view.

2 It Within Itself: Mimetic Fissures in Brakhage's Object Collage/Time Paintings

Peter Mudie

There's an old adage that has served me well over the years – it goes something like: '*there's more to this than what meets the eye*'. This is indeed true when it comes to Brakhage's painting-based films.

In the early summer of 1994 I found myself sitting in Palm Court at the film-makers' co-op in London going through their catalogue of new acquisitions. I was alone in the co-op on Gloucester Avenue, left with the task of answering the door (as the entire administration staff had gone to the pub across the street to share a few drinks with a departing colleague). The doorbell rang and (unexpectedly) there was Stan, standing larger than life carrying an armload of film canisters for deposit into the legendary collection of films at the LFMC. Many of the films he had brought at that time were his new 'hand-painted' works. Sitting in Palm Court, wearing his large dark sunglasses, Brakhage and I talked for a long time about the new work and his concerns around the medical problems he was having with his eyes (after suffering a recent fall on black ice in addition to the removal of cataracts). The concern over his vision (at the time) predicating the detail he discussed his new works that he had brought to London.[1]

A large part of our discussion was around the painted works – it was my introduction into his thinking around the painted works discussed here. Yet there was a level of inadequacy at the base of our discussion – as one would expect, a degree of searching for adequate terms (or phrases) that could describe and summarise the films verbally between us. Noticeably his manner of speaking towards the painted works was quite different than when he spoke of the new camera-based print he had brought to London as well.[2] Similar to the manner that a painter would discuss a blank canvas before them, Brakhage repeatedly referred to the frame as an 'empty space' to which light could be 'worked'.

Across the hundreds of films that Brakhage would complete in his lifetime were literally dozens of 'hand-made' works (especially during the last two decades of his film-making). These works form a rich vein within his oeuvre, they are particularly intense and carefully formed compositions by Brakhage, quite dis-similar to the paratactic form of constructions that are a feature of most of his camera-based works across his life.[3] In contrast to many of his camera-based films, Brakhage's painted works are carefully shaped condensed constructions that individually (and collectively) epitomise Copland's notion of forming 'la grande ligne' of traditional musical composition missing from his camera-based works.[4]

It is simple to recognise that this particular form of film-making was important to Brakhage – it would be impossible to note any other artist or film-maker that would spend so many years completing as many works of this type. They are easily recognised, sharing many similarities and traits with his other films – from the miniscule, nine seconds long, *Eye Myth* (1967), to his longest purely 'painted' work – the elaborate 57 minutes trilogy based around the American Constitution (*I Take These Truths*, *We Hold These* and *I …* , all completed in 1995). Despite their various lengths, forms and themes these painting-based works are unmis-takably Brakhage films, they share the 'optical signature peculiar to the film-maker'.[5]

Severing a representational connection between a pro-filmic situation (in front of the lens) with its form as a filmic event, was a particular quality embodied within most of the films Brakhage would make across his life – to varying degrees, and through a vast range of approaches. Suffice to say, Brakhage spent a lifetime investigating every conceivable manifestation that might free cognition from a dependency based within models of representational linkage (hence codification). The almost boundless field of exploration offered by putting aside his camera and working directly with the film substrate itself (in a sense) freed Brakhage's film-making. It permitted him to determine fields of concern not necessarily conditional upon the properties of the camera 'eye' to stand-in for the 'I' within his works.

This discussion will explore Brakhage's pursuit to uncover fissures within the structure of mimetic representation in a number of his object collage/time painting films over the *Mothlight* (1963) to *Lovesong* (2001) period. Making a distinction between the object collage films, like *Mothlight* and *The Garden of Earthly Delights* (1981), and his post-1990 time painting works, such as *Naughts* (1994), this investigation will discuss various approaches that Brakhage explored to sever literalised references and similarity within his films – in effect, extracting 'it' from being interpreted as something other than 'itself'. As much as there can never be a dismissal of the potent symbolism inherent within many of Brakhage's hand-painted films, the proposition of seeking a unique position for his time paintings is underscored by a progressive releasing of 'the image' from forming into anything other than what it is. The premise of this discussion is that this was the point he attained before his passing in 2003: he reached a point where he had successfully extracted 'it' from being anything other than 'itself'.

Brakhage stated many times that film could construct a unique experience, freed from representation and analogy. His purely painted works epitomise his lifelong attempt to explore that space of the purely filmic.

> How many rainbows can light create for the untutored eye? How aware of variations in heat waves can that eye be? Imagine a world alive with incomprehensible objects and shimmering with an endless variety of movement and innumerable gradations of color. Imagine a world before the "beginning was the word".[6]

The 'non-representational films', the 'hand-made', 'hand-painted' or what some have referred to as his 'abstract' works (though there is very little that is abstract about them) are often referred to as intuitive or gestural works; works remarkable for their 'beauty' or the 'aesthetic values' that they perpetuate. There appears to be a general difficulty with approaching these works, the commentary surrounding them are often based upon outlining subjective impressions of the work. It is difficult to trust any of those generalisations, despite the notable legacy of Brakhage's exploration of the non-representational, the remarkable compositional constructions that they indeed are. I believe them to be quite determinist works that progressively extend out of the objectives of 'pure film' from the film avant-garde's rich historical past. Similarly, they pursue many of the same objectives of the Abstract Expressionist painters that he had admired during his lifetime. Like an expressionist painter, Brakhage was intensely focused on the compositional challenges of his works, within his works. The frame was where those challenges were worked out.

There are two fields of this specific endeavour in Brakhage's legacy: the object/collage (or assemblage) films, and those largely formed by colour, hue and form (for the most part, painted works). *Mothlight* and *The Garden of Earthly Delights* reside on one side of that field – both are formative films that are universally regarded as contemporary masterpieces. Those formed by colour, hue and form are commonly referred to as Brakhage's 'hand-painted' films, and they can be distinguished from his many other forms of film-making by the overwhelming aggregation of painterly materials and methods used in their development.

Mothlight was completed just a year after *Blue Moses* (1962). *Blue Moses* stands as a bit of an oddity in Brakhage's extensive film repertoire: the exasperated tone of the diatribe within the film is strangely out of place with the considered form (conceptual or compositional) indicative of his other works. There's a passage within *Blue Moses* in which the actor states:

> Actor (within the film): "Look, this is ridiculous. I'm an actor, you see what I mean? Look, you see what I meant by all that? This is ridiculous – I'm an actor, you're my audience. You see what I mean, you see what I meant – all that? You're my audience, my captive audience. This whole film is about us. So, don't be afraid - there's a film-maker in back of every scene, in back of every word I speak. Now, don't be afraid – there's a film-maker in back of every scene, in back of every word I speak. In back of you too, so to speak. No, don't turn around it's useless! You see? You see my back, but if I could really turn myself around and see, there would be nothing … "
>
> Actor (as the bare chested film-maker - in front of a screen): " … but empty black space and that glaring beam of illumination, those moving screens pulling … "
>
> Actor (as a sound, off-camera): "Don't be afraid, there's a film-maker in back of every scene".
>
> Actor (as the bare chested film-maker – in front of a screen): " … pulling, pulling … No, it's impossible! It'll be you. How do I know? I know, it's impossible! You know?"[7]

It could be that the freedom discovered with the form of *Mothlight* grew out of the polarised frustration engendered within *Blue Moses* – but that is simply conjecture. A particular passage from *Blue Moses* (noted in the above quotation) provides a significant suggestion to the manner of Brakhage's thinking towards the peculiar pictorial properties offered within a cinematic event:

> " … if I could really turn myself around and see, there would be nothing but empty black space and that glaring beam of illumination, those moving screens pulling … "[8]

I have always viewed a symbiotic relationship (albeit a dialectic one) between those two Brakhage films (*Blue Moses* and *Mothlight*). Although the title of *Mothlight* (when referred to in a written form) is persistently presented as a compounded singular term, the form it takes as a title sequence at the beginning of the film is quite different: the word 'MOTH' is clearly suspended above the term 'LIGHT' in the frame. My understanding of the film is based upon this configuration – that is, the suspension of 'figure' above 'ground'.[9] The material base upon which Brakhage placed the various objects in the film was clear film. When 'activated' into a durational experience the material base becomes projected light – the material base becoming reflected light off the screen. The various seeds, pods, pieces of vegetation and the wings of dead moths provide a graded scale of shapes formed by tones relative to their level of opacity – from silhouettes to translucence. That scale of tones form into perceived layers (or stratas) that position the various objects in relation to the light – from total opacity (forming the immediate foreground) to barely perceptible translucence (that appear closer to the base of light). When the film is projected the various levels of perceived objects form a peculiar 'depth' of developments established perceptually within that '… empty black space …' – that is, between the reflective two dimensional surface of reflected light coming from the screen and the '… glaring beam of illumination …' emanating from the projector. The effect of *Mothlight* is an orchestration of objects suspended between lux (light in its source) and lumen (reflected or radiated light).[10]

That unique space between projector and screen is where the cinematic event occurs – the 'shadow play' of cinema. Many expanded cinema events would propose an exploration of that space in a variety of manners – perhaps none are more articulate that Malcolm Le Grice's *Horror Film* (1973) where the film-maker positions his body between multiple projectors projecting coloured loops of film and off-set frames of reflected coloured light. Source, effect and activity in Le Grice's *Horror Film* collapse into an elemental articulation of the event itself.[11] Whereas Le Grice's exploration was based in the physical presence of machinery and maker and the defined parameters of actual space (and actual time) – Brakhage's field would be largely pictorial in shape, determined within the perceptive activity of rendering illusory form. Without doubt, his focus was upon (and within) the frame itself: 'that empty black space' for Brakhage (as noted in *Blue Moses*) was the empty white canvas sitting before a painter.

Brakhage's *Mothlight* worked apart from the conventions of Cartesian pictorial orientation – that is, the 'in-frame' arrangement of objects/characters/or values along a perpendicular axis of orientation determined by the vertical 'x' and the horizontal 'y'. This perpendicular alignment forms a logical illusion of spatial volume within the frame – in effect, proposing a 'z' axis of depth. So laboriously worked out centuries before, this orientation has become a habitual convention of representational cinematic form, it promotes and sustains a sense of believability in the values of photographic representation to form a logical illusion of 'spatial realism'.

The expansive field of (what has been termed as) 'pure film' in the avant-garde is full of examples where the dimensions of perspectival illusion have been tested and found to be malleable. Richter, Fischinger, Ruttmann, Lye, McLaren are some of the many film-makers that explored the unique opportunity that the cinematic form offered non-representational construction (via its temporal base). The simple geometric forms that appear to protrude and recede within Hans

Richter's *Rhythmus 21* (1921) for example, cumulatively defy the rendering of an illusion based on the premise of a Cartesian based perspectival logic. Larger and lighter shapes, which should note the immediate foreground, are contradicted by smaller/darker tonal shapes that move in front of them (within the 'black' field of negative space). In turn, these create composite shapes/tones where the two overlap. The movement, or more specifically, the organisation of movements within the parameters of the frame, effectively present a constant renegotiation of the 'z' axis within the duration of the film.[12]

The fixed position of the frame in *Rhythmus 21* does not present a perceptual complication for this as the stasis formed by the frame retains a simple single point perspectival form for the viewer. The viewer's point-of-view (pov) is fixed with geometric forms either protruding forward, receding backward, entering or exiting laterally before the ground. Therefore the viewer's pov, or more accurately a viewer's perceptual orientation to the developments, is not challenged in relation to the frame – at no point in Richter's *Rhythmus 21* do the developments alter single point perspective into multiple point perspective (two, three, four or otherwise).

Len Lye's exquisitely simple *Free Radicals* (1958) provides an illustration of how perceptually active 'negative' space within the frame can be. The entire film was fashioned by engraving (scratching) linear forms within an opaque emulsion upon the film's surface. The resulting linear forms are shaped by light on a black field defined by the frame – a black void of absent light. In the beginning, Lye's scratched lines of light appear to simply be what they are: linear 'signatures' scratched on a two dimensional surface that appear to undulate with a synchronicity to either the human chant or the percussive elements of the accompanying Bagirmi tribal music.[13] This changes dramatically when it is understood that the 'signatures' swivel on their 'x' axis (or laterally accumulate on their 'y' axis). In effect, when this realisation occurs the former flat field of negative space perceptually swells and acquires depth – the linear 'signatures' effectively become sculptural forms. Importantly, this is not simply an 'imagined' space but one determined through an active perceptual engagement in relation to the evolving events within the frame.

In *Mothlight* the figures appear suspended between the reflected field of incident light coming off the screen in front of the viewer – the absence of an orientating horizon line replaced by an attentiveness to the frame boundary of the leading edge. For most of *Mothlight* this is either the top or the bottom of the frame: objects placed upon the surface of celluloid appear to largely 'fall' from the top to the bottom of the frame. This forms an expectation that the top of the frame (as the leading edge) coordinates a form of rectilinear grounding for the flow of material to pass in relation to.

The most remarkable of all the objects are the translucent moth wings referred to in the title. Interspersed throughout the film, their elemental form, the structure of their placement across the durational length of the film, positioned in relation to the field of transmitted light that forms the ground of all the objects in the film. In effect, they are the 'figure' in the eternal pictorial 'figure/ground' relationship. The range of tonal values extends from silhouette to translucence – there is a counter-representational formation of volume that extends forward from the foundation of transmitted light. The closing sequences of wings 'fluttering to life' (as more than one commentator has stated) defies that passage – the *objet trouvé* of translucent wings moving upwards and out of the frame (left and right). The separation of incident and interval are wonderfully composed – passages of pure transmitted light separating the illusion of movement. The *objet trouvé* in Brakhage's formulation in *Mothlight* never diverges away from what it is: it is what it is.

The Garden of Earthly Delights resolved many of the pictorial conundrums illuminated by *Mothlight*. Brakhage applied his pronounced vocabulary to structure an attenuated composition that utilises object silhouettes as masking tools, and frames the film by bleeding a middle section of transmitted light out of the rich opening sequence of organic objects staged in bas relief. The form of the objects is intensified with this treatment – an isolating line of white defines their shape distinct from the negative field surrounding them and flattens their overall shape. If nothing else, Brakhage reinforces the complex architecture of organic form with those thin lines of defining light and intensified the hues of the photographic representations against the dark ground that surrounds them (that is, within the night sequences, or their silhouetted form during the day passage in the middle of the film). The alteration of pace is effectively a form of orchestration, an important tool that controls the constant shifting of one pictorial field above/below the other. There is a plethora of compositing and post-production manipulations used in *The Garden of Earthly Delights*: freeze-framing, step printing, travelling matts and other methods of optical work are used throughout the film. These assist the various movements Brakhage orchestrates with a complex field of characterisations. The complexity of the compositing throughout the film (not necessarily overwhelming per se) is really underscored by Brakhage's basic structure – night is followed by day, which is again followed by night – a simple structural alignment of organic forms to the consistent passage of time that (in effect) governs all life.

Many of Brakhage's painted works during the latter 1980s (and through the 1990s) would operate on the same set of principles as *The Garden of Earthly Delights*, except there would be few literal references made within the works. The breadth of Brakhage's heuristic propositions would expand considerably within his painting-based films – the fluid forms and multitude of compositing methods would lead towards a type of reconciliation with the rectilinear confines determined by the frame. Arguably, his best works of this ilk occurred in the middle 1990s and extended with greater clarity towards the end of his life.

Increasingly complex methods of optical compositing passages of material within his work would occur during the late 1980s and 1990s, his complex perceptual/cognitive explorations within film-based forms would parallel the medical problems he was confronting with his vision during this period. The aberrations in his eyes, spoken of in Colin Still's *Brakhage On Brakhage* (1996) video discussions, would lead to him rapidly parsing fragments of images together in his mind and developing intricate post-production methods to accomplish his films (almost as a by-product of his difficulties with sight).[14]

The painted works are deeply grounded in the unique attributes of film; they are distinctively similar to the reflexive explorations previously questioned in various mannerisms of contemporary painting (especially American Expressionism). The challenge was a considerable one – that is, how is it possible to embody a relationship of sensibility within works that refrain from using literalised representational form? These were determinate works, not random intuitive gestural constructions that evolved from 'chance operation' (refer to Brakhage's colourful story of how Jackson Pollock hurled a ball of paint at his studio doorknob for the art critics in Colin Still's video interview).[15]

Brakhage would employ an extensive range of strategies during this period within his painted films. Certainly there is a plethora of referential works that related specifically to various philosophical, religious and cultural parcels of thought that would fuse together his elaborate visual vocabulary with a conceptual thinking extending from any given source. The rich density of developments are a particular quality of his painting-based films, they are unmistakably Brakhage films. Many of these concern themselves around concepts of life and death and forms of mythology – the films champion areas of thought with a diverse range of approaches developed specifically to embody the subject of a work. The mannerisms are formed from the concerted conceptual approaches Brakhage used, typifying an astute understanding of the subject that any given film approaches. The range of conceptual tactics increasingly display a precision with his use of the various formal strategies developed during this period – disputably, the painting-based compositions display a greater willingness to explore speculative post-production methods than those of his camera-based works. Increasingly complex forms of optical compositing formed into mannerisms that extend across a number of films (such as those that were finished with Sam Bush during the 1990s).[16] Some of these would replicate basic tactics that had been used on his camera-based films – such as his use of handwritten inter-titles that predicate developments within (and between) sets.[17]

Irrespective of the many internalised mannerisms within the works, Brakhage contains his compositions within quite specific fields. These may be self-referential – in one way or another, it could be said that all of the works are – but each specify a perspective indicative of the material within the film. Almost all of these are alluded to within the titles he assigned to each of the works – they ground a specific sensibility (or perspective) with the viewer at the beginning of each film (albeit with varying levels of relevance). Ironically, this is incongruous with his conclusive statement from *Metaphors on Vision* ('Imagine a world before the beginning was the word') and a desire that he expressed during the 1990s to 'have the good sense to give up titles altogether'.[18] Notwithstanding those reservations, Brakhage would simply summarise that his film titles were meant to 'open people to seeing the film'.[19]

The titling of Brakhage's predominantly painted film works from this period are particularly important – at times they specify the inimitability of source, such as his remarkable *The Dante Quartet* (1987), or the *Chartres Series*, and, on occasion, framework, such as the seasonal changes that organise alterations of hue within *Autumnal* (1993). Some titles present a defined perceptual perspective, such as *Black Ice* (1994) – noting a barely visible state of matter that presents a clear physical danger; or only reiterate basic formal relations of equivalence, such as *Stellar* (1993) – rarely would a title assigned to a film only offer a descriptive understatement, such as *A Study in Color and Black and White* (1993). Other titles would note an emotional framework that governs the reading of the construction – in effect providing a title that collapses an expressive state with a predominant form within the film, such as the dark vertical column within *The Dark Tower* (1999).

Musical frameworks are noted unambiguously in a number of film titles, often in correspondence to psychological states, such as the wonderful condensation of sorrow in *Night Music* (1986); religious thought, *Jesus Trilogy and Coda* (2001); yet also noting a reference that is antithetical to the basic theme, such as the 'Haydenesque complexity' of *Ephemeral Solidity* (1993). The persistence within Brakhage's thinking towards the relations between music, poetry, art and cine-

35

matic form would condense within his wonderful treatise *Three Homerics (for Barbara Feldman)* (1993).

Three Homerics (for Barbara Feldman) was one of the most explicit of Brakhage's quest for a pure time canvas of painted form that distinguishes itself from musical form (yet in relation to that form directed from that of classical poetry). The film, dedicated to the innovative Canadian composer, is formally dominated by orchestrating the directional form of brush strokes within the frame – in time, in relation to time and the boundaries of the frame. Although resembling the temporal pacing and structure of Feldman's choral composition, Brakhage modeled his three sections of the film that 'was created to accompany a piece of music (by Barbara Feldman) on a Homeric poem'.[20] In effect, a triple *entendre* (or three-phased feedback loop) of structural form that brings together music, poetry and vision. There are considered progressive movements between frozen frames and step-printed dissolves that accentuate the depth of merging of hues – these provide a rich ground that angular characterisations work in relation to across the film. The surface marking of resists and crystalline forms, that provide punctuating points of pure light upon the surface within the second section, extend the elaborate descriptive mapping of pictorial depth within the field of the frame. They form an immediate foreground within the complex density of material within the frame that lead to the addition of a matrix of coloured brush strokes (introduced with large areas of fluid colour) – the merging of different 'voices' within the compositional frame. The final sequence, constructed as a form of 'recapitulation' sequence, brings together infused forms of colour, fluid shapes and kinetic linear figurations 'recurrently interrupted by the "blush" of soft suffusing reds'.[21] Balancing the interplay between three expressive compositional 'types' – music, poetry and film – outlines the relevance of *Three Homerics* in Brakhage's extensive repertoire.

The relations between pacing (interchange), spatial levels (stratas) and accumulated passage in all of his painted works endorse the persistent referral to musical form made in commentaries surrounding Brakhage's painted works (including his own). As complex as the optical manipulations became in these works, the equivalence between painted form, musical form and the compositional structure of temporal form disclose the uniqueness of his works from this period. Brakhage's formation of an embodied sensibility, similar to one extending from musical composition, would be enhanced by the impressive multitude of production/post-production methods used.[22]

Indeed, if a musical equivalence is considered in relation to Brakhage's temporal modelling within these films from the latter 1980s and 1990s, there can be a number of useful parallels drawn: frozen frames are analogous with sustained notes; superimpositions establish chords; pacing/interchange form arpeggios; alterations of hue standing in for changes in pitch, tone and/or volume. In effect, many of Brakhage's time paintings (from late in his life) were predominantly constructed from his inimitable structure of creating visual 'arpeggiated chords'. These are chords that are spread within (and across) time, creating and aggregating into a set of organisational fugues, often fugues within fugues. Although rarely acknowledged by Brakhage during this period, thinking of his painted compositions in this manner permits the viewer to position and configure the structure of developments occurring. Most of the films contain separations of developments (via interval or other forms of temporal separation) that assist with distinguishing one set of occurring developments from a previous set in the film (and those that follow). In *Three Homerics* the handling of material 'disharmonies' (such as the embedded crystalline shapes in relation to the angular brush strokes) differentiate passages that lead into changes of pace that can be distinguished as forming a set. These accumulate across the film with internal developments (framed within a set) positioned in relation to the others (that is, positioned within the order of sets across the composition). In general terms, albeit quite specific on occasion, many of Brakhage's painted films are formed on a similar three-part structure as that of a musical fugue – the exposition, a set of developments and then the recapitulation (often including, or extending into a form of coda).

Extending beyond the temporal structure are other analogies with music and art (or painting) that are useful to consider – such as the spread of values between harmony and disharmony. Painters (or artists more generally) are consistently occupied with the challenge that harmonious/disharmonious tensions present within a composition (during the process of formation or otherwise). Musical composition similarly so – positioning, blending, compositing or integrating those values across a piece of music to construct compositional movements and passages. Brakhage was particularly adept at collapsing distinctions that separate painting and music within many of his films, almost intuitively so. The density of the works can easily disguise certain developments that are repeated within passages or relocated into other areas of the film. On occasion, certain developments are represented in another form – for instance, sections of fluid movement are broken apart and recharacterised as a set of staccato frozen frames (or 'blended pictures'). As much as these signify a closer association with forms of music (especially when considering the formation of rhythm and the pacing of interchange), the specific values worked within most of the films are resolutely pictorial. In fact, all of the fully paint-based works are silent films – the modelling of consequence (or sensibility) resolutely temporal. The division of time within the films, often distinguished by intervals, appear as lyrical (or intuitive) decisions and not necessarily determined by the consistent metrics of a musical score.

The inability to form a stable understanding of temporal rhythm is a consequence of Brakhage's paratactic forms of construction. The basic premise of 'reading' a temporal structure from most of Brakhage's film works is overwhelmed by the constant flow of compounded image events – frequently layered into multiple pictorial planes, often changing, at times completely unexpectedly, filled with visual complexity. This is similar to the frequent shifting of angle, rapid camera movement and the shooting of reflections or through distortion devices within his camera-based works. In effect, forming an understanding of apperceptual continuity within a Brakhage film is hard work – as Bruce Elder summarises: 'One is so intensely involved in acts of perception that one has little energy left over for engaging in apperceptive acts'.[23]

Yet merging the symbolism integral to the source of a painted work into the eventual form that the film construction assumes (temporal or otherwise) presents a particular challenge – one cannot be separated from an expectation of representational mimesis without extending the work into a different range of perceptual acts (apart from nodes of distinguishable representation per se) or apperceptual considerations. Two painted films by Brakhage are noteworthy when considering the challenge of representing sensibility extending beyond a given conceptual origin: *The Dante Quartet* and the *Chartres Series*.

The *Chartres Series* is one of the richest of all Brakhage films from the 1990s. Built on the structure of a fugue (with an added coda), the four passages are separated by sections of interval that distinguish between one set of developments and the next. The three intervals positioned within the film define the four 'series' related to in the title; they also reiterate the importance of the black 'negative space' as an orientating space for the viewer. The absence of light within the field (of the frame) intensifies the hues and isolates the shapes of colours as distinctly separate from each other. The first set of developments is largely formed around suspended fragments of colour – minute in relation to the expanse of the void, the spinning movements of the coloured fragments mapping a form of simile for the three large rose windows of the cathedral (the north and south facing transepts and the larger western facing composition of the Last Judgement). The 'ink-blot' symmetrical forms of the second phrase compositionally leads the viewer into the middle of the frame – a distinct movement inwards – before a set of counter-clockwise rotations reaffirms a recognition of the frame parameters. The third phrase begins with a sense of serenity that counterbalances the preceding two phrases of kinetic activity. In this section, coloured shapes appear/dissolve quietly upon the black field before leading into the final section which builds a more literalised formation of the architectural forms that define the cathedral interior (repeatedly passing vertical columns that often expand to lead the viewer through, and Gothic arches that outline openings and the separation of space within). Knowing that the representational forms position a passage within an enclosed interior space, Brakhage forms/reforms these shapes during the final section of the film. In effect, he plots the passage through developing an imagined form of the rectilinear 'x' / 'y' perpendicular coordinates that lead the viewer pictorially through movements (or the depth of spaces) within the film.

Throughout the *Chartres Series* the rich indigo blue areas of colour dominate the range of hues Brakhage uses in the film, mirroring the abundance of it that was used as a background that surrounds and isolates figures pictured within the narrative/symbolic stained glass compositions of the medieval cathedral. Indeed, the indigo blue coloured shapes provide a continuous mapping device that links together the various passages in the composition. The recapitulation sequence that leads into the conclusion of the film, particularly rich with explosions of indigo blue, returns to the initial subject – the full-frame flashes of white light that appear before/after the title and at the conclusion of the film. The unadulterated flash of white light assails the viewer by reiterating that light (itself) is the subject (and contains the composition by bracketing the duration at the beginning and end).[24]

Brakhage's treatment of the material parallels the experience one might feel within the twelfth century Notre-Dame de Chartres cathedral, as much as encountering all the Christian mythology and symbolism as passing through a dark Gothic interior illuminated by coloured light passing through the large medieval stained-glass windows. A sense of spiritual sensibility is instilled throughout the breadth of the *Chartres Series* via a formal framework defined by colour, structure (compositional and temporal) and through the passage within, and between, phrases of the film. The astute construction positions the viewer within a spiritualised space leading through a series of colour orchestrations. As a result, there is an exquisitely shaped balance between lyrical impression and fleeting moments of implied formal resemblance.

Brakhage's form of mimesis attempts to limit imitation and the representational values that have formed a habitual dependency to view such works as gestural formal pieces. Certainly they use important formal strategies within their construction that are difficult to dismiss (such as the precise positioning of the colour yellow within *The Garden of Earthly Delights*), yet many test the framework of values that elicit simile and metaphor. The conundrum this presented Brakhage would be partially resolved by off-setting 'values' – at times Brakhage would employ photographic forms and quasi-representational fields to instil 'sensibility' into the films.[25]

A good example of this would be the infusion of snow covered shots of the Rocky Mountains into the pale blue areas of light that form within the dense indigo blue forms during the first section of the *Chartres Series*. Barely discernible, the liminal landscape appears to infuse Brakhage's spiritual place into the elaborate study of light within the Gothic cathedral of Chartres – an infusion that is felt (as opposed to seen). This is a subtle and highly personalised inference noting a type of signification peculiar to Brakhage (the uncertainty of which is also a particular trait).[26] It also notes an understanding of the dilemma of limitation faced when using a representational image within a representationally based vehicle that attempts to free specific association within itself.

The 'theme' of Brakhage's *Chartres Series* however is not simply that of a set of passages through the medieval French cathedral – despite all the rendering of forms, colours and other indicators that would suggest it is. Rather, the basis of Brakhage's *Chartres Series* is the corporeal nature of coloured light within a spiritualised interior space (in the broadest possible understanding of the term). Similar to Claude Monet's thirty some-odd different paintings of the Rouen Cathedral (1892–1894), the subject is one of changing coloured light that defines a spiritual relationship with a particular place. In considering Monet's master-pieces in relation to Brakhage's, one question comes to mind: would it have been possible for Monet to render spiritualised light (with paint upon a canvas) without the façade of Rouen's cathedral? If so, would that rendering be capable of referring specifically to all the particular attributes of that place (aspect, scale and position) that make it unique? The quandary proposed is full of similarities with the challenges that were faced by Brakhage towards making representational equiva-lence, yet one that he would intuitively comprehend from his pronounced understanding of 'sensibility'. In extension, if one were to remove 'sensibility' from this consideration (Brakhage and Monet) the conundrum can be clarified with yet another question (and one that I have considered in most of my thinking around the film avant-garde): would it have been possible for Peter Gidal to have made his formidable anti-illusionist treatise *Room Film 1973* (1973) firstly without the room; and secondly, without a camera?

The example of Gidal's *Room Film 1973* is an important one. It has nothing to do with the 'values' of photographic based representation, yet it also concerns itself directly with the assumption that those values would aggregate into a defined 'something'. The entirety of Gidal's film is constructed within the interior space of a room – the bulk of material structured into a progressive set of stuttering progressions across forms within that space – soft lit forms reveal themselves as surfaces, dimly lit linear forms revealed as edges to pieces of furniture, books, etc. Across the fifty-five minutes of structured progressions within the dimly lit space it is assumed that the entirety of the room has been scrutinised by Gidal's meandering camera (and reiteratively examined via his structural schema). Yet, setting aside the dialectics (Structural/Materialist or otherwise), the film viewer is unable to form an understanding of the room, the interior space, or even an impression of it. The dimly lit room (which could be plural) in Gidal's film is progressively exposed to the viewer in forensic representational detail – yet it is not understood (and certainly not 'felt'). Which is the point: understanding has nothing to do with representational determinism; Gidal's accumulated linear passages (across surfaces and areas) aggregate into a deconstruction of space.

As much as Brakhage's 'hand-painted' works simply avoid the problematic of reconciling a resemblance based within representation codes, they also tend to prompt a search for internalised references suggestive of mimicry. Often these are suggested (or inferred) via the titles Brakhage assigned to a film (as discussed previously) or become imagined out of formal developments within the films (such as the architectural forms that appear in the *Chartres Series*). The relevance of an association between framework and resulting effect certainly ebbs and flows across a number of films (and a variety of approaches) – perhaps his purest distillation between the two was the film *Naughts* (1994).

Naughts presents a form of axiom that signposts the decisive revelation embodied in *Lovesong* (2001). With *Naughts*, Brakhage makes a distinction between figures (or figurations) of coloured light and stratas (or levels) of activity that form spatial fields within the frame. The title of the film, although undermined by Brakhage's own musings, notes a simple game (known more widely as 'checkers') played by two opposing players on a board equally divided by squares of black and white.[27] The contest of the game pits one set of markers consuming another through forward and lateral steps in linear and diagonal moves (forward and across the board).

Containing five 'phrases' (or subsets) the film closes and separates each phrase with a soft flare-out to flash frames of white light and a few seconds of pure black interval – opposites that close and open each set of development. The first phrase begins with soft-edged coloured washes that emerge from the black void, appearing to rest behind a veil of dark forms that obscure the field. As the two stratas develop definition the section ends abruptly in a flash of white light. The second

41

phrase opens with a series of held coloured shapes that move outward in the frame – a form of 'zooming inwards' (from the middle of the frame to the periphery) that prompts a sensation of constant movement into the black void continually opening in the middle of the frame. The second section is the shortest of all five phrases in the film – it ends with an identical flare-out/flash-frame of white light as the section preceding it. The third phrase is largely formed by a series of textured colour fragments that appear to 'spin' within the frame, clockwise movements that swirl within the rectangular frame. In effect, the spinning motion of the coloured fragments reaffirm the confines of the frame edges – the fixed boundaries that had been (in relative terms) negated by the passage of material in the previous section. Occasionally frozen-frames (or held areas of a frame) randomly appear within and dissolve into the kinetic activity occurring in this section. There are two layers of moving coloured shapes within the frame each moving in different patterns. Both spatial fields are applied yet they retain their own unique spatial and temporal characteristics – the scale and durational passage of the textured coloured shapes would be modelled by an elaborate optical treatment, they form movements in relation to each other (and in relation to the ground of negative space and the definitions of the frame). Yet, almost lost within the array of coloured fragments and movement within the frame, are small delicate areas of protruding light – emanating from the emerald green and orange/red areas of colour, the light creates soft flares across other areas of the frame. In effect, these define a new pictorial foreground and serve to distinguish the other two stratas apart from each other.

Those soft light flares are the bridging device between the pictorial planes defined in the first three sections and come to dominate the two remaining sections. In the fourth phrase the light flares become more prevalent – they extend vertically through the frame, clearly providing soft veils over the multitude of colour fragments that are step-printed and phased underneath them. As these enlarge they dominate the frame, obscuring all the movement beneath them. Extending from the top to the bottom of the frame they move in and cross the frame from the left and right. Similar to a fog that covers a windowpane, the flares of light obscure what lies beneath it and simultaneously notes the flat uniformity of its surface. It is here that the nature of the 'contest' (noted in the title) becomes clear – that is, between the imagined deep space of the void (that the moving fragments of colour move within) and the flat surface that the veils of light define. In other words, between material surface and pictorial depth.

The durational form of a film construction (its length in time) prefigures a perceptual process of forming relations that accumulate into a form of understanding. During viewing this increasingly aggregates into something while the composition progresses. In *Naughts* the first three sections familiarise the viewer with different configurations of the spatial depth within the frame. Towards the end of the third section the soft light veils are introduced – they appear to emanate from beneath the textured coloured shapes (inferring a base layer of light). The crescendo of *Naughts* leads to one of the most spectacular conclusions of all his painted works: the musical notion of reaching a crescendo followed by a collapse reaches full visual maturity in this often overlooked gem.

Naughts predicates the resolution of a particular problematic that Brakhage would face with his painted films (perhaps all of his works). The film sets out, then collapses distinct pictorial fields (and movements within those fields) into the distinctly specific (and unique) material context of film. That is, surface and illusion – or, as the previous comparison between Brakhage's *Mothlight* and Le Grice's *Horror Film* – between the actual and the imaginary. As impossible as removing mimetic expectation may be for a film-maker (or any artist for that matter) – especially one with such a personified (and pronounced) stature as Brakhage – it appears clear that he reached a point of resolving a conundrum that he had been working around for decades. Perhaps more so than any other film artist, Brakhage understood the problematic of blending the act of expression within a cinematic based construction. In a sense, the problematic of imitation became the problem – whether perceived or perpetrated, the suspicion of mimicry was inescapable.

Shortly before his untimely death I believe Brakhage resolved the problematic of mimetic expectation (at least partially so, in as much as it could ever be). He resolved the basic problematic of the perceptual functions that engender notions of imitation. This does not 'symbolise Brakhage's turning away from the objective world, towards a hermetic realm of optical phenomena where illusory objects are conjured out of light',[28] but rather a grounding of filmic light with the material. With *Naughts* he would build and then collapse a resemblance of spatial depth – the formation across time (and a series of developments) of an illusionistic field that would eventuate into a collapse upon itself. With *Lovesong* Brakhage would present an illusion, followed by a representation of the material that had formed that illusion.[29] By using two distinct sources of light to distinguish one from the other, Brakhage would incorporate 'it' within 'itself', in effect by extracting 'it' from being interpreted as anything other than 'itself'.

Lovesong begins with an internalised presentation of 'it' – undulating painted forms that move through the frame in a series of step-printed fields of evolving form on a clear field. Brakhage repeats the first sequence and internalises an external aspect of 'itself' – by off-setting the values of light, effectively overpowering the transmitted light with incident light to note the material topography of 'it'. Long fluid lines and shapes that had formerly appeared as black silhouettes in the frame are given colour and form when the incident light strikes the topography of the paint on the surface of the celluloid (transforming them into three-dimensional forms). In effect, linear silhouettes are illuminated and re-formed into sculptural shapes (with resplendent highlights, middle tones/colours and shadows) – consequently, the formerly vivid colour washes/marks become muted. 'It' is material (paint/ink) upon a surface (the clear base of the filmstrip – in itself, a material).

As much as this discussion may appear to be a glib semantic interplay, it certainly is not: determining the specific characteristics of it, within and upon itself, is (indeed) the point of *Lovesong* that Brakhage insistently makes throughout the film. 'It' is a persistent iteration of 'itself'. This is it – it is what it is and only that (whether 'it' is within, or of, 'itself'). The recapitulation sequence combines the two – superimposing the extreme surface highlights of the paint/ink surface upon the translucent colour of light that articulates the presence of form from material. By the end of the film material and effect become unified.[30]

In 1993 Brakhage would state (my capitalisation):

> … all my life I've been trying to pry film loose from all forms of usage, whether it's drama, illustration, propaganda or modes of visual thinking. I've come to a point where I believe that if a film reflects anything that is nameable then that limits the fullest possible aesthetic of film – it's not film anymore. That is why I was on red alert when I heard Whitman's praise for Shakespeare – as a mirror held up to nature. Film should not refer to anything in the world, IT should be a thing in ITSELF. My new handpainted work tries to achieve this.[31]

Notes

1. Brakhage was in London to attend the large R. B. Kitaj retrospective held at the Tate Gallery and to present his new works at the parallel *Art Into Film* screenings and discussion at the National Film Theatre.

2. By memory, this was *A Child's Garden and the Serious Sea* (1991).

3. A generalised statement, but a useful distinction to make. Discussing the form of Brakhage's film construction (in relation to D. H. Lawrence, Ezra Pound and Charles Olson in particular), Elder notes: '… Brakhage employs paratactical forms of construction. His films often give the impression of picking up and using certain images or clusters of images, that are sometimes repeated and thus acquire additional richness and significance through this repetition – working with them and then leaving them behind'. (See Elder, 1989: 45.)

4. A point that also Elder makes; see ibid. The great American composer Aaron Copland wrote: 'But whatever form the composer chooses to adopt, there is always one great desideratum: The form must have what in my student days we used to call la grande ligne (the long line). It is difficult adequately to explain the meaning of that phrase to the layman. To be properly understood in relation to a piece of music, it must be felt. In mere words, it simply means that every good piece of music must give us a sense of flow - a sense of continuity from first note to last'. (See Copland, 2009: 26–27.)

5.   Sitney, 2008: 255.

6.   Brakhage, 1963: not paginated.

7.   From *Blue Moses* (1962).

8.   Ibid.

9.   Despite my reservations, I recognise the universal acceptance of the compounded term *Mothlight* and have used it when referring to the film.

10. Latin terms used by Robert Grosseteste within his treatise *De Luce (On Light,* 1225). For this distinction, and an English translation of the treatise, see Reidl, 1942: 5.

11. See Le Grice, 2001: 302.

12. The moving forms expose (and become embedded within) successive sequences of Richter's re-filming structure – noted through the gradual 'bleaching' of the negative space within the frame. The base (so to speak) becomes a form of marker, a variable that reveals Richter's structural schema for the film.

13. 'Signatures' is an apt description of the linear forms made by David Curtis; see Curtis, 1971: 49.

14. Now in Brakhage, *By Brakhage: An Anthology*, DVD (Criterion Collection, 2003).

15. Ibid.

16. Such as the films *Naughts*, *Black Ice*, and the *Chartres Series* (all finished in 1994). Brakhage states in the concluding credits on each of the films: 'This film is to be considered as a collaboration with Sam Bush, and optical printed at Western Cine, in the sense that I was the composer, he the visual musician'.

17. Such as the *From: First Hymn to the Night – Novalis* (1994), a homage to the early German Romantic poetry of Georg Philipp Friedrich Freiherr von Hardenberg within *Hymnen an die Nacht* (1800) – or more specifically, to the concept of the night symbolising a threshold between life and death. The inter-titles used within this film lead a viewer progressively through connected (and emotionally rich) passages – similar to the position of inter-titles used to lead into separate passages within the camera-based *I … Dreaming* (1988).

18. Ganguly, 1994: 38.

19. See Fred Camper in http://www.fredcamper.com/Film/Brakhage3.html (accessed 09/03/2016).

20. See the liner notes of Brakhage, *Stan Brakhage: Hand-Painted Films*, VHS (Paris: Re:voir, 2007). The *Infinite Other* (1992) was the composition by Barbara Monk Feldman Brakhage's film was meant to accompany – a choral piece with an accompanying piano, flute, clarinet, two violins, a viola and a cello.

21. Ibid.

22. When asked what he felt was central to his thoughts about his film-making during the 1990s, Brakhage replied: 'That I believe in song. That's what I wanted to do and I did it quite selfishly, out of my own need to come through to a voice that is comparable with song and related to all animal life on earth. I believe in the beauty of the singing of the whale; I am moved deeply at the whole range of song that a wolf makes when the moon appears, or the neighborhood dogs make – that they make their song, and this is the wonder of life on earth, and I in great humility wish to join this'. (Brakhage quoted in Sitney, 2008: 257.)

23. Elder, 1989: 46.

24. Many of the exquisitely complex compositions that Brakhage completed during this time begin and end in this manner – all were made in collaboration with Sam Bush (Western Cine).

25. For instance, the barely discernible photographic material from Billy Wilder's *Irma La Douce* (1963) used as a base layer below all the painted forms in the *Purgation* section of *The Dante Quartet*; see Sitney, 2008: 253.

26. If taken literally, the change of hue intensity (that alters the dense indigo into a gradated pale blue) might be a form of acknowledgment to central motif of the Virgin Mary contained in the *Sedes sapientia* composition of the *Notre-Dame de la Belle-Verrière* (perhaps the most famous of all twelfth century windows within Chartres).

27. Various phonetic forms of 'naughts' form these musings – as Brakhage would note: 'A series of five

hand-painted step-printed films, each of which is a textured, thus tangible, "nothing". A series of "nots", then, in pun, or knots of otherwise invisible energies'. See liner notes of Brakhage, *Stan Brakhage: hand-painted films*, VHS (Re:voir, 2007).

28. Hamlyn about Brakhage's *The Text of Light* (1974), in Hamlyn, 2003: 91.
29. This discussion is based entirely on the first film in the *Lovesong* cycle of five films.
30. In effect, the epistemological and the ontological collapse into each other.
31. Brakhage in Ganguly, 2002: 150.

3 Bottom-Up Processing, Entoptic Vision and the Innocent Eye in the Films of Stan Brakhage

Paul Taberham*

Stan Brakhage's concept of the 'untutored eye' and the constructive theory of perception marks one of the clearest convergences between the concerns of avant-garde film-makers and cognitive scientists. Constructivists argue that perception is indirect in the sense that we usually depend on internal processes instead of direct perception.[1] They suggest that the reason the world appears to be stable as we encounter it, even though our sensory information is in constant flux, is because we apply schemata – arrangements of knowledge already possessed by the perceiver – to almost everything we encounter, using them to predict and classify new sensory data. According to constructivist doctrine advanced by Hermann von Helmholtz and later elaborated on by psychologists Jerome Bruner, Ulric Neisser and Richard Gregory,[2] perception is an active, goal-orientated sense-making process. Because sensory information is incomplete and ambiguous, it cannot determine a percept alone. The perceiver, then, makes a perceptual judgement based on a series of inferences.[3]

*An earlier version of this essay was published in *Projections: The Journal for Movies and Mind*, Volume 8, Issue 1 (Summer 2014): 1–22. It is also due to be published in *The Avant-Garde Filmmaker as Practical Psychologist* (Berghahn, 2018).

Inference proceeds on a continuum between two poles. It can be developed from the bottom-up, meaning that sensory information provides the details necessary to make the appropriate inference. This occurs when the sense data alone determines perception without transformation in light of stored information; for example, touching a hot stove tells you that it should not be handled. When the inference is made from the top-down, perception is guided by expectations, background knowledge and problem-solving processes.[4] Face recognition would be one example of top-down perception. In both top-down and bottom-up processing, inferences are involuntary and virtually instantaneous, but most percepts involve both top-down and bottom-up processing.

Like our interactions with the natural world, film spectatorship involves both top-down and bottom-up processing. Bottom-up visual perception such as edge, colour, depth, motion, and aural pitch detection is employed, without recalling associated memories and creating only immediate impressions. Cinematic story-telling, however, cannot be defined by bottom-up categories as objects contained therein are referential and thus depend on prior knowledge and unconscious inferences. Because avant-garde film invariably problematises narrative comprehension and sometimes puts a greater emphasis on surface detail, this suggests that bottom-up and top-down processing are employed in a manner distinct from conventional narrative-dramatic film-making.

Of all film-makers from any aesthetic tradition, Stan Brakhage perhaps made the clearest call for the possibility of a cinema that depends solely on bottom-up processing, in which the work is to be engaged by virtue of its surface details, without relying on prior knowledge and expectations. With this creative ambition, Brakhage studied his own perceptions and intuitions rather than using constructivist language or making direct reference to it. Nonetheless, there is a direct convergence between his creative concerns and this theory of perception.

The pervasiveness of the following passage written by Brakhage demonstrates how widely it has been used when understanding his aesthetic:

> Imagine an eye unruled by man-made laws of perspective, an eye unprejudiced by compositional logic, an eye which does not respond to the name of everything but which must know each object encountered in life through an adventure of perception. How many colors are there in a field of grass to the crawling baby unaware of "Green"? How many rainbows can light create for the untutored eye? How aware of variations in heat waves can that eye be? Imagine a world alive with incomprehensible objects and shimmering with an endless variety of movement and innumerable gradations of color. Imagine a world before the "beginning was the word".[5]

Although this declaration was considered liberating for film-makers in its time, it was only radical insofar as that the sentiment had not yet been fully articulated in a written statement for film-makers. Film scholar William Wees traces

Brakhage's declaration back to a variety of other writers who pre-date the above passage from *Metaphors on Vision*. In J.D. Salinger's *Teddy* for instance, the title character claims that if children are taught that grass is green, 'it makes them start expecting the grass to look [that] way', rather than 'some other way that might be just as good, and maybe much better'.[6] J.R.R. Tolkien suggested in a 1947 essay titled 'On Fairy Stories' that we need to 'clean our windows; so that the things seen clearly may be freed from the drab blur of triteness or familiarity – from possessiveness'.[7] Aldous Huxley used the psychoactive drug mescaline to inhibit his interpreting mind. Describing his experience in *The Doors of Perception* he commented that 'Visual impressions are greatly intensified and the eye recovers some of the perceptual innocence of childhood, when the sensum [is] not immediately and automatically subordinated to the concept'.[8]

Looking further back, the term innocent eye originates with the art historian John Ruskin, who comments in *A Joy For Ever* that 'one of the worst diseases to which the human creature is liable is its disease of thinking. If it would only just look at a thing instead of thinking what it must be like … we should all get on far better'.[9] For Ruskin, one of the greatest barriers to true visual sensitivity is that people see what they think they know to be there, rather than what they actually see. In constructivist language, Ruskin would say that our ability to attend to the world from the bottom-up is inhibited by the non-conscious reflex of applying top-down processing (although his theory pre-dates constructivism by about a century). In *The Elements of Drawing*, he commented 'The whole technical power of painting depends on our recovery of what may be called the innocence of the eye; that is to say, of a sort of childish perception of these flat stains of colour, merely as such, without consciousness of what they signify – as a blind man would see them if suddenly gifted with sight'.[10] Brakhage's famous passage, then, should be understood as part of a longer tradition, and his 'untutored eye' can be understood as continuous with Ruskin's 'innocent eye'.[11]

How might the viewers switch off their interpreting mind in the natural world, and attend to their visual surroundings without engaging them for their semantic content? As Ruskin suggested, newborn babies are not yet equipped to interpret their surroundings, and giving sight to the blind through surgery also offers a form of innocent vision. Unlike a baby, the newly sighted child or adult can articulate his experience. The earliest report of this came in 1728 by the surgeon William Cheselden, who removed cataracts from a 13-year-old boy who had been blind from birth. Reportedly, once given sight, the boy could not make any judgement with regard to distances, nor could he discern objects as being separate. Subsequent reports suggest similar cases in which the newly sighted individual perceived coloured patches, indistinctly separated from one another.[12] What Cheselden came to believe, then, is that the optical field (i.e., vision for the subject not yet in possession of a visually interpreting mind) resembles an arrangement of coloured patches for everyone in early infancy. It is only over the course of time that these sensations take on shape, solidity, distance and identity.

Although newborn babies, or those who have just been given sight might serve as a utopian model for the experience of 'innocent' vision governed solely by bottom-up processing, current constructivist research suggests that those with ordinary vision are unable to return to such a visually naïve state. Top-down processing and the application of schemata to our visual field is always present and we have a spontaneous, uncontrollable reflex towards experiencing our surroundings as solid, three dimensional, and nameable. Psychologist Richard Gregory characterises perceptions as hypotheses, suggesting that perceptual information is always 'cooked' by prior knowledge and expectations; and in summarising this position, he comments: 'if past experience, assumptions, and active processing are important, there can hardly be raw data for vision'.[13] Cognitive psychologist Donald Hoffman describes the human facility to process and construct one's visual field as a form of 'creative genius' when detailing early developmental stages of visual construction. He explains how quickly we lose our visual 'innocence':

> By about the age of one month, kids blink if something moves towards their eyes on a collision course. By three months they use visual motion and construct boundaries of objects. By four months they use motion and stereovision to construct the 3D shapes of objects. By seven months they also use shading, perspective, interposition (in which one object partially occludes another), and prior familiarity with objects to construct depth and shape. By one year they are visual geniuses, and proceed to learn names for the objects, actions, and relations they construct.[14]

The period when a newborn child can be said to possess innocent vision, then, is short-lived. In *Art and Illusion*, art historian Ernst Gombrich drew from the constructive theory of visual perception in an effort to argue that the artist's eye is never 'innocent' by demonstrating how artists are guided by prior knowledge and expectations when painting scenes. Comparing the artwork of an 11 year-old child next to the work of the English romantic painter John Constable, Gombrich observes that the child misses or underestimates the modifications that various objects undergo when seen from different angles, or in different light. In addition, when painting a pastoral landscape, the objects that would interest a child like swans and trees, tend to be oversized.[15]

The child, then, depends heavily on pre-existing top-down conceptual frameworks for each object in the painting. Gombrich also observes that medieval artists operated in a similar way to modern-day children in the sense that they also have single, generic templates for painting objects of interest. He comments, 'The medieval artist, like the child, relies on the minimum schema needed to "make" a house, a tree, a boat that can function in the narrative'.[16]

Constable, by contrast, does not solely draw from a set of generic assumptions about how a tree, a swan or any other object is painted; he also makes allowances for the transformations that colours and shapes undergo depending on lighting and the position of objects. Did he attend to his surroundings with an 'innocent eye' when recreating them on canvas, addressing solely his bottom-up perceptions? Not necessarily. According to Gombrich, Constable represents a heightened state of accomplishment as an individual artist and, in the collective evolution of fine art in the West, he was an exemplar in his ability to reproduce what appeared in front of him. His ability to observe his surroundings without reverting back to a pre-existing set of schemata for each object might be understood as the application of 'innocent' vision – a visual sensitivity working from the bottom-up, unguided by pre-existing concepts. However, Gombrich suggests the contrary. Constable draws from more schemata, and thus, more prior knowledge, in order to reproduce his visual field, rather than less. This type of vision comes from years of training and learning the variables available to the artist, not from a return to innocence. Gombrich explains:

> Whenever we receive a visual impression, we react by docketing it, filing it, grouping it in one way or another, even if the impression is only that of an inkblot or a fingerprint. … It is the business of the living organism to organize, for where there is life there is not only hope, as the proverb says, but also fears, guesses, expectations which sort and model the incoming messages, testing and transforming and testing again. The innocent eye is a myth.[17]

In applying the conventional constructivist position on visual perception, Gombrich claims that Ruskin's innocent eye (and Brakhage's untutored eye, by extension) is implausible. Top-down processing cannot simply be switched off. If the innocent eye is to be considered a myth, however, there may be a simple way of shifting the terms by which we are to define innocent vision to make it a plausible concept again. The problem may lie in calling Constable's mode of vision 'innocent' or 'untutored', which implies naïveté and pure bottom-up processing.

Visual psychologist James J. Gibson, a contemporary of Gombrich, accommodated the idea of a mode of seeing that is comparable to the notion of an innocent eye. He distinguishes between the visual world and the visual field, and these might be comparable to 'tutored' and 'untutored' vision. Gibson compares these two different modes of visual attention by asking the reader to imagine a room they might inhabit. In the first mode (the visual world), one sees a familiar and stable scene of floors and walls, and a variety of objects with relative distances between them. The book at the far end of the room looks like it is the same size as the book next to you. Square objects look square, and horizontal objects look horizontal. This is a commonplace, familiar way of engaging one's visual surroundings that draws explicitly on top-down processing, as the viewer recognizes that the visual impression of the various objects is informed by their spatial distance, and the angle at which they are being viewed. Gibson then asks you to imagine looking at the same room and attending to the visual field as if it consisted of patches of coloured surface, divided by contours:

> The attitude you take is that of the perspective of a draftsman (that is, seeing that, as on a flat picture plane, "square objects" are really trapezoid, "horizontal surfaces" are inclined planes, the book across the room is much, much smaller than the one lying in front of you, and so on). … You may observe that it has the characteristics somewhat different from the former scene. This is what will be called here the visual field. It is less familiar than the visual world and it cannot be observed except with some kind of special effort.[18]

What we need is a compromise between Gombrich's acknowledgement that we possess a natural impulse to file and categorize visual stimuli, and Gibson's distinction between the visual world and the visual field – both of which require top-down processing, even though the visual field is loosely comparable to the bottom-up visual array that newborn infants experience. The conflict between the two theories perhaps arises from describing the visual field as innocent or untutored vision, which implies strict bottom-up processing, and is considered an implausible claim today. We might instead call it *retutored* vision, which requires more schemata and 'eye training' for engaging with the world, and is in this sense radically top-down. Gombrich and Gibson agree that attending to the visual field requires a special effort. Engaging with the visual field, like draftsmen do, or Constable did when he painted his surroundings, is a radically top-down activity, while the newborn baby and the 13-year-old boy who had his cataracts removed engaged with their visual fields radically from the bottom-up. The newborn baby and the painter ultimately reach a similar place, so to speak, but they approach it from different directions.

Sense as Muse

Up to this point, I have explored the possibility that a person can attend to their surroundings with an innocent eye, experiencing the most immediate and unmediated form of visual perception. Existing research on visual perception suggests that returning to this naïve state is an impossibility. Although existing top-down perceptual facilities cannot be discarded, I have suggested that viewing habits may be retutored so that the viewer may attend to the visual field instead of the visual world. They do so with the use of a specialised effort that depends on top-down inferences, rather than bottom-up data-driven perception.

For Brakhage, the 'untutored eye' represents a primal vision of the world, as if it is being seen for the first time. He was, however, aware of the top-down dimension to visual perception (although he did not use that term). Paul Arthur suggests that Brakhage's aesthetic is designed to drive toward an ideal, rather than attempting to attain an impossible goal:

> Although he readily admits that any actual return to a state of "innocent", childlike vision is impossible, the persistent project throughout his vast oeuvre has been to guide the eye in a journey of "untutoring", using every possible cinematic tool as leverage for that journey.[19]

As such, we as viewers do not experience innocent vision itself when viewing his films. Instead, we see Brakhage's representation of innocent vision that should sensitise us to a richer and more varied visual life. The argument advanced so far has been that while it may feel like we are discarding prior visual habits, in reality we are expansively developing new skills and sensitivities. Engaging with Brakhage's films, I suggest we retutor our visual skills, instead of untutoring them.

Because cinema has traditionally exploited the ordinary human perceptual habit of focusing on the visual world instead of the visual field, Brakhage sought to develop an expressive style that compels the viewer to pay attention to the visual field in his films, retutoring the spectator's visual sensitivities by drawing attention to the surface details, rather than their semantic content. I will next consider how Brakhage retutors the viewer's eyes.

Brakhage wrote his famous passage about the untutored eye at the same time that he was working on *Dog Star Man* (1961–64; henceforth *DSM*), a film that invoked responses in his audience that alluded to the possibility of a cinema that could expansively sensitise the viewer to the visual field over the visual world. The poet Robert Kelly famously summarised his reaction to *DSM* with the phrase 'mind at the mercy of eye at last'.[20] Kelly's image of the mind at the mercy of the eye may not hold in the strictest sense for reasons already detailed; yet it serves as an evocative metaphor for a film that subdues the viewer's tendency to attend primarily to the semantic dimension of the imagery on-screen.

One of the ways in which Brakhage accomplished this effect was by attempting to refamiliarise the viewer with the actual experience of seeing, rather than the idealised conception of vision expressed in traditional film-making with the conventional use of tripods, focusing, tracking dollies, steady panning, and zooming. In a 1965 letter to Jonas Mekas, Brakhage wrote, 'I find myself feeling that it is the total physiological impulse of a man must be given form in the making of a work of, thus, called, art'.[21] A year later, Brakhage commented that his goal as a film-maker was to create a filmic equivalent to the act of seeing, stating 'film is, thus, premised on physiological sense – *takes* Sense as Muse'.[22]

How might the physiological impulse of man be captured in film? How might sense serve as a muse? In addition to filming point-of-view shots and emulating saccadic eye movements by hand-operating the camera, Brakhage also found inspiration by paying attention to entoptic phenomena – visual experiences whose source is within the eye itself. This is one characteristic of human vision that the conscious mind learns to ignore as it is of no adaptive benefit – visual information is distinguished from visual noise.[23] Marilyn Brakhage comments:

> beginning in the early 1970s, a major shift was developing in a parallel strand of Brakhage's work, as "vision" was increasingly presented as "thought process" – as the ... feedback of the nervous system in response to the incoming light being "spanked" in upon it (as he would say) were given equal weight to any exterior sights.[24]

One example of the entoptic effect includes 'floaters' or muscae volitantes, transparent blobs that slowly drift across our visual field. These can be caused by swollen red blood cells suspended above the retina, which become most visible if you lie on your back and look up towards the sky. Treating the film directly with intermittent marks on the film strip, Brakhage appears to add muscae volitantes to the mechanical vision of the camera lens with speckles of light on the film frame (see plate 20). Craig Dworkin makes a similar observation:

> the dust, hair, and scratches visible after that printing – like the surface manipulations of paint flicked from a brush onto the surface of the film or scratches etched into the emulsion – all simulate the flinch and drift of entoptic imperfections which cast shadows on the retina as debris floats through the vitreous fluid.[25]

The purkinje tree is another entoptic effect. This is a reflection of the retinal blood vessels in one's own eye, which becomes most visible if you sit in a darkened room, close one eye and shine a light back and forth in the other eye, such as one is likely to see at the optician's during an eye examination. In *DSM*, trees are a recurring motif, which at times loosely resemble the purkinje tree (see plate 21).

Phosphenes are another visual experience not provoked by information provided by the outside world. Patterns of light are perceived in the visual cortex without light entering the eyes; these can be caused by electrical or magnetic stimulation, or simply by rubbing one's closed eyelids, which stimulates cells on the retina, producing 'pressure phosphenes', speckles that can create the impression that you are moving through a star field or a darkened tunnel. They might also be caused by a blow to the head (hence 'seeing stars'), a vigorous sneeze, or standing up too quickly with low blood pressure. The treated film in Brakhage's *The Dante Quartet* (1987) resembles phosphenes (see plate 22).

In addition to phosphenes, the visual system also produces a persistent low level of grainy light, referred to as visual 'noise' even when there is no stimulation of the eye by light.[26] Visual noise is most easily discernible when we close our eyes or sit in a darkened room. Once sensitised, visual noise can be registered in full light as well. Generally, as with phosphenes and various entoptic effects, we typically ignore these visual impressions. Gregory comments:

> Imagine some neural pulses in the brain: are they due to light entering the eye, or are they merely spontaneous noise in the system? The brain's problem is to 'decide' whether neural activity is representing outside events, or whether it is mere noise, which should be ignored.[27]

Brakhage once said that he was inspired by human vision, and was 'involved with a process so naturally always existent its workings have been overlooked'.[28] It might not only be the persistence of visual noise that compels us to disregard it; the brain itself appears to be geared to do so.

In *Desert* (1976) Brakhage emulated the impression of shimmering beams of light that appear when one squints, as well as the visual distortions that occur when you are in an intensely hot environment. Flash blindness is another visual phenomenon that can serve as an inspiration; this is where the retinal pigment is bleached and over-saturated by a bright light (e.g., a flash photograph) that causes temporary visual impairment. As the pigment returns to normal, so too does sight. Brakhage's underexposed images, as featured in *DSM* for example, resemble this effect. All these visual experiences and others take the 'sense as muse' for Brakhage, reawakening the viewer to the subjective dimensions of human vision that we typically ignore.

Dworkin suggests that Brakhage's films reawaken the viewer to the physical nature, the corporeality of human vision rather than conceiving it as an objective, unmediated window to the outside world:

> Brakhage's films, in short, momentarily replace the illusion of the eye's transparent clarity with a clear view of its obstructions. His films, like the bodily experiences they imitate, frustrate the idealization of vision by documenting the obstructions and impediments that the eyes themselves present, and they remind us of the corporeal ground for resisting those ideologies that have attended myths of unmediated transparency.[29]

When Brakhage aspired to 'sound the depths of all visual influence',[30] he sought to represent all visual information that reaches the visual cortex, and not just light that enters the eye. Training as a draftsman would be one method for retutoring the eyes, observing the visual field in a similar manner to the way Constable observed Wivenhoe Park. Attending to entoptic phenomena and other subjective dimensions of vision provide another route, which extends and builds on Ruskin's original conception of the innocent eye.

Here, I draw from Wees's account of Brakhage in *Light Moving in Time* (1992). Wees argued that Brakhage is best understood as an artist who attempted to capture undiluted vision, freed from mental embellishments. Though my own work is influenced by Wees's discussion, I place the topic in a constructivist context, propose the less problematic term retutored eye, elaborated on claims set forth by Gombrich and various perceptual psychologists, and also elaborated on entoptic vision, illustrating Brakhage's use of it in his films.

'Bad Practice' and Flattening the Screen

Brakhage developed a series of methods in *DSM* and other films to inform human vision with novel experiences that have been traditionally understood as 'bad' practice with the camera. For example, he resisted traditional aesthetic values of 'good' composition, compelling viewers to engage his images with 'an eye unprejudiced by compositional logic' rather than traditionally appealing standards of visual composition. The image reproduced in plate 23 can be taken as an example of one of Brakhage's hand-held shots that would traditionally be considered poorly framed. Other techniques include letting the 'wrong' amount of light into the lens according to commercial standards through overexposure or underexposure. Objects might be stretched out of shape with attachable lenses, or out of focus. All of those effects occur in *DSM*.

In adopting putatively 'bad' practice with the camera, Brakhage compels the viewer to appraise his visual style according to a unique set of aesthetic criteria. Nicky Hamlyn offers a rationale for this, and ties Brakhage's approach to the broader practice of avant-garde film-making:

> in discussing these films one inevitably resorts to expressions like "out of focus", yet such expressions are already problematic. First, and most obviously (and not just in relation to Brakhage's oeuvre), the phrase is value laden in ways that will be familiar to anyone who is familiar with experimental film. It assumes a normative and narrowly drawn understanding of vision as focused and stable. In questioning the instrumentalism of dominant cinema's use of film technology, experimental filmmaking must involve a rejection of ostensibly technical terms that turn on unexamined or assumed correlations between focus, clarity, objectivity, and good practice/craft. Such questioning is not unique to Brakhage's oeuvre, of course, but his work constitutes, with a few exceptions, a consistently sustained attack on the dichotomy of focus versus unfocused.[31]

Coming into focus can be understood as the process of textures sharpening with lines or edges forming rather than reaching a discernible, idealized form. Focused and unfocused was one dichotomy Brakhage rejected, along with over- and under-exposed. In order to produce the work he did, Brakahge also refused the dichotomy between representation and abstraction, commenting: "'abstract', 'non-objective', 'non-representational', etc. I cannot tolerate any of those terms and, in fact, had to struggle against all such historical concepts to proceed with my work'.[32] Denying such a distinction, Brakhage sensitises the viewer to the visual field by gliding and shimmering across images that contain discernible and indiscernible objects in the same manner and fluidly cutting between them, without treating the referent images as if they need to be contemplated any differently to the non-referential imagery.

One of Brakhage's other central strategies when drawing the viewer's attention to the visual field rather than the visual world is 'flattening' the cinematic image, following the lead of modernist painters that had preceded him. Clement Greenberg explains:

> Realistic, naturalistic art had dissembled the medium, using art to conceal art; Modernism used art to call attention to art. The limitations that constitute the medium of painting – the flat surface, the shape of the support, the properties of the pigment – were treated by the old masters as negative factors that could be acknowledged only implicitly or indirectly. Under Modernism these same limitations came to be regarded as positive factors, and were acknowledged openly. … It was the stressing of the ineluctable flatness of the surface that remained, however, more fundamental than anything else to the processes by which pictorial art criticized and defined itself under Modernism. For flatness alone was unique and exclusive to pictorial art.[33]

Applying a Modernist sensibility to cinema, Brakhage commented that 'we have an eye capable of any imaginings. And then we have the camera eye, its lenses grounded to achieve 19th-century Western compositional perspective'.[34] In essence, Brakhage suggested that the film camera is tailored to emulate principals of visual perspective that were developed during the Renaissance, which create the illusion of visual depth on a flat canvas.[35] To undermine the illusion of depth, Brakhage developed a series of specialised techniques, for instance, 'flat' paint was placed over 'deep' photographed imagery. He also tried 'spitting on the lens [and] wrecking its focal attention',[36] and using extreme close-ups so that that the viewer cannot discern what they are looking at, or how shapes and objects relate to one another spatially.

In emphasising the flatness of the cinematic screen, Brakhage sought to dispel the impression that the cinematic image is a 'window' into a three-dimensional environment. Near the inception of cinema, in the Lumière Brothers' *Arrival of a Train at Ciotat* (1896), the illusion of visual depth is vividly exploited as a train approaches from the distance and moves past the camera. For Brakhage, the screen can be understood more productively as a flat canvas on which novel and exploratory visual experiences may take place, rather than a window through which you see into a three-dimensional space. The window analogy in reference to the cinematic screen remains inadequate for Brakhage in the sense that we cannot look through the screen in the way we can look through a window. Instead, the cinema screen becomes a canvas on which the true nature of human vision may be reawakened. In *A Moving Picture Giving and Taking Book*, Brakhage commented (quoting Blake) that the film-maker must see "'*with, not through*, the eye" … *with*, rather than thru, machine'.[37] As Wees explains:

57

> The "machine" is no more a "window" than the eye is. Both eye and "machine" make what is seen; hence, cinematic equivalents of seeing cannot be divorced from the materials and processes of filmmaking, any more than human sight can be separated from the body's visual system.[38]

Again, Brakhage highlighted the corporeality of the 'physical eye' rather than the idealised form of vision advanced by traditional conceptions of cinematic vision. In highlighting the constructedness of cinema by flattening the screen, he alerted us to the parallel constructedness and materiality of human vision.

Conclusion

Two principal lines of discussion have been proposed in this article. First, the concept of the untutored eye has been placed in a historical context and reassessed in the context of cognitive theories of visual perception, suggesting that it might instead be called the 'retutored eye', which carries less problematic implications. Following this, the way in which Brakhage went about retutoring the eyes was considered, with the suggestion that he reintroduced the corporeality of visual perception by approximating entoptic vision and phosphenes. He also exercised 'bad' film practice, compelling viewers to re-evaluate traditional aesthetic standards. In addition, he alerted the viewer to the true nature of the cinematic image by attempting to collapse cinematic illusions of visual depth.

There are other dimensions to Brakhage's aesthetic that invite an appraisal from the cognitive perspective. In the later part of his career, Brakhage argued that one of the most significant expressive potentials of film was its ability to recreate that which he came to call '"moving visual thinking" – a non-verbal, non-symbolic dimension of thought that verges over "into the un-nameable or the ineffable"'.[39] Marylin Brakhage explains:

> Perceiving the mind's movements as being in constant interplay with both visually and sonically received and experienced rhythms, he theorized further that the aesthetic creation of either visually ordered or sonically ordered rhythms could present meaningful equivalents of those inner movements, and he created works in constantly renewing visual forms that would not only respond to a variety of sights seen – while simultaneously manifesting an interior life and documenting complex layers of optic feedback, or "closed-eye vision" – but that would give to the eyes (and mind) something analogous to what music gives to us through hearing: "visual music".[40]

In *Rage Net* (1988), Brakhage created an equivalent to his inner movements while being in a state of anger by painting directly on the celluloid. In *Lovesong* (2001) he created an equivalence to his inner movements that occur during lovemaking. He went as far as to state 'if science comes up with a machine so you could tap into people's actual thinking process and then project whatever they're thinking as vision and put it up on a screen, I'm doing that laboriously by painting, because we don't have any way to do that'.[41] This may seem like a promising line of discussion for a film-maker who mines his own cognitive facilities when producing art. Neural oscillations may be the closest phenomena in cognitive science that parallels the idea of ineffable movements in the mind that interact with the 'rhythms' of the exterior world that can then be approximated through film. As such, the mind does respond rhythmically to the outside world. Evidently, this is a complex topic that has to be considered in more detail in another discussion that does not focus directly on visual experiences. Note, however, that aside from bearing a loose parallel with research from cognitive science, the concept of moving visual thinking relates directly to Romanticism and the 'intellectual' or 'imaginative eye'. According to M. H. Abrams:

> The preoccupation is with a radical opposition in ways of seeing the world, and the need to turn from one way to the other, which is very difficult, but works wonders. "Single vision", the reliance on the "bodily", "physical", "vegetable", "corporeal", or "outward eye", which results in a slavery of the mind to merely material objects, a spiritual sleep of death, and a sensual death-in-life to this way of seeing [Romantic] poets opposed the liberated, creative, and resurrective mode of sight "throe' and not with the eye", the "intellectual eye", the "imaginative eye", or simply, "the imagination". The shift is from physical optics to what Carlyle in the title of one of his essays called "Spiritual Optics", and what Blake and others often call "Vision".[42]

According to Malcolm Turvey, Brakhage articulates a powerful version of the 'human subjectivity theory', in which various forces in modernity such as science, technology, and 'instrumental reason' altered the way that the average person's mind works, enslaving modern consciousness to rational, instrumental imperatives which are 'intrinsically divorced from the senses, the body, and nature in general'.[43] Because we cannot *see* in the fullest sense of the word, the artist can compensate for our flaws in normal vision by, for instance, looking inwards to attain visual knowledge that is free from rationalistic consciousness, via moving visual thinking. Alternatively, as in the case of Brakhage, they might evoke a cinema that recreates vision with saccadic movements, phosphenes, and entoptic vision.

According to existing cognitive theory, it is not modernism that alienates us from attending to the full richness of visual experience, it is the nature of the brain itself to mentally organise objects encountered, and ignore non-utilitarian visual experiences such as phosphenes and entoptic vision.[44] Brakhage is an exemplar of the model of the film-maker who explores his own cognitive capacities and draws inspiration from them while expansively engaging the viewer in a novel way. It is not the goal of this article, however, to justify all of Brakhage's intuitions about the mind or visual perception by finding a direct correlation in the field of cognitive science. Brakhage was inspired by the idea of providing an antidote to modernist consciousness, of returning to a pre-linguistic visual utopia, of refusing the distinction between figurative and abstract imagery, and attempting to express an ineffable visual correlation to the movements of the mind. These concepts enabled him to produce a prolific and evocative body of work. Their value as theories can be measured in large part by the art they inspired, rather than whether they run directly parallel with existing scientific research. The interactions between human perception and thought with its corporeality, limitations, and idiosyncrasies, productively served Brakhage as a creative muse.

Notes

1. The indirect processing theory advanced by constructivism was counterpointed by James Gibson's theory of direct perception. Gibson argued that there are no internal representations involved. For my discussion, I focus on the more conventional constructivist approach.
2. See Eysenck and Keane, 2000: 54.
3. See Bordwell, 1985: 31.
4. Ibid.
5. Brakhage, 1963: not paginated.
6. Salinger, [1953] 1970: 299.
7. Tolkien quoted in Pearce, 2001: 166.
8. Huxley, [1954] 2009: 25.
9. Ruskin, [1857] 2007: 106.
10. Ruskin, [1865] 2013: 45.
11. Note that Ruskin suggested the artist should attend to their visual surroundings with an innocent eye, while Brakhage's idealised untutored eye was framed as a perceptual idyll not just for film-makers or artists, but for all people gifted with vision.
12. See Wees, 1992: 59.
13. Gregory, 2004: 9.
14. Hoffman, 2000: 12.
15. See Gombrich, 2002: 247–248.
16. Ibid., 248.
17. Ibid., 251.
18. Gibson, 1950: 26–27.
19. Arthur, 2003: not paginated.
20. Kelly, 2005: 32. Kelly's comment was originally made in reference to Brakhage's extended version of *DSM*, titled *The Art of Vision*.
21. Brakhage, 1982: 32.
22. Brakhage, 2001: 129. Brakhage may, in fact, have been extending a long-lost tradition. Lewis-Williams and Dowson speculated in their article 'The Signs of All Times' (1988) that entoptic vision served as the basis for images in Palaeolithic art. Richard Bradley made a similar claim in 'Deaths and Entrances: A Contextual Analysis of Megalithic Art' (1989).
23. See Blom, 2010: 174; and Helmholtz, 2005: 323.
24. Brakhage, Marilyn, 2010: not paginated.
25. Dworkin, 2005: 135.
26. See Gregory, 2004: 93.
27. Ibid.
28. Brakhage, 2001: 40.
29. Dworkin, 2005: 136.

30. Brakhage, 2001: 13.
31. Hamlyn, 2005: 115.
32. Brakhage, 1993: 11.
33. Greenberg, 1993: 86–87.
34. Brakhage, 2001: 15.
35. See Huble and Livingstone, 2008: chapter 7.
36. Brakhage, 2001: 18.
37. Ibid., 112.
38. Wees, 1992: 84–85.
39. Brakhage, Marilyn, 2010: not paginated.
40. Ibid.
41. Taken from a video interview available at http://www.youtube.com/watch?v=EFDQfHvyzGI (accessed 15 May 2016).
42. Abrams, 1972: 377; also quoted in Turvey, 2008: 105.
43. Turvey, 2008: 104.
44. See Gregory, 2004: 93.

4 The Eye and the Hand: Brakhage's Challenge to Ocularcentrism

Gareth Evans

The eye can become affected by a cultural languor. In fact, this is the habit of vision that pervades our transition into adulthood. Such is the fearful warning implicit in Brakhage's writings fuelling one of the key political attributes of his engagement with film.[1] Our visual experience will stagnate when determined by a consensus on how reality should be seen and understood. Brakhage wants us to see, but seeing must be personal, emancipatory and a perpetual 'adventure of perception'.[2] He believed that as we age our vision comes increasingly into conflict with general consensual determinations of perceiving reality, and it is against these that personal visual experience must assert its singularity. This political aspect of Brakhage's aesthetic practice is oriented around the freeing of the eye from such a languor; to offer a touchstone in the expression and sharing of his own singular vision through film that may provide a basis from which to begin one's own adventures.

Yet the eye holds a complex conceptual place in both Brakhage's writing and film-making. James Boaden has warned that the way we position the eye in Brakhage's work can lead to a 'misreading' of the power accorded to it in relation to the rest of the body. He writes that,

Brakhage recognised the power of the eye – but wanted to take it further, make it do more. In his texts he recognised that the opposition between mind and body (an opposition that pivots around questions of vision) was a false division and that the eye worked in tandem with the rest of the senses. Brakhage's films aimed to stimulate those other senses located across the body and through vision.[3]

Positioning the eye at the top of a pentalogical hierarchy of the senses, understanding vision as the principal means by which the world outside the body is perceived and internalised, has historically dominated Western thought and its organisation of the body.[4] Although Brakhage came to define the art of film solely in accord with the possibilities of vision, his aesthetic approach was supported by an ever-growing mistrust in the cultural hegemony of sight. This essay explores one such relation between vision and other sensory stimuli in Brakhage's filmmaking: the relation between the eye and the hand, between vision and touch.

Brakhage's writings and comments about his films are strewn with references to the importance of 'the whole organic system' in producing visual experience through the vibrancy of cells, the pulp of meat and pulses of the living body.[5] For instance, discussing *Dog Star Man* (1961–64) in an interview with Colin Still in 1996, Brakhage said that the hopefulness expressed by the film emerges out of 'the beauteousness within the rigours of this life, and the power and joy of the sensuosity, and the "meat joy" as Michael McClure would put it, a poet who understood this work I felt better than any other poet'.[6] And in his 1992 essay 'Credo', Brakhage wrote of the necessity of the mind maintaining a sensuousness in its thought processes, a need to remain in contact with '[t]remors [that] arise along the whole length of the body', so that the visual manifestations of touch produce an 'object reflectively worthy of the moving lights of the mind which made it'.[7] Brakhage liberates the eye by establishing its sensuous dependence upon a body always in states of change and in continual contact with the world.

For Brakhage, film offered the possibility of documenting the 'lights of the mind'. He sought equivalencies through unconventional appropriations of cinematic technology to record visual experiences he called 'closed-eye', 'hypnagogic' and 'moving visual thinking'. Closed-eye vision refers to the movements and colours of light seen when the eyes are shut. They are typically shifting swarms of visual noise produced by stimulation of the photoreceptor cells in the retina. Hypnagogia are hallucinatory experiences that occur in the transition from wakefulness to sleep. For example, Brakhage recalled the spectral transformation of his first wife Jane as he drifted in a semi-conscious trance state whilst she read.[8] Moving visual thinking is what Brakhage termed the constant stream of colours generated by the body as manifestations of emotional and sensational states. These cellular illuminations are not caused by external receptions of light but by impulses of the nervous system. Brakhage believed these to be the ground of all sight and thought.[9]

As well as examining Brakhage's attempts to represent such phenomena, this essay will explore other relationships between the eye and the hand in his film-making. The application of paints, dyes and materials directly to film stock appertains to a tactile and manual investment in Brakhage's working process. This intimate connection to the material of film can be found across his career, from the scratched titles (that would become a signature for much of his film-making) in *Desistfilm* (1954) to his last completed film *Chinese Series* (2003) in which he made fragmented ideogrammatic marks with his fingernails, scratching off emulsion from the surface of celluloid. Brakhage's gestural use of camera movement also attests to a proprioceptive engagement with technology in making images. He spoke of practicing holding and moving with devices 'so the camera could become one with my body. It wasn't to increase control so much as to increase the possibilities of emoted feeling that might have moved through me into that camera when I was shooting'.[10]

All of these different approaches to film-making show a continued involvement with relationships between vision and touch. These relationships were important to Brakhage's commitment in emancipating personal vision from an ocularcentric bias dominant in cultural understandings of sensory perception: an understanding that determines and appropriates the function of sight as corroborating a reality known through the rationality of logocentric thought. This essay will show that the relationships between the eye and the hand active in Brakhage's work are not limited to a specific period of his film-making. Rather, they were strategies he returned to frequently as a way of resisting a cultural dominance of ocularcentrism in the organisation of the body's senses, and to a logocentric dichotomy in which the mind is separated and privileged over the body. His work explores experiences of knowledge and perception attained through perpetual sensuous and material interactions of bodies, both one's own and others. For Brakhage, this type of knowledge realised the beauty of an ever-changing interaction between things and the constant opening of possibilities to new ways of seeing inherent in perceptual experience.

Criticism of, and resistance to, ocularcentrism in some ways reaffirms the broader aesthetic tradition of Romanticism that writers such as P. Adams Sitney, R. Bruce Elder and David E. James have identified in Brakhage's film-making. Yet it also offers a new approach to the way we view this tradition. As Martin Jay finds, criticism of ocularcentrism began to emerge in thinkers of the Enlightenment and continued in the writings of Romantic poets and philosophers. In the twentieth century it came to be one of the key concerns of French philosophers, such as Jean-Paul Sartre, Jacques Derrida and Michel Foucault, whose denigration of visual hegemony circulated around questions of power and control in cultural and social practices. Underlying this concern lay a wariness towards the normalising function to which vision could be appropriated, making it valorise a specific ideological view of the world to the detriment, repression and negation of that which did not conform to this view.[11]

It is in this light that the chapter draws upon developments in recent French philosophy, which continue to criticise the dominance of ocularcentrism, as well as illuminating relationships between vision and touch that offer new approaches to Brakhage's film-making. In his writing on Francis Bacon's painting, Gilles Deleuze proposes four ways in which the eye and the hand form a relationship in regard to the production of the work of art and the encounter of the viewer with the work of art. Firstly, there is that which Deleuze terms the *digital*. In this relationship the eye dominates over the hand, the finger acting only as an identifier of objects for vision that are already coded in accord with the recognition of a logocentric thought. Secondly, the *tactile*, where the eye retains its dominance in identifying things but incorporates textural elements into vision. Deleuze gives examples 'such as depth, contour, relief', but these are still part of a coded optical representation of space. The *manual* is the third relation that Deleuze identifies. The hand and touch dominate over the eye and vision, with the eye being unable to focus, get bearings or rest. The eye experiences a purely textural space that exceeds its foveal normativity. Finally, there is the *haptic*, in which neither the eye is subordinated to the hand nor the hand to the eye, but where the eye takes on a quality of touching that does not rely on the hand yet does not impose an optical coding on that which is visible.[12]

Deleuze's writing does not oppose a digital visuality in favour of a haptic one as such. Rather, his writing shows a multifaceted and shifting nature operative across these four relationships in Bacon's work and his practice of painting. Undeniably Bacon's approach to painting counters the traditional dominance of representation in portraiture and landscape generally. The mingling of sensuousness implicit in the operations of the eye and the hand through haptic relations are also certainly privileged as a way to emancipate a particular visibility of figures from this tradition. But Deleuze also writes of Bacon's use of figures operating between two extremes: on the one hand, this 'exposition of a purely optical space', and on the other hand, 'the imposition of a violent manual space', correlating with contemporaneous practices in the work of painters such as Jackson Pollock, Mark Rothko and Willem de Kooning.[13] In his practice of making images Bacon was forced to develop and work through these tendencies in Western painting in order for a haptic relation to emerge. This is a relation that contrary to assertions of modernity, both Deleuze and Bacon traced to Egyptian hieroglyphs.

Similarly, Brakhage's engagement with ways of seeing does not denigrate a digital or tactile form of seeing in favour of manual or haptic relations between vision and touch. Brakhage believed that the pictorial representation of perspective in Renaissance painting, which utilised a tactile colouration in its representative rendering of three-dimensional space, had come to create a normative model for the way the world should be seen. He also believed that this dominance pervaded the technological development of film technologies in the nineteenth century, and continued to be reinforced by mainstream narrative cinema. Brakhage's attack is levelled at the normalisation of scopic distance rather than Renaissance perspective itself, which for him is merely one among an infinitude of possibilities of visual experience. In his essay 'Geometric versus Meat-Ineffable' he wrote:

> There is an almost endless variety of perspectives represented in human drawing and painting. It is difficult to realize that each of them is as [sic] sure corollary of what, eventually, their culture's people saw as Reality, as it is to recognize Renaissance perspective as but *another*, among many, realities …[14]

This essay will closely explore a selection of films across Brakhage's film-making practice, from his first film *Interim* (1952) through to his late films *Lovesong* (2001) and *Chinese Series*. This will show that relationships between vision and touch were not limited to a particular period of his film-making but were an aspect of a sustained attempt to emancipate vision from cultural strictures that Brakhage believed determined, negated and repressed possibilities of visual experience. A closely related criticism of ocularcentrism through relations of the eye and the hand in writings by French thinkers like Deleuze provides new approaches to exploring this relationship in Brakhage's film-making. His influence on film theorists such as Laura U. Marks and Laura McMahon, and Deleuze's own exploration of touch in cinema developed through the films of such directors as Robert Bresson, also opens up Brakhage's work to a dialogue with other film-makers working both within and outside the industry mainstream that his film-making has typically been distinguished from. It is in this sense that approaching Brakhage's work in terms of touch and vision offers a new way to connect his film-making and writing with broader themes within film studies.

Interim

A boy (Walter Newcomb) trudges along a highway between two distant urban areas. Vehicles cruise past on the smooth asphalt. He pauses in his journey to light a cigarette and looks out over the railings. The perspective cuts from a shot in third-person viewpoint to a shot in first-person, and we survey the scene through the boy's eyes. Panning across the grey urban horizon he sees its meeting point with the highway in the distance. Here his vision lands on a closer object, a staircase that descends to a space removed and different from the highway and the urban areas it adjoins. Below the highway exists a wasteland with unkempt grass, weeds, small broken wooden shacks that are barely standing, and the concrete structural supports of the road above. The boy, instead of continuing his trudge toward the high-rise buildings, steps down into this other world.

From the highway the surveying gaze allows the different spaces to be united and mapped together. It provides spatial distance from, and between, areas and objects that allows them to be oriented and individuated as parts making up a whole in the field of vision. Yet, once the boy descends into the wasteland space this type of seeing is no longer possible. Rather than being surveyable the adjacent spaces of concrete and scrub feel disconnected and different from one another. The revelation of each space is not available from a static viewpoint and through a distanced vision, but can only be encountered by moving through this space. The boy meets a girl (Janice Hubka) in the concrete underpass. The couple wander through a maze of concrete supports, crossing train tracks, following the course of a river along its bank, before escaping a downpour by running across a field and seeking shelter in a dilapidated shack. Their journey through this space is not and cannot be mapped out by vision, putting it in stark contrast with the way of seeing that makes the journey possible on the highway.

It is this contrast that disrupts ocularcentrism in *Interim*, aided by a growing intimacy between the boy and girl as they wander through the wasteland space. The surveying gaze is determined by the dominance of the eye positioned at a static and distant vantage point to the world it views. There are movements between a tactile and a digital dominance of the eye over the hand in the opening sequence. The digital allows for the mapping out and identification of spaces in relation to one another, uniting them and making them function in relation to one another: the highway connects the urban areas making the wasteland below a space to be passed over in haste. But the perspectival depth, a tactile object of vision, gives the road a sense of claustrophobia in relation to the openness of the wasteland. The boy's gestures figure his aversion to the confines of the road, and his surveillance shows him a way to escape to a different type of space.

The journey through the disconnected spaces of the wasteland no longer operates through surveillance, and the domination of the eye in its digital and tactile relationships oscillates with a vision that, as Deleuze writes, 'makes touch an object of view in itself'.[15] Deleuze makes this comment about Bresson's *Pickpocket*

(1959), in which a passage around the Gare de Lyon is presented in fragments connected by three thieves circulating stolen objects. These images, framed closely on the hands of the thieves, display the dexterity of their movement in procuring wallets and watches from commuters in the station. But the thieves also traverse the space through the touching of objects and the exchange of these objects between each other. As viewers we circulate around the space, which is shown by these close framings whose primary object is the touch of fingers, without gaining any overall description of the station or identification with the characters in the space. Deleuze writes that in this scene 'it is the whole eye which doubles its optical function by a specifically haptic one'.[16] Contact becomes the object of the scene and that which makes our eyes glide around the Gare de Lyon connecting people and things.

McMahon, in her analysis of *Pickpocket*, draws upon Bresson's own conception of fragmentation to demonstrate how the isolation of hands through close framing, and the type of contact the thieves' hands make with others in the Gare de Lyon scene, creates a dependency between people, objects and spaces situated in the fleeting acts of touch.[17] In *Pickpocket* this dependency is made visible in a touch that must simultaneously make contact with parts of others, yet be so slight and localised as to go undetected. As McMahon writes, 'what interests Bresson is perhaps not so much the reunion of souls as *l'entre nous* [the between-us], the simultaneous contact and spacing of the in-between'.[18] Michel (Martin La Salle) describes the dexterity of the touch of thieves as a grace, and it is this grace that is figured in 'an emphasis upon surfaces in contact rather than identificatory bonds' with a represented character.[19] For McMahon, the limits of a body to be both in communion with and yet separate from another are made visible in *Pickpocket* through this graceful touch, creating 'a tension between the spiritual and the corporeal, between the ineffable and the material'.[20]

Interim, as its title suggests, is a film that also draws attention to in-betweens: the wasteland as an in-between space, appropriated as purposeless by the utility of the highway to connect the urban areas; the in-between of a destinationless walk with another, rather than spending one's time on a commute or errand; the break of a rain shower in an otherwise dry day; and, like *Pickpocket*, the in-between of contact between people, the limit of touch and separation of two bodies. Unlike *Pickpocket*, the disconnected spaces of the wasteland in *Interim* are not given a dependence and orientation by the movements and fragmentation of the hand and their touch. The bodies of the boy and girl together enter and leave the areas of concrete, the river bank, scrub land and the shack, connecting these areas that feel separate yet adjacent. In the opposition between the highway's surveillance and the proximity of vision in the wasteland, the whole body plays an initial role. On the highway bodies are marked by their separation: the boy is alone, and people are divorced from one another travelling in private modes of transport in the same direction. The possibility of contact with another is limited by this privatised technology following a determined course. But in the wasteland bodies are marked by the growing intimacy between the boy and girl. It is in showing this growing intimacy with another that hands play an important role in *Interim*.

There are four key points where touch becomes the object of vision. Firstly, the girl touches the boy's shoulder before pointing towards birds fluttering under the rafters of a bridge. The importance of the touch affects the digital function of the other hand directing the gaze, and the fluttering of the birds metaphorically captures something of this first contact between the two. There is a pause, a realisation of intimacy, which is immediately sullied by the boy's response to nonchalantly turn aside. Secondly, the boy places his hand on top of the girl's while they sit by the river. The body is fragmented twice by close framings in this sequence, unlike the first touch which we see in a medium framing of the couple. These two close framings, the first of the eyes and brow of the girl then the boy, and the second of the boy's hand lying on top of and caressing the girl's hand below, echoes the tension McMahon finds in Bresson's film-making between an ineffable contact and material sensuosity. The boy has an attraction to the girl, a desire to touch her. She does not shy from the contact. But there is also a touching with the eyes, a looking at one another, a desire to make contact with the other's thoughts, an ineffable spiritual contact. In the earlier contact between the boy and girl this tension is figured in one image, but by the bank of the river the eyes and the hands are fragmented from the body as the sites where the affects of physical and spiritual contact are located. Close framings of the eyes and hands are separated by images of the river's waves lapping one another, a movement mimicked by the boy's caress. Thirdly, the couple embrace in the shack, holding and kissing one another in medium and close framings, whilst rainwater leaks through the building's wooden structure. Like the rainwater through the slats, some of the girl's warmth and closeness seeps through the last lingering coldness of the boy's demeanour. There is an eroticism in the montage of the imagery of these materials and the couple's intimacy, a relation and mingling of textures given as the object of vision. Finally, there is a close framing of the girl's hand catching a droplet falling from a window frame. The shower has ended and so has their embrace. The boy has become frigid and the warmth of their being together turns to separation and a distancing from one another. Separated at the tracks by an oncoming train, the boy decides to rejoin the highway leaving the girl alone in the wasteland space.

Touch and its relation to vision distinguish spaces in *Interim*. The highway constitutes a space of separation, a distance of view, whereas the wasteland is a space where contact with others is possible and necessary. The space of the highway is determined and organised by this separation and distance from people and things. But the wasteland, in opposition to the highway, makes relations between people and places indeterminate and adventurous in its requirement that people must make contact in order to understand one another.

Interim is not an isolated example of making the touch of hands the object of vision in Brakhage's early films. In *Desistfilm*, for example, the close framings of hands at the beginning show the activities of a group of several teenage friends in a small apartment. One plays a mandolin, another smokes, some are reading, a cat's cradle is being weaved from string, and a tower of books is being built. The tightly framed images attest to the group's lethargy in their idle manual perform-ance of these solitary activities together in the same room. The need to become closer is catalysed and erotically charged when a couple kiss and the activities become energetically communal and participatory: drinks are poured, a circle is formed by holding hands and the group dance by spinning around together. A boy (Walter Newcomb) runs around the room laughing before he is hoisted in the air on a blanket held by his friends. Hands play an important role as isolated objects depicted throughout the film, capturing a sense of touch that is both a joy in the proximity of people and mutual activity, yet at the same time a claustrophobic anxiety in the need for separation following prolonged intimacy with others. Another such example appears in *Reflections on Black* (1955), which also creates a tension between closely framed images of hands performing domes-tic tasks, whilst in the hesitancy of their gestures expressing a nervous eroticism between a couple considering an affair.

Laura U. Marks in her book *Touch* (2002) discusses haptic visuality in terms of an erotic visuality: a visuality that reduces the distance between bodies to become a touching of the surface, the skin, of another. For Marks, haptic visuality is a close vision, where the ability to discern contours and delimitations of objects gives way to an encompassing visual surface. As she writes, 'haptic looking tends to rest on the surface of its object rather than to plunge into depth, not to distinguish form so much as to discern texture. It is a labile, plastic sort of look, more inclined to move than to focus'.[21] Although she builds on Deleuze's discussion of both digital and tactile relationships, bringing them under the concept of optic and haptic visuality, Marks questions Deleuze's understanding of the role of touch in *Pickpocket* because the hand retains its identification and delineation as an object for view. The eroticism of haptic seeing, for Marks, is generated through what could be termed an aporia of identification between one's self and another. The eye does not act to give a person spatial bearings in relation to others and things but explores mingled surfaces of contact where bodily separation becomes problematised. For Marks, the representative mastery of the eye in optic visuality that enables identity to be determined upon others by one's objective separation from them is effaced in haptic visuality by the eroticism of an embodied perception.[22]

Deleuze, on the other hand, makes a distinction between two different types of relationship between the eye and the hand where the hegemony of optical visuality is diminished. The emphasis on bodily surfaces and an eye stripped of its capacity to define and delineate seems to coalesce Marks' idea of the haptic with Deleuze's conception of a manual vision in which texture dominates over sight. For Deleuze, the eye does not settle in manual vision, rather it is continually put in movement by a type of space foreign to it.[23] The eye does not achieve a function of touch as it does in haptic visuality because it cannot rest or focus on anything. The eye is without an object or subject, lost and tractionless in a space ruled by the touch of the hand, a space composed of texture, and a duration of seeing without any stable visual forms. For an eye to gain a sense of touch independent of the hand, the relationship between vision and touch that Deleuze terms haptic, the eye must make touch an object and subject of vision whilst retaining an indeterminacy between the two.

The separation and distancing of bodies elicited by the surveying gaze at the beginning of *Interim* is countered by the affects of contact between the couple in the wasteland spaces. These affects alter vision by forcing it to cede its mastery and enter into an erotic unknown adventure of perception with another. However, this impact of touch upon sight is still metaphorically figured in *Interim*'s story: the montage of images connecting first contact to the fluttering of birds, the caress of a hand as the lapping of water, water seeping through wood as sexual excitement or the capturing in the hand of a single drop of rain as a memento of a lost moment of intimacy. The love affair forged in the in-between space, in this in-between time, relies on touch but it is not touching that makes the spaces of the wasteland dependent on one another as in *Pickpocket*. Yet there is still a haptic sense of touching with the eyes for the viewer in the connection of materials and surfaces, the relations of flesh upon flesh, of flesh with water, and of wood with water. The eye still has a sense of objects and is not lost in a surface, but vision is more textural than optically coded.

The next section looks at the importance of relations of touch in Brakhage's consideration of the developments of visual experience in childhood. Contact and separation are once more integral for Brakhage to show the ways children encounter the world and begin to form social relations with others. Yet, the foveal acuity, which Brakhage bemoans for its dominance and normalisation of vision, is not yet physiologically developed in the newborn baby. Brakhage explores the beauty and terror of this vision in two of his best-known works, *Dog Star Man* and *Scenes From Under Childhood (Section One)* (1967).

Dog Star Man and *Scenes From Under Childhood (Section One)*

Brakhage's film-making and images do not present us with a primordial pre-linguistic eye that could be considered the true reality of vision stripped of logocentric impositions of identity and delineation. As Fred Camper notes, the conception of Brakhage's images as a pure and innocent vision is one of the fundamental misunderstandings that 'dogged his work for decades'.[24] Brakhage himself wrote that 'one can never go back, not even in imagination' in reference to a vision before one has encountered language.[25] In his films such as *Dog Star Man: Prelude* (1961), *Dog Star Man Part 2* (1963) and *Scenes From Under Childhood (Section One)*, Brakhage attempted to remember and imagine childhood by empathetically engaging with his own children's developments in familial life. Filmically presenting this process makes vision into an experiential loosening of the bonds of language that for him determined the transition from childhood into adulthood. It is in such a context that manual and haptic relations between vision and touch play a key role in Brakhage's film-making that orients around epistemological reflexivity and revelation.

In the opening sequences of *Dog Star Man: Prelude* and *Scenes From Under Childhood (Section One)* red tones pulsate and fill the screen. These hues are warm and fleshy, making the texture of the image appear like the transparency of sunlight permeating the skin of the eyelids. The beating and throbbing of this luminous tonal range creates a manual visibility that alludes to a close womb-like spatial envelopment. The screen is filled with warm shifting surfaces of granulated colour, which help to generate this sense of texture and enclosure. These images do not provide anywhere for the eye to grasp onto a delineated object, but they are images that feel tactile through the pulsation of warm red tones. Brakhage's meditation on the transition from the warmth and safety sensed from these fleshy fields of colour to other forms of relationship between vision and touch are developed differently in each film.

In *Dog Star Man: Prelude* the pulsing red tones give way to a sequence of flashes of white streaming from the centre of the frame to its outer edges, street lights casting blue streaks, flames flickering, the corona of the sun in silhouette, a pale moon and closely framed images of parts of the Dog Star Man's face, particularly his eyes and forehead. The sequence combines fast cutting rhythms and super-impositions of two layers of images. As P. Adams Sitney writes of this beginning of *Dog Star Man: Prelude*, 'the eye is teased by the speed and shifting focus of these initial elements, it becomes apparent that the montage is in the service of a double metaphor; the opening of the film seems like both the birth of the universe and the formation of the individual consciousness'.[26] The teasing of the eye that Sitney locates in this sequence is evinced by the continual movement that vision is made to make across the frame area, in the shifts of scale of objects, the obscure framing of objects and in a fleeting duration in which to grasp the changing images. An oscillation between warm red tones and colder blue and white tones creates a sensation of expansion and contraction that draws us into a microcosmic vision of embodied human birth and a macrocosmic expansion of the universe. The montage of these elements nullifies the measure that would allow identifica-tion of scale between the macroscopic distancing of celestial bodies and the proximity of the microscopic or closely framed images of terrestrial or biological bodies that will appear later in the film. The screen becomes a surface of equality between these images. The effects of montage are dependent upon a rapid recognition of objects that pushes the powers of a digital visuality. Yet the recognition of objects is continually disrupted by a manual visuality of an eye at times aswarm in an onslaught of non-objectifiable imagery; in fractions of a second visuality touches and moves from the warmth of a womb to the coldness of the moon. Between the textural sensations of a manual vision where the eye is in constant movement unable to grasp an object and the disoriented perception of recognisable objects through a quashing of their proportion and framing, Brakhage creates an imagistic metaphor of the birth of a universe in which the mastery of the eye over the world is subsumed in a frantic viscerality or plunged into the dark iciness of space.

Montage in *Dog Star Man*, across all five of its parts, forms a schema from which the generation of metaphorical meaning is both encouraged through links formed in the juxtaposition of bodies in images, and problematised by the indetermina-tion of these linkages. Over the duration of the whole film, the linking of metaphors gives rise to the mythic narrative of the Dog Star Man's journey to destroy a spiritual tree that connects man with the forces of the universe. Non-objective images of colour-fields, like the red tones at the start of *Dog Star Man: Prelude*, continue to be spliced and superimposed with images that feature recognisable things throughout the film. The manual disorientation of vision interferes with the meaning making process of the montage schema, blocking the determination of any absolute meaning and any dominance of logocentric thought in synthesising the images into a coherent narrative. Instead, the manual relation of the eye and the hand incorporates an aspect of sensual embodiment not reducible to the cause and effect of the narrative. This ensures that ambiguity is retained in any meaning making drawn from the montage of images.

Brakhage wrote that *Scenes From Under Childhood* can be regarded as 'a shattering of the "myths of childhood" through revelation of the extremes of violent terror and overwhelming joy of that world darkened to most adults by their sentimental remem-berings of it'.[27] Red tones once more open the film, but here they fill the frame and take on much greater vibrancy, duration and colour saturation than the slow pulsing of dark patches of red that begins *Dog Star Man: Prelude*. The full-frame fields of red in *Scenes From Under Childhood (Section One)* fade in and out of black like waves. These undulations are eventually broken up by frames of white, then frames of white and blue, which strobe before being superimposed with an outward zoom of blurry red amorphous moving objects. In this opening sequence there is a transition from the manual visuality of the colour fields to the visual recognition and gradual emergence of objects. The amorphous objects, with their blurred contours that blend with one another making the distinction between objects and between the objects and their environment largely indiscernible, rely upon a haptic relation of vision and touch where a dependency is being forged with the outside through a touching of the eyes. The eye caresses these dilated forms, drawing us to indulge in the beauty of the colour and the liquidity of movement whilst evoking the struggle to give more identity to the world through a vision that separates and delineates. This is a transition from a manual vision in which the eye is in a state of agitation and anxiety at being unable to identify objects, subordinated fully to a space known only through the textural play of touching, to a growing recognition of objects and figures that can be individuated, identified and delimited. Rather than the sudden birth of world and consciousness in *Dog Star Man*, there is a slow process across the whole of *Scenes From Under Childhood (Section One)* to those digital and tactile relations between the eye and the hand that allow for the identification of objects as separate from one's self within a three-dimensional space.

Throughout *Scenes From Under Childhood (Section One)* there is a sense of vision in a state of transition. The film's opening images attest to a vision that is ineffably incommunicable, idiosyncratic, and yet at the same time inhibits the differentiation of bodies from one another. For instance, the rhythmic flicker between red and blue fields is like the vital pulse of optic nerve receptors trying to adjust to light. There is the sense that there is a world obfuscated by an inadequacy of the eye to settle, focus and control the reception of light. This is the vision of someone separated from others by their, as yet, inability to see normally. It is an inability that fuels an anxiety in being separated, a fear at being vulnerable in a world that can be sensed but not yet perceived. Yet, the emergence of figures is cast in these same red colours. The figures are skewed flat across the frame, stretching across the visual field. Like the sensation of the full frame colour fields of red warmly enveloping the body, these amorphous figures feel connected to the body. Growing in domination throughout the film, however, is a vision that segregates one's self from others, and in doing so allows for what is visible to be communicated with others through a language that can identify and express what is seen.

Brakhage by no means denigrated the acquiring of a vision that can identify and delineate. Much of the fear experienced through the lack of comprehension manual vision produces subsides with the recognition of scenes in which siblings are seen eating and wandering about the family living spaces. There is a familiarity founded through the transition to a vision dominated by the eye: both a familiarity of space, the safety of a territory known through a shared recognition of objects and orientation, and a familiarity of those around us upon whom we depend, a safety provided through a shared environment. This extends to the mutual sense of care we witness in the film's final image of one child helping to feed another. Being part of a community, in this case the social cell of a family, necessitates the ability to see in such a digital and tactile way. As Marks writes, 'obviously we need both kinds of visuality: it is hard to look closely at a lover's skin with optical vision; it is hard to drive a car with haptic vision'.[28] And this is also the implication from Brakhage's film: that the societal and biological transition of our bodies through childhood, in which optical visuality is developed, is imperative to living with others. Yet the film also suggests that this development should not be experienced as a progression to a more correct way of seeing the world, nor as a negation of manual and haptic visualities in which our sense of self as separation dissolves in a sensuous mingling with other bodies. Like *Dog Star Man*, colour fields and amorphous streams of moving light in *Scenes From Under Childhood (Section One)* will continue to be superimposed and juxtaposed with images that describe objects with more solidity and delineation. And even though optical visuality becomes more conspicuous towards the end of the film, the emphasis is not on privileging one type of relation between the eye and the hand over another. Rather, the superimpositions and juxtapositions of both types of image attest to an incommensurable visual tension between different relations of vision and touch that Brakhage believed to be experienced in childhood, yet are repressed in our inauguration into adulthood in favour of a visual hegemony that establishes the sovereignty of optical seeing.

76

The two films organise the tension between an optical mode of vision and a manual or haptic vision in different ways. In *Dog Star Man: Prelude* the womb-like textural red frames enter into a relationship with recognisable images of the moon, the sun, streetlights and the protagonist's face. The tension is metaphoric, the birth of consciousness is the birth of a universe and vice versa: perception and sensation are entwined with cosmic forces, and it is the Dog Star Man's separation from these forces, and need to make contact with them once more, that propels the narrative of the film. In *Scenes From Under Childhood (Section One)* the tension is focused on the development of childhood vision, in the growing sense of oneself as individual, yet at the same time the necessity of contact to feel social. In the film, one's sense of individuality emerges out of a visual indistinction between ourselves and others, but this separation that lets us orient the world and feel less vulnerable becomes then that which must be struggled against in order to allow contact with others. The organisation of images is not one of metaphoric relation, but of an imagined document that finds equivalencies in the filmic image for the visual development Brakhage perceived in his children's interactions with each other and their environment. In order to expand upon this idea the next section focuses on the way in which Brakhage attempted to find filmic equivalencies for his own entoptic visual experiences by making direct marks upon the film strip, eschewing the use of cameras, to document these visual phenomena generated by bodily sensation.

Lovesong

> I use brushes at times, but basically it's paint on fingers, a different colour on each finger. Usually I prepare the film first with chemicals, so that the paint can dry and form patterns, then during the drying I use chemicals again to create organic shapes and forms. Finally I go over it a frame at a time to stitch these patterns into a unified whole. If you watch me do it, it looks as though I'm playing the piano – it's very quick, very deft.[29]

Lovesong is the first and longest, at eleven minutes, of five films that Brakhage called a 'visualisation of sex in the mind's eye'.[30] Themes of love and sexuality have a recurring role throughout Brakhage's career as a means to explore the shifting relationships between vision and touch. For example, *Loving* (1957) finds Brakhage recording the sexual activity of his friends Jim Tenney and Carolee Schneemann, which she described as being motivated by Brakhage's 'fascination with the erotic sensitivity and vitality that was between Jim and me'.[31] *Lovemaking* (1968) is comprised of four sections, the first frequently shown independently of the others, in which Brakhage documents different loving relations: sexual intercourse between a man and woman, a pack of dogs copulating and interacting, sexual intercourse between two men, and the naked play of his own children whose ideas of sexual difference and identity are emerging through their interactions. As Ara Osterweil writes 'Lovemaking is about what it feels like to bring the camera so close to the other bodies that you can touch them'.[32] Lovemaking draws out two different ideas of making love in interacting with others. On the one hand there is the sexual intimacy of bodies, and on the other hand social and psychic bonds of caring, friendship and fidelity as well as desire. Touching is crucial in these films as a site where the physicality of bodies in love mingles with social and psychic forms of love, the distinctions between the two frequently becoming indeterminate. Other examples of Brakhage's film-making in which sexual intimacy fuels a relation between vision and touch include the Sexual Meditations series (1970–72), Sexual Saga (1996) and Coupling (1999).

Lovesong can be understood as an attempt by Brakhage to represent his entoptic visual experiences by painting directly on 16mm film stock. Entoptic visions are those generated from within the eye and its connection with the brain. They are derived from light activity within the body rather than light received from an external source, such as the shifting colours and visual noise witnessable behind closed eyelids, phenomena caused by photosensitive receptors in the retina being stimulated in their connection to the brain. One of Brakhage's uses of hand-painting upon film stock was to capture and represent his entoptic visual experience and emphasise the importance of these phenomena as experiences of light. Lovesong is made in an attempt by Brakhage to document phosphenes generated during sexual activity. Bodies in contact, mingling together, becoming close and separating, produce entoptic effects through the sensations they generate. Brakhage, having spent his adult life meditatively honing his ability to allow these effects to elude their typical neglect in visual experience, saw these phenomena during the full intensity of sexual intercourse. In this sense Lovesong would seem to be a metaphoric rendering of these inner lights, which elude actual capture by any imaging technology. Yet by painting onto film stock, and utilising the motion of cinematic technology, Lovesong provides the possibility of conveying sensations connected to the event that gave rise to these images. Colour and movement, as qualities of light, are given a sensuous existence by the film, which can be felt in the body through viewing the film. In this sense, sensation is not metaphorically figured but literally figured in Lovesong. It is this relation of touch and vision, which resists the sovereignty of the eye and the separation of the senses, that this section draws from the film.

Lovesong has two distinct palettes of colour. It opens with white, yellow, peach, lavender and red hues overlaid with ragged globs and veins of black. But this colour scheme descends quickly into a different palette of aquatic blues and greens in which darker tones and the black marks become denser and dominate the frame. These two palettes transition into one another but do not begin to mingle until approximately halfway through the film. Before this mingling, one colour in a palette may become more prominent than another, however the two palettes of colours retain their own distinction. Once they begin to mingle, the colours become more saturated and they blend from one to another in each frame much more intricately than earlier frames in which larger patches of yellow and lavender, for example, kept their own distinct amorphous areas without bleeding into one another.

Brakhage's technical application of paint is emphasised throughout the film. The amorphous patches that open the film bear the traits of dried fluid with shifts in opacity where pigment has collected or dried thinly, with some of the irregular curving contours hard and some softly blurred. The black globular marks sometimes wisp across the frame in quick liquid strokes; sometimes their application looks roughly dragged with the streaks broken and trailing from the solidity of a large bead of black. Brakhage also plays with the visible texture of the paint's thickness, layering frames with carefully positioned flecks of white light in such a way as to give patches a glazed tactility, a relief off the surface of the film stock that makes areas of lavender or red glisten with a sticky congealed texture. The relief of thickly applied paint is also created by stepping up and down exposure levels of the image to move visible information in and out of darkened areas, giving the impression of certain patches emerging or submerging quickly out of or into the screen. When the two colour schemes begin to mingle in the latter half of *Lovesong* the black begins to form thick webbed terrains of paint that vein the image creating plains and pools where the colours of both palettes blend and break each other up. The two palettes elicit affects belonging to two different sensations. On the one hand the red, lavender and peach are soft, warm and, with the flecks of light, feel sticky. On the other hand, the blues and greens feel wet, marine and cool. As two bodies of light they interact and mingle together making the shifts in sensation belonging to each palette felt throughout the film. Sometimes the warm colours dominate and sometimes the cool, but there is a continued modulation between the two, which produces a rhythmic affect of these sensations on the body of the viewer.

This rhythm that modulates colours in *Lovesong* is constructed through an intricate and complex form of montage. The montage of images is cut at the level of individual frames. The film runs at twenty-four frames per second, but rather than an image having the same number of frames before passing on to the next, *Lovesong* builds the intensity of sequences through the rhythmic shifts in the number of frames a particular image is given. For instance, the opening twenty second sequence of white, yellow, peach, lavender and red patches overlaid with black marks, begins and ends with the prominence of quick staccato rhythms, and a smoother legato rhythm briefly dominates the montage in between. The staccato rhythm emphasises the discontinuity of the composition of images by giving irregular durations to each image. To break down the first second of *Lovesong* for example: the first image appears for one frame, the second for two frames, then images three and four both appear for three frames, before image five appears for two frames, images six, seven and eight get four frames each, and image nine two frames.[33] Images make an abrupt hold on the eye, whilst the composition and application of painted elements in these images, the patches and marks, are too detailed for the image to be surveyed in its entirety with the brief durations they have on screen. The groupings of images given the same duration, such as images three and four with three frames and images six, seven and eight with four frames in the opening second, increase towards the legato section. It is in this legato section that the images keep much greater visual continuity. There are larger groupings of images with the same duration, for example image seventy-six to eighty-two appear for three frames each, and images one hundred and four through one hundred and seventeen appear for one frame each. The consistency of the rhythm allows the eye to find continuities of mark and patch movement across the images in motion, letting the eye briefly hold onto elements before being once more interrupted. Rhythm is then not a separate element to the affects of the palettes of colour but integral to the sensations that *Lovesong* produces. Rhythm makes speed an intensive quality for the eye. It controls whether a smooth modulation between the palettes of colours can be seen and felt, or whether the affect is one of discontinuity. The legato rhythmic sections allow the eye to catch brief animations of amorphic figures that alter their shape and size, and smooth modulations between palettes, but the staccato rhythms produce disjunctive jumps across frames that break or arrest figures in movement. In these latter rhythms the eye holds to no forms, and it is in such sequences that sensation can either dissipate, through the sudden break in touching that the eye has been performing, or build in bodily anticipation toward another legato sequence.

As with Brakhage's other hand-painted films, the techniques by which paint and dyes are applied to strips of film in *Lovesong* has a deep affinity with painters like Pollock. In the quote which introduced this section Brakhage describes the importance of putting his fingers into action in order to make marks, controlling the distribution, layering and textured drying of these materials to create an image. Brakhage discusses the influence of American abstract expressionism, and

Pollock's work in particular, upon his own practice in an interview with Scott MacDonald. Here Brakhage conceptualised the image making process of Abstract Expressionists as capturing 'shapes related to nerves, to cells, to the honeycomb of the bones, to the synapse system in the brain'.[34] For Brakhage there was an emphasis on biological visualisation in this technique of applying paint. Pollock's use of gesture in his practice, the controlled throwing of paint onto canvases stretched over the ground of his studio, resonated for Brakhage as a way of bringing the body into the image. The movements and nervous energies of a lived body could be harnessed through a manual technique to produce images. But where artists like Pollock may not have recognised their paintings as correlating with actual visual experience, Brakhage's attention to his entoptic sights and the way these changed with affectations of the body provided him with a way to explore Abstract Expressionist painting techniques through film.

Deleuze writes of Pollock's practice of painting as liberating the hand from its subordination to vision.[35] This liberation, according to Deleuze, was a way Pollock averted acculturated figurative clichés in painting, which imposed a coding upon visible forms. Similarly, it was just this type of struggle Brakhage found himself facing with painted film, often leading him to scrap images that resembled landscapes or objects too closely.[36] Yet Brakhage's hand-painted films tend to implement a resistance to the eye being totally lost to a chaotic image where the hand has been freed to make gestural marks not guided by the eye. For example, in an interview with Suranjan Ganguly, Brakhage described his final application of paint as a stitching together of the frames of the film.[37] The legato sections of *Lovesong* exemplify this technique of allowing the eye to grasp a smooth transition or transformation of colour, shape and movement in time. The cost of creating a solely textural space is that the eye is put into a maelstrom of constant, tractionless movement over the surface of an image. This is what Deleuze finds in Pollock's work, where the marks made through gesture extend to the entire surface of the painting, and the typical bearings of the eye with a horizon, spatial depth and identifiable forms are unanchored in an all consuming ground. Brakhage did not wish to make a film where the eye could not follow a transformation of qualities of light in time and this is what the interplay between staccato and legato rhythms provides in *Lovesong*: a transformation that touches the body through vision and ensures the sovereignty of the eye is diminished with regards to sensory experience, whilst saving the eye from being chaotically lost in a manual space where it can only encounter textures, movements and surfaces that hold it in a perpetual state of disorientation.

Much of *Lovesong* certainly still imposes a manual visibility upon the eye. The irregular rhythmic montage and short durations of images jar their visibility and disrupt the continuous movement of colour patches and marks. Coupled with the intricacy and density of paint application in each image, this jarring of the eye makes it almost impossible for it to rest in the staccato sequences that dominate the film. This restlessness was something that Brakhage not only explored through painting but through the gestural use of holding, moving and manipulating the light reception of the camera during recording. Writing on Brakhage's *The Roman Numeral Series* (1979–80), Nicky Hamlyn highlights that 'Brakhage films are restless and animated' and that the relation between 'the apparatus and its subject … is always precarious and unstable'.[38] Hamlyn draws attention to several techniques used by Brakhage in the recording of images for the series, such as defocusing and aperture changes whilst filming, which he believes challenge the tendency to interpret Brakhage's images as solely representative of his subjective vision. Rather, these techniques allow colour to find 'a relative independence from form and function to become a thing in itself'.[39] Hamlyn also finds that Brakhage's use of these techniques 'raises productively ambiguous questions about the place of vision in a hierarchy of the senses'.[40]

The denigration of the sovereignty of sight by making colour and its movement the object of filmic experience (colour independent of its function as coded either symbolically or as an element of normalised renderings of spatial representation) is connected to shifting relations brought into play between vision and touch. For example, the physical operation of stopping-down the camera aperture in a sequence from *Roman Numeral Series: VII* (1980) simultaneously performs both the operation of increasing the focal clarity of the amount of visual information in spatial depth and reducing the amount of light available to the film stock, making the image increasingly engulfed in black which restricts and re-shapes that which is becoming more clearly visible.[41] On the one hand, Brakhage's handheld manipulation of the aperture during filming challenges the orthodoxy of standard and stable light measurement to achieve consistent film exposure, an act usually considered preliminary to recording. On the other hand, the changes in the image that this causes, Hamlyn writes, can be considered as a device 'in effect altering the hierarchy of elements within the scene, or "leading the eye around", to borrow a phrase from painting'.[42] There is, within this short sequence, a multifaceted exchange between different relations of the eye and hand – an increasing focal depth akin to spatial representation where the eye dominates, a manual operation of the camera that imparts something into the image that is foreign to the eye, and a haptic affect that makes the eye move around the image and grasp at the disappearing light and its changing colours as the visibility of images alters over time. These relations between the eye and the hand draw us into the consideration of colours and their production within the film, and also to the consideration of perpetual variance in our own visual experience.

Conclusion

Relationships between vision and touch are integral in considering the ways Brakhage challenged the dominance of linguistic thought over how we see the world throughout his career. In *Interim* the need to find contact with others, abandoning a way of seeing that restricts this possibility in its organisation of the world, propels the protagonist's journey. *Dog Star Man: Prelude* metaphorically ties together the birth of consciousness with the birth of a universe, but both emerge from the swelling fleshy womblike textures of red colour fields: evoking a bodily relation of vision. *Scenes From Under Childhood (Section One)* documents the shifting relationships of vision and touch in infancy, from haptic and manual forms of vision where everything is close and concomitant with one's self to a vision that can delineate forms, encounter spatial depth and recognises one's individuality from others. And *Lovesong* makes the eye touch light in its qualities of colour and movement, as two bodies interacting that produce in us sensations that Brakhage harnesses in his film from his own bodily experience. Brakhage's use of cinematic technology also shows the ways in which he resisted a purely optical notion of the medium in his practice. Gestural movements with the camera and direct manual marks made onto film stock are two ways that Brakhage channelled his bodily energy into the images he produced.

Brakhage's films do not denigrate vision in favour of promoting a truer experience of the world through touch. His films simultaneously resist vision's determination by words and show that our senses continually mingle in our experience and understanding of the world. A key concern within Brakhage's film-making is the way multifaceted and shifting relations of vision and touch counter the normal-isation of vision as a sovereign sense determined solely by the mind. As a final example, his last film, *Chinese Series*, turns the very idea of language's dominance over vision on its head. Through its finger scratched shards of light carved into spit softened black filmstrip, light jaggedly appears 'lying on the cusp' writes Fred Camper, 'between abstractions, symbols, and pictures that hint at Chinese ideograms'.[43] Our eye is led around the frame by the bolts of light and thin shards of ochre and green moving flittingly and discontinuously across the screen. Every so often they form a broken and temporary linguistic symbol. It is no longer the light marks that seem abstract, but the language itself that is an abstraction of the moving visual thought process generated by our bodily engagement with the world. A language is created out of the sensations of being in the world, and the visualisation of those sensations. This is what Brakhage achieves in so much of his film-making through the haptic visuality of light, its colour and movement.

Notes

1. This sense of politics confronts its traditional conception as the governance and ordinance over territories and communities. Following Jacques Rancière's revitalisation of the concept, politics is an operation that disrupts the order of governance by making perceptible something belonging to a territory and community that is ignored by its current organisation.
2. Brakhage, 2001: 12.
3. Boaden, 2013: not paginated.
4. See Jay, 1994: 24.
5. Brakhage, 2003: 15.
6. Brakhage, 'Brakhage on Brakhage', in Brakhage, *By Brakhage: An Anthology*, DVD (Criterion Collection, 2003): Disc One.
7. Brakhage, 2003: 16–17.
8. Brakhage, 2001: 32–33.
9. Ibid., 205.
10. MacDonald and Brakhage, 2003: 5.
11. See Jay, 1994: 587–590.
12. Deleuze, 2005b: 108–109.
13. Ibid., 88.
14. Brakhage, 2003: 74.
15. Deleuze, 2005a: 12.
16. Ibid. Although the translators Hugh Tomlinson and Robert Galeta use the word 'grabbing' instead of 'haptic' the original French is 'haptique', the same word used by Deleuze in his book on Francis Bacon and translated as 'haptic' by Daniel W. Smith in accordance with the tradition from which Deleuze draws the term.
17. McMahon, 2012: 40–41.
18. Ibid., 40.
19. Ibid., 42.
20. Ibid., 36.
21. Marks, 2002: 8.
22. Ibid., 4.
23. Deleuze, 2005b: 109.
24. Camper, 2003b: not paginated. Camper finds that the other two myths that have limited understandings of Brakhage's film-making are: a narrow and dogmatic conception of the role of subjectivity in relation to the perspective of the image; and a misunderstanding of the 'social engagement' in Brakhage's film-making, which too often denigrates the contemporary relevance of his work by brandishing it as apolitical.
25. Brakhage, 2001: 12.
26. Sitney, 2002: 194.
27. Brakhage's notes for *Scenes From Under Childhood*, in Stan Brakhage, *By Brakhage: An Anthology Volume Two*, DVD (Criterion Collection, 2010): Disc Two.
28. Marks, 2002: 2–3.
29. Brakhage in Ganguly, 1993: 21–22.
30. Brakhage's notes for *Lovesong*, in Stan Brakhage, *By Brakhage: An Anthology*, DVD (Criterion Collection, 2003): Disc Two.

31.   Schneemann in MacDonald, 1988: 142.

32.   Osterweil, 2014: 115.

33.   In the absence of access to a film print of *Lovesong*, I have based these frame counts upon the fantastic digital transfers produced for the 2003 *Criterion Collection* DVD anthology *By Brakhage*, which allows step framing through the images.

34.   MacDonald and Brakhage, 2003: 5.

35.   Deleuze, 2005b: 74.

36.   Brakhage, 'Brakhage on Brakhage', in Brakhage, *By Brakhage: An Anthology*, DVD (Criterion Collection, 2003): Disc One. Brakhage here discussed also an excerpted piece of film from *The Dante Quartet*.

37.   Brakhage in Ganguly, 1993: 10–11.

38.   Hamlyn, 2003: 127.

39.   Ibid., 114.

40.   Ibid., 115.

41.   Ibid., 126.

42.   Ibid.

43.   Camper in the booklet accompanying Stan Brakhage, *By Brakhage: An Anthology Volume Two*, DVD (Criterion Collection, 2010): 35.

Colour Plates

Plate 1.

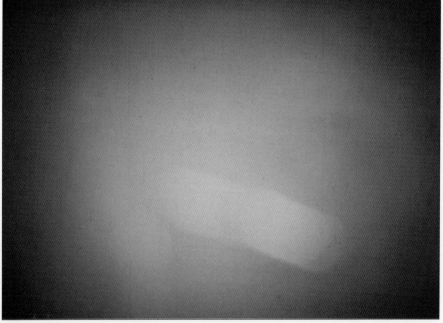

Plate 2.

Plate 3.   *Plate 4.*

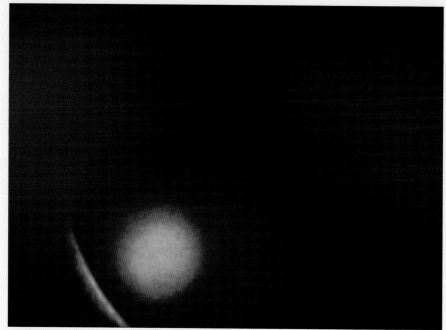

Plate 5.

Plate 6.

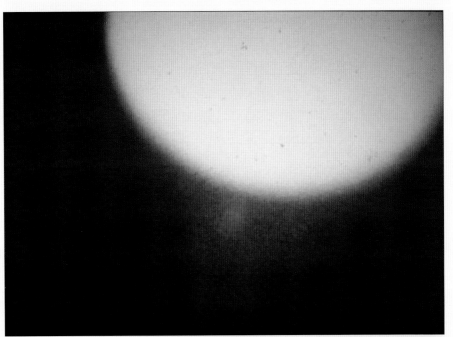

Plate 7.

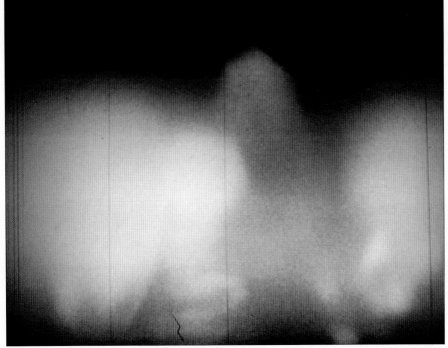

Plate 8.

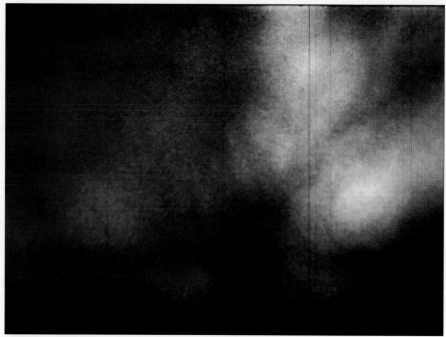

Plate 9.

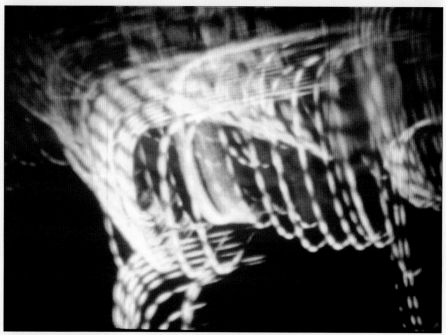

Plate 10.

Plate 11.

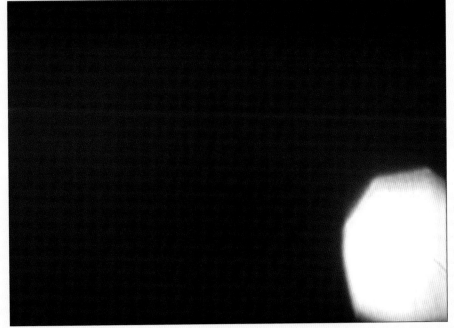

Plate 12.

Plate 13.

Plate 14.

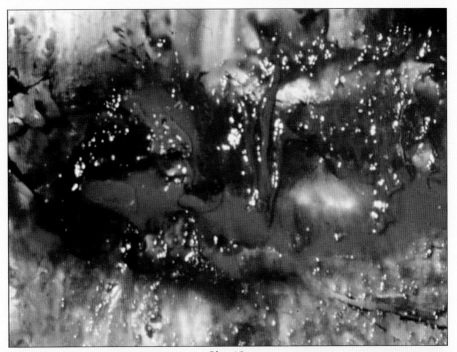

Plate 15.

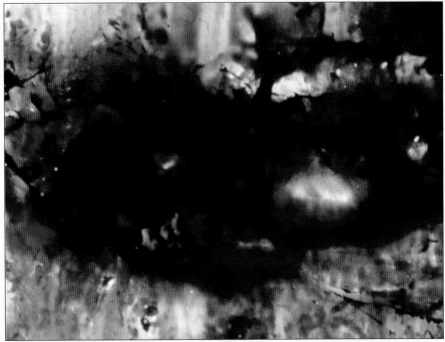

Plate 16.

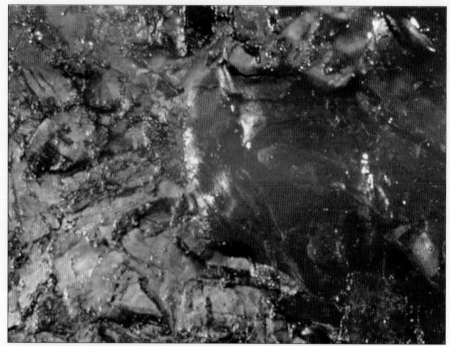

Plate 17.

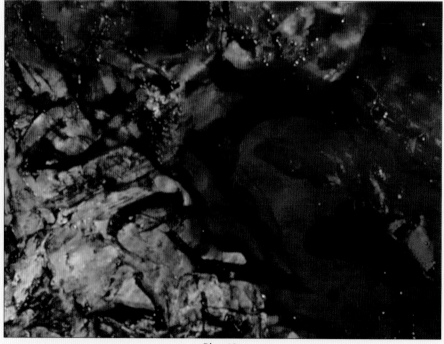

Plate 18.

Plate 20.

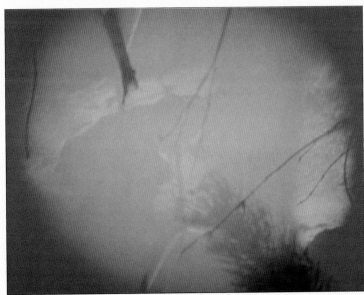

Plate 19.

Plate 21.

Plate 22.

Plate 23.

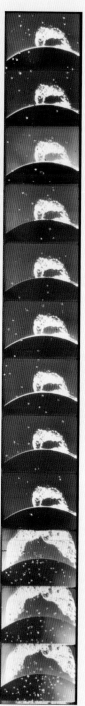

Plate 24.

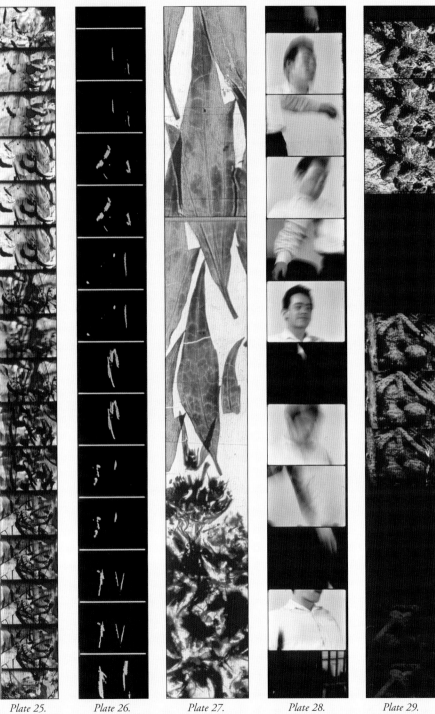

Plate 25.   *Plate 26.*   *Plate 27.*   *Plate 28.*   *Plate 29.*

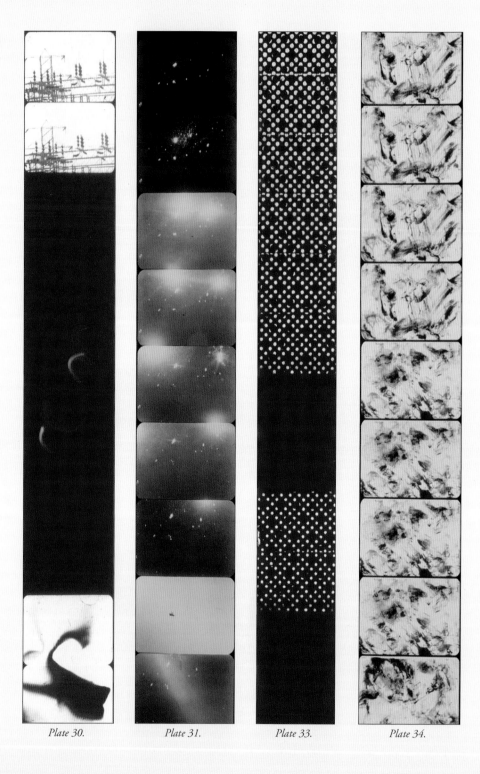

Plate 30. Plate 31. Plate 33. Plate 34.

Plate 35.

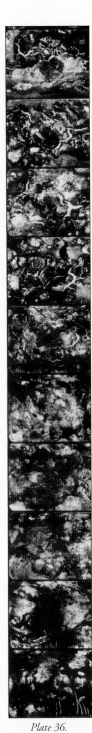

Plate 36.

Plate 37.

Plate 38.

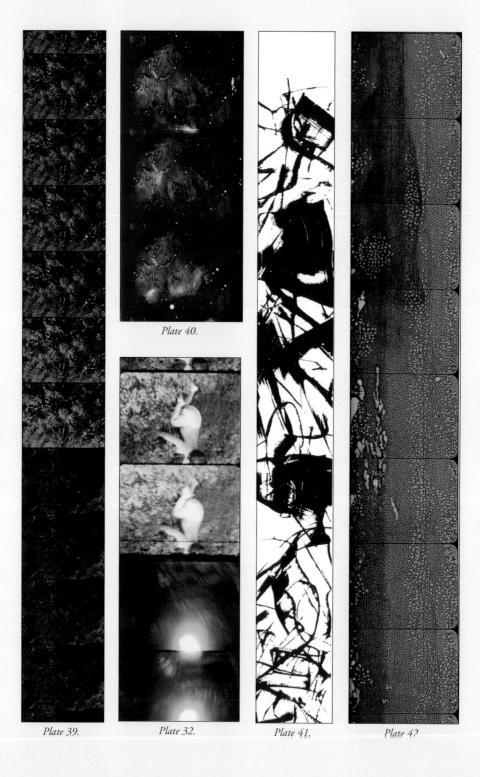

Plate 40.

Plate 39.

Plate 32.

Plate 41,

Plate 42

5　The Renewed Encounter with the Everyday: Stan Brakhage and the Ethics of the (Extra)ordinary

Rebecca A. Sheehan*

For a number of years, the late work of Ludwig Wittgenstein has surfaced in debates about the future of film theory and the possibility of a film philosophy. This essay asks whether Stan Brakhage's conception of Wittgenstein can offer an example from film rather than philosophy of how we might picture the future of film theory and even 'film-philosophy'. In pursuing the question of what a film-philosophy might look like by returning to the late Wittgenstein and by locating there an affinity with certain philosophical practices and methods at work in the lyrical avant-garde films of Stan Brakhage, I hope to illuminate how Brakhage's films practice and deploy renewed encounters with the everyday as an ethics of spectatorship and thought. Brakhage's films philosophise in a way similar to Wittgenstein's *Philosophical Investigations*. They offer a model for thought that replicates the autonomy of linguistic meaning heralded by the late Wittgenstein, and they open that autonomy into a practice (on the part of film-maker and spectator) of interrogating what we already know, visiting and revisiting our own

*A slightly different version of this essay was published in *Screen*, Volume 53, Issue 2 (Summer 2012): 118–135; with the title 'Stan Brakhage, Ludwig Wittgenstein and the Renewed Encounter with the Everyday'.

perceptual condition, its limits and its possibilities: or, as Wittgenstein put it in his *Philosophical Investigations*, solving problems by 'assembling what we have long been familiar with'.[1]

Brakhage's work performs and incites the kind of investigation Wittgenstein in his late work imagined as a replacement to theory through three primary avenues: a repeated engagement with the ordinary or the common; his employment of the fragment; and his subsequent investment in the immediacy of the present (an extension of the meaning-making which occurs at every step of the journey of thought for the late Wittgenstein). The philosophical inquiry that Brakhage's films perform owes its genesis to the work of poets whose experiments with the linguistic fragment and with notions of means as meaning were foundational to Brakhage's understanding of film. Brakhage's translation of Gertrude Stein's puns into a process of visual fragmentation and assembly are central to the renewed encounters with the everyday that we find in many of his films, and also at the heart of Wittgenstein's later writings. The minimalist poetics of Robert Creeley, whose work inspired Brakhage's writing and conception of the image, also stems in part from the inspiration of the *Tractatus Logico-Philosophicus* and other writings by Wittgenstein, and for this reason is helpful in articulating the poetic underpinnings of the thinking that Brakhage's films provoke.

The greater stakes of articulating the debt to, and coincidences with, Wittgenstein's *Philosophical Investigations* performed by Brakhage's films and writings relate to recent invocations of the late Wittgenstein to call into question the necessity and use of theory in the Humanities and in film studies in particular. Malcolm Turvey and Richard Allen, who have argued that the *Philosophical Investigations* and other late writings of Wittgenstein should serve as a 'prophylaxis against theory',[2] explain that Wittgenstein shifts from a theoretical conception of language in the *Tractatus* which doubts that language users know the real meanings of their words, leaving philosophy the task of discerning 'the hidden essence of meaning by logical analysis',[3] to a rejection of theory in *Philosophical Investigations* and a replacement of this claim with one in which meaning is open to view, with nothing for philosophy to explain. In his 2007 essay, 'An Elegy for Theory',[4] David Rodowick characterises a crisis in the field of film theory as it was denatured by contestations advanced in the 1990s on the part of cognitivists like David Bordwell and Noël Carroll and by recent attacks by philosophers who accuse theory of an 'epistemological atheism'. That is, many philosophers see film theory as having strayed from making claims based on the realities of the object. Rodowick's essay calls for a setting aside of 'theory' to examine what a 'philosophy of the humanities' or a 'film philosophy might look like', going on to explore the work of Gilles Deleuze and Stanley Cavell as 'exemplars of the twinned projects of ethical and epistemological investigation'.[5] Indeed, Cavell, Deleuze and, as many contemporary film philosophers have suggested, Wittgenstein can help bridge the divide between theory's ethical objectives and philosophy's concern with returning film studies to an epistemological grounding.

By pursuing an investigation of the fragment and the commonplace in works by Brakhage and in the *Philosophical Investigations*, I hope to reveal that through investing in the meaning gleaned by everyday language users, a model of meaning embodied by the provisional and the fluid, and figured by the journey rather than the path, emerges; and that this replaces the model of completeness and deficiency upon which Wittgenstein's perceived rejection of theory rests. This model of meaning has been illuminated in the *Philosophical Investigations* and elaborated upon by recent Wittgenstein scholars like Simon Glendinning, who argues that the *Investigations* encourage and engage what he calls a 'philosophical nomadism'.[6] This concept shows that Wittgenstein is less interested in giving us in his work a map that takes us 'from A to B' than in showing us how to accept that neither such a map, nor absolute clarity, are required at points in the journey where we are puzzled. Glendinning's illumination of Wittgenstein's tendency to have us 'take some breaks along the way', a way that sticks to 'natural paths', has influenced contemporary views on Wittgenstein's relevance for film criticism. Andrew Klevan has shown how the *Philosophical Investigations* inflects Stanley Cavell's writings on film, focusing in particular upon how Cavell's work conspicuously revolves around 'film moments' which Cavell permits to 'stop him, hold him, and prevent him from going on'.[7] These moments, Klevan suggests, are similar to the 'breaks' we take with Wittgenstein on the 'natural path' of the *Investigations* upon which Glendinning charts Wittgenstein's 'nomadic' philosophy. As Klevan has pointed out, Cavell's tendency to dwell upon the most 'ordinary' moments in films shows how he finds within film, because of its particular ontology, an ability to present the mysterious or the unknowable within moments that can seem quite common and quotidian – or, as Cavell calls them, 'missable'. Klevan shows that for Cavell 'the ordinary lucidity of film dramatization means significance may be readily available but not immediately easy to see (or hear)'.[8]

If narrative film presents the conditions for the nomadism of Wittgenstein's *Investigations* through the ordinariness of its 'dramatization', it is necessary to understand how Brakhage's non-narrative films perform and incite this kind of thinking by engaging the ordinary through alternative means. The ordinary might be said to play a more immediate role in Brakhage's films, where documentary footage of his everyday world permits him as a film-maker to perform the mode of dwelling and return to the familiar, therein to locate significance that may have been available, but is not seen or known, in a vein similar to the 'missable' in Cavell's treatment of narrative films. Brakhage's experimental films involve the same fundamental ontology that plays a critical role *vis-à-vis* narrative films for Cavell, as both kinds of film permit access to 'apparently insignificant moments'. As this essay shows, if anything Brakhage denies us moments that would be deemed significant in narrative films. Rather, his films invite encounters with the everyday through a series of immediate images presented without narrative emphasis or explanation, images which lead the spectator on a journey similar to the one the *Investigations* takes its reader on, the former through particularities of the visual world, the latter through the particularities of language. That is, Brakhage's films explicitly crowd our viewing experience with the everyday and the mundane in images that, shot through filters or projected out of focus, painted over on the editing table or captured at an unnatural angle, make us look differently at such everyday things as a tree, a house cat, a shadow, a vase, kitchen wallpaper. Through repetition and an absence of narrative suspense, Brakhage's films are also able to hold us in these moments, just as the *Philosophical Investigations* holds us and makes us puzzle over sentences that comprise ordinary language. The model of meaning as nomadic, returned to without the 'apocalyptic desires for clarity' to which Simon Glendinning argues the *Investigations* makes us less prone, is precisely the model within which Brakhage's films work. The figure of nomadism also best describes how Brakhage reads Gertrude Stein and Ezra Pound; returning to the same poems time and again, and there finding and re-founding meaning through a process of re-encounter. It is this very journey that he envisions for his spectator.[9]

As Malcolm Turvey and Richard Allen explain, for the late Wittgenstein, '… meaning cannot be explained by postulating something invisible to those who actually use language, something exterior to the practice of using language that determines meaning in advance of use. Instead, linguistic meaning in this sense is "self-contained and autonomous".'[10] By looking at the similarities between Brakhage's films and Wittgenstein's philosophy, I would like to concentrate on the autonomy Wittgenstein imagines for language in the *Philosophical Investigations* in the context of the operation of fragmentation and the fragment through Brakhage's films. I will also consider the renewed significance of common language and the ordinary that emerges in Wittgenstein's later writings through Brakhage's interest in his family, his pets and his natural and domestic environs as he employs his camera to help picture the interstices of the everyday. It is indeed an autonomous encounter with Wittgenstein's language that Stanley Cavell has argued characterises the act of reading the *Philosophical Investigations* – whose fragmented composition as a collection of short paragraphs is resonant with the encounter that Brakhage envisions for his spectator.

While there is a paucity of critical investigation into the philosophising nature of lyrical avant-garde films like Brakhage's, there have been numerous investigations of this kind into the nature of films by structural film-makers such as Hollis Frampton, Ernie Gehr and Michael Snow. P. Adams Sitney's famous characterisation of structural film-making as 'cinema of the mind [rather than of the eye]'[11] is reflective and, for better or worse, prescriptive of the overt consciousness experienced by the spectator of a film like Snow's *Wavelength* (1967) or Gehr's *Serene Velocity* (1970). Extending the descriptions of these films and their performance (as opposed to their depiction or representation) of philosophy to the lyrical film-making of Brakhage necessitates asking not just how film can philosophise, but also how the kind of philosophising advanced by film-making is activated by ways of thinking particular to the poetic. In a 2006 essay, 'Philosophizing through the Moving Image: the case of *Serene Velocity*', Noël Carroll offers a description of Ernie Gehr's 1970 film which Carroll admits, '… may be said, unequivocally, to be an example of doing philosophy through film'.[12] I agree with Carroll that '… in order to make it an instance of moving-image philosophizing, a specimen must develop an original philosophical idea – rather than merely illustrate, recount or record one – and it must do so in such a way that the art of the moving image plays some role in the articulation of the philosophical point at issue'.[13] However, I would like to push even further into Carroll's emphasis on film using its means to perform philosophy rather than simply to depict or display it. It should be acknowledged here that the concern with finding ways to philosophise film without 'disenfranchising' the latter has been the focus of recent work by film-philosophers like John Mullarkey, Robert Sinnerbrink, Rupert Read and Jerry Goodenough. Mullarkey even articulates the affinity between philosophy and film by voicing the 'envy' the former has for the latter in its proximity to 'reality itself' as well as for the general popular interest in the realities it creates.[14] Evident in many recent discussions is a concern with philosophy relating to film in a way that seeks to theoretically clarify, reveal or analyse what films are trying to say themselves. The application of Wittgenstein to film aesthetics seems, then, not only appropriate to film's ontology in the ways Cavell demonstrates and Klevan has illuminated – that film presents the 'missable' in a manner similar to the *Investigations*' revisiting the ordinary. There remains as well a fundamental sympathy between a belief in film's independence of expression, its lack of a need for critical translation, and the late Wittgenstein's notion that language bears nothing not already open to the view of its users.

Carroll's concern, then, with films that 'philosophise' is less unique to the field of film-philosophy than his explicit engagement with the philosophising of structural experimental film as opposed to narrative film. Structural films deal with subjects that tend towards the interests of philosophers, treating issues of representation, reality, language and paradox. I use Carroll here not only to show that structural films philosophise in a way more similar to Wittgenstein than to, say, John Rawls; but also to break down an enduring divide that has artificially separated structural film-makers like Gehr from lyrical film-makers like Brakhage, a separation based on the extent to which each could be said to be 'doing' philosophy.

The philosophising that happens in Gehr's films (as well as Snow's and Frampton's) is not aimed at the articulation of a singular 'point' as Carroll suggests but, like its location in the means of expression, is interested precisely in means as meaning. This is something, as I will argue, it shares with Brakhage's lyrical vision, but I would like to challenge Carroll's analysis here to think of the ways in which Gehr's films create a kind of thinking on the part of the spectator that encourages a re-viewing of the known world, opening the possibility of renewed encounters with the familiar. Carroll acknowledges the reliance of many philosophers upon what he calls 'thought experiments' which work by 'guiding the reasoning of the listener to the desired conclusion, ineluctably …' and parallels this with the 'recognition of movement' towards which Gehr's films manage to transport the mind of the prepared viewer.[15] Wittgenstein's thought experiments function similarly for Carroll but it is necessary to make a distinction between the linguistic experiments the late Wittgenstein uses in the *Philosophical Investigations* and those made by philosophers like John Rawls. As Carroll himself acknowledges, Wittgenstein's thought experiments (and this is as true of the *Tractatus* as it is of the *Philosophical Investigations*) left their ramifications or conclusions unstated, to be worked out by his readers. This openness to view and review is more descriptive of the kind of philosophising we see at work in Gehr's films which are not just meditations on film, as Carroll argues, but models for thinking and for the work of philosophising with which the late Wittgenstein is also experimenting.

Wittgenstein's case for philosophy as an alternative to theory is based upon autonomous linguistic meaning, a concept, as David Rodowick explains, '… exemplified in the distinction between reasons and causes. In a causal explanation, each effect is presumed to have a cause identified by a hypothesis, which may and must be rejected or revised in light of further evidence.'[16] Causal explanation is ill equipped for human action and behavior because agents can explain and justify their actions. Rejecting causal explanation as a model more fit for scientific inquiry which can test its hypotheses against an external world than for philosophy which must rely upon self-investigation, Wittgenstein's rejection of theory brings into question the linear and binary nature of cause and effect in its application to philosophical reasoning. Since nothing about language's use remains hidden from view for the late Wittgenstein, there is no epistemological task left to the philosopher. Ernie Gehr's films focus on the means of image and thought production while disrupting binaries similar to those that structure the relationship between cause and effect. In a recent interview with the L=A=N=G=U=A=G=E poet Charles Bernstein, Gehr describes always feeling an irritation with films that could manipulate his emotions, an irritation that got him interested in '… spending more time with the phenomena of the projection of the film and the environment in which the film was being shown … things peripheral to the cinematic event, the rectangle'.[17] The rectangle of the screen is illuminated by Gehr for what it suggests of the possibilities of off-screen space, with which Gehr was interested in focusing his spectator's attention as he describes getting the viewer to 'pay attention to how things work along the edges or at the borders of the rectangle'.[18] This space at the edges which are not necessarily represented or described by the film itself but happen in the darkness between audience and screen extend Gehr's interest in the 'in between' evident as much in his explanation to Bernstein of how time functions in *Serene Velocity* as his disruption of binaries in his 1991 *Side/Walk/Shuttle*. We can imagine that the edges of the rectangle are also pointing to the cinematic apparatus' mediation of what takes place between the image and the eye. His interest here emphasises the medium as a means that determines and may interrupt the relationship between the cause of the image and its effect or its reception by a spectator. Bernstein notes that Gehr makes time feel as if it has stopped in *Serene Velocity*, as if it is 'opening up', to which Gehr responds,

> There is a linear movement in time [in film] regardless of any other factor – at the same time I work counter to that … I have this problem with leaning forward, with suspense – How is this going to resolve? I'm interested in the present, with staying in the present as much as possible. Many of these strategies are meant to work counter to [suspense] to keep you in the present … that this is a strip of film or to make you aware of the artifice that has been constructed is part of pulling you out of this ongoing thing and bringing you back to the present, is a way of making you present … In *Serene Velocity* … there are different developments that will take place, but I'm not saying that that takes place in time … the idea of infinite space, the idea of something that may go beyond the space that we've been looking at all of this time starts to bleed into this space …[19]

Gehr's later film, *Side/Walk/Shuttle*, gestures to a similar disruption in the linearity of time, not just through the repetition that also characterises *Serene Velocity* but also through a disruption of spatial and temporal continuity. Just as he interrupts the continuous space between the rectangle of the screen and our perception of the image, Gehr's work to 'keep you in the present' opens up a moment of time and separates it from the film's continuous duration. The present, dislodged from the continuity of the film's duration (and its future-oriented suspense), as well as the space of the rectangle's edges, dislodged and illuminated from the continuity of projection and representation become points suggestive of the undetermined, places of possibility Gehr suggests as an 'idea of infinite space'. If we imagine Gehr's emphasis on points of discontinuity as points in between two spaces or two moments, we can better understand the affront of his aesthetic to the binary relationship between cause and effect: Gehr's notion of the 'present' challenges that relationship temporally while the edge of the rectangle upsets an epistemological causality by positing the unthought on the edge, between the illumination of the visible and the darkness of the unknown. Gehr's engagement of these peripheries wherein time and image are linked to the infinite is suggestive of the disruption to the binary of cause and effect evident in the late Wittgenstein's description of the autonomous linguistic meaning that comprises philosophical inquiry. Wittgenstein's claim that linguistic meaning is autonomous rests on the breakdown of invisibility: if nothing about meaning is not visible, there is no epistemological task left for philosophical inquiry. As Rodowick suggests though, the realm between cause and effect does not disappear but multiplies: it is that any human agent can offer a causal explanation of his or her action or behaviour which makes a scientific inquiry that tests its hypotheses against external phenomena unsuitable for philosophy. Wittgenstein's late work explodes the distance between cause and effect into contingencies akin to the 'present moment' and its infinitude upon which Gehr's films dwell in resistance to suspense.

With its panoramic vistas of San Francisco *Side/Walk/Shuttle* suggests itself as an homage to the photographic panoramas of the city Eadweard Muybridge made in the 1890s. Gehr shot the footage for *Side/Walk/Shuttle* from the window of a moving elevator in one of San Francisco's downtown hotels. It consists of shots in which Gehr's camera moves us up and down with the elevator (and we are shown with each go a different angle of the city from the perspective of the elevator) followed by vertical images which move horizontally on account of a camera turned on its side and eventually upside down. The effect is the creation of uncertainty about which way is up, which way down; an effective disordering of the cinematic rectangle. The film achieves a conflation of the binaries of horizontal and vertical movement through fragmenting the 90 degree angle that structures the relationship between vertical and horizontal planes (giving us with each trip in the elevator a segment of the panorama that was not visible before).

This fragmentation is reminiscent of Muybridge's motion studies that break the movement of the animal and human body into discrete instants, always suggesting the un-pictured moments between two positions. By emphasising the possibility for locating yet another aspect of the panorama 'in between' two aspects we have encountered before or another plane of motion between the vertical and horizontal binaries, Gehr's film opens upon the 'infinite space' he describes in his interview with Bernstein. Mary Ann Doane argues in *The Emergence of Cinematic Time* that the discrete instants which comprise Muybridge's motion studies function as points of contingency where the unpredictable and the accidental generate a freedom of immediacy that counters modernity's systemisation of time and models of efficiency.[20] In *Side/Walk/Shuttle*, the hinge of up and down, left and right, vertical and horizontal, now and next, is exploded into an infinite number of possible intermediary or provisional positions that suggest just this kind of contingency. Gehr's films go beyond orienting the viewer towards realising something about film and the process of watching film, as Carroll suggests, to offering the viewer a model of thinking similar to the philosophising of the late Wittgenstein, which replaces the binary nature of causation with autonomy, an interest in the discrete which encourages investigation founded upon revisiting the known and there encountering and opening new spaces of thought.

Gehr's films move in the same direction of what Rodowick has argued is Wittgenstein's restoration of philosophy to its ancient task of self-examination rather than a quest for epistemological certainty. By denaturing binaries of space and time (the vertical and the horizontal, the before and after), Gehr encourages the provisional while finding the other or the unknown within the familiar. Given their shared affinity for prompting this kind of self-investigation, it is perhaps no coincidence that Gehr began making films in the 1960s after what he describes as a chance encounter with some films by Stan Brakhage being screened at a theatre in New York where Gehr went one day to escape the rain.[21]

As Wittgenstein's alternative to theory disrupts the binary of cause and effect with a renewed faith in the autonomy and visibility of meaning, Brakhage's emphasis on locating meaning within means extends to challenging causation at the level of film's image of reality (and, indeed, its indexical relationship with that reality). It is here that we find that Brakhage's disruption of the singularity of cause and effect also questions the unity of the linguistic signifier with an object or set of objects in reality, and that this disruption questions the relationship between language and meaning, replacing it with autonomous encounters between viewer and world (both between Brakhage and the world he films and between his spectator and his films).

The indexical relationship between the objective world and its impression on celluloid is a relationship that film's photographic history encourages us to parse down into one that is essentially between cause and effect. While the index should be distinguished from the causation of philosophical argumentation, it should also be understood as emblematic of philosophy's larger epistemological claims, particularly in the context of the greater significance that the interruption of the index bears for Brakhage's notions of thought. Brakhage's willingness to bypass the photographic process with the unmechanised marks of his own hand explicitly interrupts the causal relationship of the index in films like *Mothlight* (1963), which is comprised of moth parts glued to the celluloid of the film. This film has no photographic origin in the world, as neither do films like *Dog Star Man* (1961–1964) and the *The Wold Shadow* (1972), which involve Brakhage's painting on celluloid. He speaks about the creation of *The Wold Shadow* in a 1977 lecture on poetry and film, explaining that painting allowed him to make 'a full exposition of everything in that place [the woods] that I felt, and I reflected as I sat there painting all those things that Eastman Kodak's film does not usually accommodate. I can't put a camera inside my head to photograph my own optic system as it is seeing, so I have to paint.'[22] Brakhage goes on to describe the laborious task of painting the film frame by frame, and then makes a suggestive leap from the representational capacities of painting to those of language,

> And then as I went on painting, all such places came rich in my mind, all such places as the history of painting has brought them to us. The word "wold" is there because if you look in the *OED*, it is a wood. Originally, it was a wood and then it came to mean a flat place, and then again a wood. Along hundreds of years of the English language, and directly because of the acts of the poets, the word got shifted to mean these alternative things.[23]

Brakhage disrupts the indexicality of the film camera (which engages a causal process) with his painting of the discrete frames, just as his impressions of place interrupt the image of the wood presented by Eastman Kodak's film stock. He articulates this visionary break with causality and turn to an autonomous representation that works between world and representation through a linguistic example that describes a process of catachresis (whereby words are used which only inadequately represent what they describe, the world being far more vast in its particularities than a shared language can accommodate). Brakhage's interest in etymology's disruptions to the relationship between word and meaning and word and object interrupt the relationship between signified and signifier in a way that works against the diachronic time of language's evolution, allowing a word of the past to be employed in the present. Brakhage's emphasis on finding meaning in the means of creation and representation (as well as in the process of a language's evolution) divides the duration of his film (and its title) into discrete moments of contingency.

Brakhage's interruption of the photographic index in these films corresponds with the puns in his writing on film and his interest in the wordplay that interrupts the correspondence between world and word at work in the poetry of Gertrude Stein. In an early piece entitled, 'My Eye' Brakhage warns us, 'I deck my prose with whatever puns come my way, aiming at deliberate ambiguity, hoping thereby to create a disbelief in the rigidity of any linguistic statement, knowing only poetry immortal enough to escape the rigorous belief in any one word-world as a sense-killing finality'.[24] Brakhage's puns engender in language an intention for his films to evoke, with each projection, multiple rather than determined and singular images and perceptions for the spectator. He emphasises this wish in 'My Eye', as he juxtaposes his belief in avoiding the 'one word-world' with likening the 'life-giving' nature of the eye to a spectroscope. The figure of the spectroscope is a generative metaphor for the pun's role in literature and poetry that extends the word to the realm of the moving image. As the pun exploits semiosis, sometimes engaging a word's etymology, the spectroscope undoes the composition of light to create prismatic variation in what would otherwise, or at first glance, appear to be a singular or whole image.

Similarly to the puns that arise throughout Gertrude Stein's poetry, Brakhage's puns often find within a word or phrase a thesis and its antithesis, one meaning and its opposite. In the 'Food' chapter of *Tender Buttons* Stein writes, 'Price a price is not in language, it is not in custom, it is not in praise'. 'Food', gives us 'price', through the sounds of which Stein's prose guides us; 'Price a price is not in language … it is not in praise'.[25] As she announces it, Stein takes us beyond language ('price is not in language'), for the sound, the repetition of 'price' makes it excessive to its placement in a syntactical system. Instead, Stein's syntax points to 'price's' possible similarity in sound to 'praise'. This line in 'Food' entices the possibility of mishearing, mispronouncing and 'mis'-understanding. Stein's play upon sounds betrays that 'price' both is and is not 'in praise'. For the two, while sounding similar, present oppositional meanings: praise is a gift, often a poetic one, for which, ideally, there is no price. Yet, within their relationship as opposites and in their similar sounds we simultaneously find the sympathy that makes them relational words: both denote a transaction, one commands giving while the other offers a gift. Brakhage employs a similar tack in the puns that run throughout his writings, just as his films transform the poetic process of renewed encounters with everyday language into a visual experience. His use of phrases and words such as 'sense ability' and 'intro-spectrum', like Stein's connecting of 'price' with 'praise', acknowledges sense that goes beyond a word's syntactical meaning to indulge meanings that arise from likenesses in a word's auditory presence. Just as the process of reading Stein's puns suggests a departure from and a return to the boundaries of language (which also suggests an ethics wherein one is able to change one's mind), Brakhage is interested in placing his spectator at times outside the visual language of his films. During his 1977 lecture on poetry and film at the University of North Carolina, Chapel Hill, after projecting *Two: Creeley/McClure* (1965) out of focus and then 'straight thru', Brakhage explains:

> Speaking of the sense of meaning that is sometimes in the air around, in the film you've seen, *Two: Creeley/McClure*, the rhythmic song of being out of focus, as if it were in another language, and then seen again straight thru, and having talked a great deal about the means of how such things are made, I'd like to emphasize that just like Gertrude stumbled into means so I stumbled into those means or am forced to them.[26]

Projecting the film out of focus to make the image seem 'as if it were in another language' is similar to Stein's foregrounding of language's means, disrupting syntactical order and employing repetition to find new affinities between words and to defamiliarise meaning. For both Brakhage and Stein, disrupting the means of communication, grammar or the projection of light enables experimentation wherein different language games and directions of meaning can be tried out.

The purpose of the exile Brakhage seeks for the spectator by projecting his film out of focus recalls what has been referred to in scholarship on Stein as her *dépaysement*. Marjorie Perloff has compared Stein's situation of linguistic exile to that of Ludwig Wittgenstein when he was lecturing in English at Cambridge, in the interest of showing how exile sensitises the writer to grammar that is taken for granted by a person immersed in his or her own language. Perloff writes,

> In both [Stein and Wittgenstein's] cases, accordingly, grammar, taken for granted by most writers, who are 'at home' in their own language, and hence are likely to pay more attention to image and metaphor, to figures of heightening, embellishment, and transformation, becomes a contested site.[27]

Similarly, in making the material means of *Two: Creeley/McClure*'s production and projection opaque, Brakhage illuminates an aspect of the image that would otherwise go unnoticed, fragmenting its completeness by drawing our attention to its graphic composition. The reassembling of the film's images modelled by the repeated projection performs the philosopher's task envisioned by the *Philosophical Investigations*. Wittgenstein writes in paragraph 109, which is often invoked for its rejection of theory:

And we may not advance any kind of theory.... We must do away with all explanation and description alone must take its place. And this description gets its light, that is to say its purpose, from philosophical problems. These are, of course, not empirical problems; they are solved, rather, by looking into the workings of our language, and that in such a way as to make us recognize those workings: despite an urge to misunderstand them. These problems are solved, not by giving new information, but by assembling what we have long been familiar with.[28]

Wittgenstein's words refuting theory present a view of language and the common that is liminal. For him, we use our language and therefore it is not unknown awaiting uncovering; but there is something about our language that begs recognition and assembly, an overcoming of our potential for 'mis'-under-standing that suggests what can be learned from not taking the common for granted (for example, hearing a foreigner mispronounce price as praise or praise as price, or seeing an image out of focus).

Brakhage begins his 1977 talk on 'Poetry and Film' by telling an anecdote in which he hears Tagore poetry in Bengali at Kenneth Rexroth's house in the early 1950s, and for the first time finds it to be extraordinarily beautiful on account of its sounds. He says, 'I realized how important it was to approach poetry first thru its sounds. And then I learned, later, that was a way for some people to approach film first, just through its vision.'[29] (After this he screens *Two: Creeley/McClure* out of focus.) The fracturing of image and word into qualities of sound and visible rhythm here takes on an ethical significance for comprehending the foreign and the oppositional. Admitting his numerous aesthetic disagreements with Kenneth Anger, even describing Anger's work as that of his 'worst enemy', Brakhage goes on to use this quality of listening to work and words first through its sounds (what for Brakhage translates into film's motion of 'qualities of light') to explain how it has permitted him to become friends with Anger:

> I've nothing against homosexuality, but I did suffer from it when I was younger [being kept out of certain things in the art world by cliques of homosexuals], so I'm not moved by what Kenneth is. Black Magic! I have no interest in black magic at all. ... So there we are, Kenneth and I, yet we can hear each other's song, or see each other's song in film. We've become friends, and indeed my whole capacity for friendliness to extreme others has increased. This does not mean at all – it means quite the reverse – that Kenneth Anger's films persuade me to his interests, but only that his song persuades me there's something in it for him. So I take poetry to be that area where I would like to see the word 'communication' defined. All the forms of communication other than the arts seem to me involved with persuasion or with advertising and then I am either for or against them.[30]

The fragmentation of image and poetry into their component parts of light and sound not only pluralises meaning in a vein similar to Brakhage's and Stein's puns but also permits meaning particular to the individual to arise which may be at variance with the meaning authenticated by another. Here, understanding the autonomy of meaning becomes a way of accepting one's opposite, permitting the coexistance of self and other – a statement next to or inside its negation, as we saw with some of Brakhage's and Stein's puns. This pluralism would be refuted not only by the singular goal-oriented rhetoric of persuasion or advertising, as Brakhage notes, but also by philosophical inquiry oriented not towards self-(re)examination, provisional statements and their revision, but towards the production and refutation of falsifiable claims.

Brakhage's films and his use of puns present us with various modes of difference as defamiliarisation, the offsetting of the fragment (of meaning or image) from the whole, the disruption of causal binaries through an illumination of means, and the autonomy of 'songs' within film and poetry that can be valued in ways that challenge one another. Stein's phrase 'the difference is spreading' is instructive in understanding images within Brakhage's films that resist the certainty of picturing one thing rather than another, occupying instead a spectrum of texture, colour and light. For example, in *Wedlock House: An Intercourse* (1959), the bodies of two lovers become indistinguishable both from one another and as bodies, taking on an abstract resemblance to a number of organic forms and parts. These images of indistinction or 'spreading difference' follow the disruption of bivalent logic evident in the pun. The pun of 'intercourse' in the title of *Wedlock House: An Intercourse* points at once towards sexual intercourse, the meaning with which the film visually commences, and also to an intercourse of dialogue and communication through looks and gestures between Brakhage and his wife, Jane. The scenes of the love-making shot in medium close-up and then super-exposed makes Stan's and Jane's bodies indistinguishable from one another and disrupts the certainty of what the image represents. The 'wedlock' of the title is similarly made into a pun as it denotes both a social institution and this image of locking and tangling bodies taking place in a private act partly compromised by our viewing. Blurring the distinction between private and public, the film teaches us to view private moments in their relationship to the public interface of wedlock and the consummation of marriage, while merging Stan's and Jane's private bodies with the body of the couple. These images picture the most familiar scenes of wedlock and locate variant meanings within them: the cohabitation of two separated bodies, and at the same time the elimination of the individual in the body of the couple. The different ways that the image of the bodies can mean (as two and as one) suggests a field of vision that presents the same polyvalence of meaning as Stein's puns, and models the autonomous means of creating meaning against the linear clarity of epistemological certainty.

The alternations and exploration of the spectrum between illumination and darkness (especially through the process of super-exposure) gives us a sense of the negotiations between known and unknown as opportunities for miscommunication that occur within the communion of wedlock. The word 'intercourse' in the title locates these variations between visible and invisible as a negotiation between the self and the (albeit intimate) other. *Wedlock House* points to these binaries of experience only to suggest the productive realm of uncertainty between them, wherein Stan's camera makes meaning through moments of immediacy within his experience of wedlock as much as we are invited to assemble the fragments of illuminated and partially eclipsed images that the film offers us. As Stein's line, 'the difference is spreading', signals both the disintegration and the proliferation of difference, these visions of difference diffract the space between binaries where their difference blurs into a realm of plural meaning. The generative 'spreading of difference' in *Wedlock House*, as two bodies become one in the super-exposed image, contests the threat of the social to the experience of the private which Brakhage envisions as he imagines, 'How many colors are there in a field of grass to the crawling baby unaware of "Green"?'[31] Brakhage's binaries that give way to multiple meanings replace this possibility for the diminishment of experience in the face of social language with departure points for meaning-making produced within the uncertain space between the subjective and the objective, individual and social knowledge. Brakhage's nostalgia for 'Green' is another way in which his aesthetics invites investigation into what we already know (but not entirely); an assembly of fragments of the everyday that locate the extraordinary in the ordinary, the other within the common. Brakhage's re-encountering of elements of his everyday life with Jane creates an experience akin to Stein's taking price out of language, and his own early longing for a baby's experience of green, making us visit this everyday word from another direction, letting it incite other ways of making meaning.

In *Wedlock House*, the diffracted binaries of self and other, the illuminated and the darkened, which spread difference in the sense of blurring it (to proliferate meaning between opposites) and also in the sense of multiplying it (to proliferate meaning as the differences between opposites), mirror the production of Brakhage's puns and their rhetorical-visual structure. For example, at one point in the film, Brakhage's flashlight illuminates a curtain for an instant; the film goes black in the next moment, but when the curtain is illuminated again Brakhage pulls it away from the window to reveal Jane's and Stan's reflection. The film goes black and then we suddenly see them reflected again in a burst of light. It is as if Brakhage is staging at this moment Wittgenstein's return to the ordinary and Stein's *dépaysement* of language, revisiting the image as Stein revisits the word and finds new meaning contained within it. At first, the figures in the reflection are looking at themselves (as the curtain is pulled away), while the second time around (without the reveal of the curtain) the suddenness of their gaze in our direction implies that they are looking at us. Taken together with the previous image, this image becomes one of Stan and Jane looking at themselves from our point of view: in one moment we are watching them, in the next they are watching us and then watching us as reflections of themselves. The image means differently as Stan and Jane go from being subjects to objects of our gaze and then objects of their own.

The Act of Seeing with One's Own Eyes (1971), a film that consists entirely of Brakhage's footage of actual autopsies, demonstrates the logic of the linguistic pun by taking particular, familiar images and exploring their different possible meanings. Brakhage employs close-ups of still body parts that we at first take to be living (for we have no reason to suspect otherwise). In one instance, it is only once a moving arm enters the frame and lifts the still arm that we notice that the latter is limp, prompting us perhaps to imagine that the person pictured is asleep. Not showing us the faces of the bodies or of the coroners, Brakhage permits these familiar body parts various other meanings. It is only when he gives us wider shots that we realize that the parts we believed to be living, awake and then asleep are actually of the dead. Brakhage's film explores in these instances the multifaceted but particular meanings of an image, recalling the multiple meanings made by the prismatic function of the pun as it changes the meaning of a word by revisiting it from other directions. This recognition of the multifaceted nature of the image, evident here and elsewhere, is also demonstrative of Wittgenstein's usage of the duck-rabbit image in his philosophical fragment, *Philosophy of Psychology*, in a claim about visual recognition that functions similarly to the pun. Just as Wittgenstein first notices the head of a rabbit and later looks at the outline again and sees a duck (not recognising that it is the same outline both times),[32] Brakhage makes us first see a living body part and then returns our gaze to the same place where the actions of the coroner make use see a dead body part. Like the 'aspect' of the duck lighting up for Wittgenstein, we could have continued to view the body parts without ever seeing them as dead. As with Wittgenstein's contention that being able to see both the duck and the rabbit in the image never eliminates our ability to see only one or the other at a time, Brakhage's revelation of the body parts as belonging to corpses never eliminates our capacity to see them as living. As the meaning of the image shifts between Brakhage's shots, the knowledge of the bodies being dead never succeeds in erasing our first impression that the bodies were alive, lending an uncanny brutality to the following scenes, which picture the use of chainsaws and violent instruments on the corpses.

Wittgenstein's work arises explicitly on a number of occasions in Brakhage's writings about film and about the processes and thought behind particular films. I would like to focus on one of those instances in *Metaphors on Vision* in which he tells P. Adams Sitney that his inspiration for his 1962 *The Dead* was Wittgenstein's *Tractatus Logico-Philosophicus* 6.4311: 'Death is not an event of life. Death is not lived through. If by eternity is understood not endless temporal duration but timelessness, then he lives eternally who lives in the present.'[33] In turning to the influence of the *Tractatus* on Brakhage's films of this period, it is helpful to look at the *Tractatus*'s sway over the minimalist language of Robert Creeley's poetry and the interest Creeley shares with Wittgenstein in ordinary language and the commonplace. Brakhage made *Two: Creeley/McClure* (the film Brakhage screened twice to college students in 1977) during a 1974 trip to Placitas, New Mexico, when Robert Creeley was writing a collection of poetry entitled *Away*, which begins with an epigram from Wittgenstien's *Zettel*: 'One can own a mirror; does one then own the reflection that can be seen in it?'[34] This suggestion of the diffracted possibilities that can emerge within the known is reminiscent of the productive disruptions in the means of representation we encounter in Brakhage's meditations on word and image. As Perloff has noted in *Wittgenstein's Ladder*, Creeley referred time and again in his work to a line by Wittgenstein which he eventually referred to as his motto: 'A point in space is the place for the argument'.[35] Perloff argues that Creeley is less interested in the larger argument of this section of the *Tractatus* (dealing with complexes and simples) than in treating the statement as a terse aphorism to which he attributes his own interpretation. The content of these lines, the aura surrounding the fragment plucked from a larger text, for Creeley reflects his interpretative methodology: to fixate on this aura is to pluck from language everyday words like 'away' (which in his collection of poems under this title becomes 'anyway' and 'always'), dwelling upon their significance as it departs from their known place within a logic of grammar and syntax. It would be easy to draw a parallel not only between Creeley's interest in everyday language and Brakhage's interest in the quotidian during this period, but also between Brakhage's experiments with putting his films out of focus and poems like 'Away' which begins, 'Yourself walked in the room tonight / and it wasn't you. Your way of / being here isn't another's way.'[36] Here, the lyrical voice displaces the concreteness of 'you' (Bobbie, Creeley's wife) with an outline of passage and identity. Perloff has in fact linked this to the out-of-focus photographs taken by Bobbie Creeley that accompanied the first printing of *Away*. Finding abstract contours as one of the many facets of language and image wherein meaning may be located or pursued unites Creeley's poetics and Brakhage's film aesthetics.

Brakhage's discussion of his encounter with the *Tractatus* bespeaks an interest similar to Creeley's in the fecundity of the singular in the face of the limits of experience and language. He tells Sitney:

> I was again faced with death as a concept; not watching death as physical decay, or dealing with the pain of the death of a loved one, but with the concept of death as something that man casts into the future by asking "What is death like?" and the limitation of finding images for a concept of death only in life itself is a terrible torture …[37]

Brakhage describes this episode as having taken place after experiencing daily asthma attacks during the filming of elements that would go into *Dog Star Man*. He says, 'At that moment, I put *Dog Star Man* in cans, stuffed it away, and began editing *The Dead*. As I edited *The Dead*, I worked my way out of the crisis in which I was dying.'[38] The eternity of the present, understood as timelessness, that emerges in the line 'Death is not an event of life' is similar to the infinite space and possibility of all situations which surround the object of Creeley's motto. The influence of these lines from the *Tractatus* on Brakhage's editing of *The Dead* is telling. Much of *The Dead* consists of images taken from moving vehicles (cars and the Seine's *bateaux-mouches*) of Paris's streets and river banks, and of images of its famous cemetery, Père Lachaise, superimposed on one another so that they are moving simultaneously in opposing directions.

The containment within a single moment or frame of two or more filmic images, moving in opposite directions, suggests the fracturing of bivalence in films like *Wedlock House* and the singular direction of linguistic meaning or the indexical with polyvalence, the pun and the limitless possibilities inherent in rehearing and restating. Paris is pictured as at once a private and a public space: we see strangers walking the iconic banks of the Seine from the private eye of Brakhage's camera. *Metaphors on Vision* was published in 1963, just after the period in which Brakhage created *Wedlock House: An Intercourse*; and it is clear that Brakhage's difficulties with 'death' extend his meditations on the common and the everyday evident in a film like *Wedlock House*. Death is frustratingly both known and unknown (and perhaps unknowable). This fixation finds company in Creeley's ongoing thoughts on the commonplace, which he summed up in a 1991 lecture at the New College of California entitled 'Some Sense of the Commonplace'. Creeley begins by pointing to a dilemma that will create a fulcrum for the remainder of his thoughts: 'Commonplaces, that seemed the most apt and specific thing that I'd think to think about: the whole dilemma as to how the common-place is *ever* the case, and as to how one *ever* finds it specific, seemed to me the absolute preoccupation'.[39] A few lines later, he compares the ancient rhetoricians' definition of the commonplace as a 'passage of general application, such as may serve as the basis of argument' to Wittgenstein's 'point in space as a place for argument'.[40] Creeley's thoughts of the common as a liminal space between the specific and the general, the social and the individual, meets in his lecture with the 'common place' as a space of collection (as in commonplace books). The fragmentary nature of the commonplace book as an extension of, and remedy to, the unknown terrain between the specific or unique and the shared is comparable to the articulation of the incomprehensible nature of death exhibited by *The Dead*.

The Dead may also be viewed as a commonplace book, using each frame to stage an encounter between otherwise discrete moments from oppositional movements in space. The quality of death being at once known and unknown poses a challenge to the kind of causal explanation for which epistemological certainty may be gained. The film homes in on this quality, and invites within this ambivalence multiple meanings for the film's images, by superimposing two or more images and sometimes by superimposing images taken from two opposing directions of camera movement. For example, superimposing images of statuary from Père Lachaise over images of living people along the banks of the Seine on the one hand gives a sense of the living dead: the collective motion of the crowds becomes a bleak image out of post-WWI poetry, *The Waste Land*'s picture of the 'Unreal City' and its crowd flowing over London Bridge – 'I had not thought death had undone so many'.[41] On the other hand, Brakhage's superimposition of the cemetery's statues upon images of life along the Seine suggests an awakening of the dead. In fact the camera, in its erratic movements, takes on a Pygmalion-like quality that brings life to the staid monuments, the city's architecture, ordinary scenes of couples talking. The same scene presents two distinct images: the living dead and the deadly living. The same differences within the singular, particular image is also present within the gaze that the camera assumes. At one moment, for example, looking at the people along the banks of the Seine from the *bateaux-mouches*, Brakhage gives us the point of view of an ordinary tourist in Paris; in the next, transitioning from a grave to this same scene, the camera's viewpoint is suddenly that of a disembodied spirit, a ghost. The shots of the water have a similar effect of showing how multiple meanings are contained within the singular. Brakhage gives us a close-up of waves on water, suggesting without a frame of reference the film's placement of the spectator at the site of meaning's emergence. The next shot superimposes the water over the gravestones and statuary of a cemetery. The water has suddenly become the river Styx through which we must visually pass in order to access the dead. In the next shots, the water is recognisable beneath banks where passers-by stroll: it has become an earthly river. A few shots later, the bridges and buildings of Paris make the water refers specifically to that of the Seine. The image of water as a visual motif assumes a myriad of meanings from one shot to the next, from deadly to life-giving, a signifier of substance, a meditation on the texture of the river's reflective surface, to a signifier of place. Most importantly, like Wittgenstein's image of the rabbit (which, once its aspect is illuminated also becomes a duck), it locates within the familiar, everyday images we have seen a thousand times (headstones, water, passers-by, cars) meanings that were open to view all along but perhaps never gleaned.

Brakhage's composition of *The Dead*, as well as the experience he creates for the spectator therein, envisions thought as grounded in the collection of fragments of everyday life, the album that permits meanderings rather than progressions, concerned less with the discovery of a unifying theory (an answer to what Death *is*) than with the permission of locating meaning autonomously as a constellation between various points that can be replaced or rejoined. Brakhage speaks of generating an encounter between film and the everyday that resonates with a 'vibrant immediacy' when he describes his film-making process to a student at the University of North Carolina Chapel Hill in 1977:

> In the case of the film *Hymn to Her* I was just shooting some film, in that case of Jane, as I do around the house, and it fell later into this portraiture.
>
> [Question:] *Do you concentrate in the camera or on the printing?*
>
> [Answer:] Both, whatever is necessary. Preferably in the camera because it's cheaper. It also has a higher energy level usually. It's less interfered with – it just has the vibrancy of immediacy that's hard, very much harder to get later, editing or printing.[42]

Brakhage's attraction to dwelling on the immediate aspects of the everyday (aspects that threaten to become unretrievable in the editing or printing process) puts him into further conversation with the late Wittgenstein, in particular with Wittgenstein's image of the thinking that takes place in the *Philosophical Investigations* as 'long and meandering journeys' through overlooked components of everyday language.[43]

This kind of thinking evident in Brakhage's films is also indebted to what P. Adams Sitney has recently argued is the influence of an Emersonian aesthetics on modernist poetry and avant-garde film.[44] Stanley Cavell's *This New Yet Unattainable America* and *In Quest of the Ordinary: Lines of Skepticism and Romanticism* put the philosophies of Emerson into conversation with the late Wittgenstein in a way that may help illuminate how Brakhage's films can be understood as philosophising, and indeed shed light on the image of thought they exhibit.[45] Cavell notes that Emerson and Wittgenstein share an interest in the common that structures their respective images of philosophical thinking as being responsible for 'finding the journey's end in every step of one's gait'.[46] Wittgenstein begins the *Philosophical Investigations* by admitting:

> The best that I could write would never be more than philosophical remarks; my thoughts

> soon grew feeble if I tried to force them along a single track against their natural inclination – And this was, of course, connected with the very nature of investigation. For it compels us to travel criss-cross in every direction over a wide field of thought – the philosophical remarks in this book are, as it were, a number of sketches of landscapes which were made in the course of these long and meandering journeys.[47]

The nature of investigation Wittgenstein attempts here finds sympathy with the mode of becoming that Emerson advocates in his essays, perhaps nowhere so much as in his oration 'The American Scholar', in which he writes that the materials for the upbuilding of man can be found 'strewn' along the ground.[48] Indeed, Wittgenstein's *Investigations* could be said to be the gathering of materials that had 'occupied' him for the 'last sixteen years', proceeding from thought to thought in a 'natural, smooth sequence'.

Brakhage creates a similar experience of collecting and assembling for the spectator of *The Dead*. Superimposed images challenge the spectator to pay attention to two simultaneous yet distinct planes of motion, challenging her to constantly collect and assemble images between the planes. These superimposed images also create a tangible artifact of collection as they consist of footage stacked and layered as it might be in an actual album. While we are tempted to try to discern what objects belong to what plane and which to the other, the film eventually encourages a unified field between these contrasting images that is suggestive of the kind of gathering Wittgenstein describes in the Preface of *Philosophical Investigations*:

> The same or almost the same points were always being approached afresh from different directions, and new sketches made. Very many of these were badly drawn or lacking in character, marked by all the defects of a weak draughtsman. And when they were rejected, a number of half-way decent ones were left, which then had to be arranged and often cut down, in order to give the viewer an idea of the landscape. So this book is really just an album.[49]

He later notes that he would like these writings to 'stimulate someone to thoughts of his own'. Here, the temporality of assembly focused on the present creates a further disruption to the temporality of causality by which we might characterise the singular argument that would, for Wittgenstein, 'spare other people the trouble of thinking'. *The Dead* offers similar points of assembly for its spectator (whose thinking may be autonomous from that of other spectators), transferring the generative fragment of the whole evident in the pun and the out-of-focus image to the temporal instant of an encounter free from unifying or pre-conditioned structures. Brakhage's films lend themselves to renewed encounters with the everyday, employing a mode of self-investigation that suggests what a film-philosophy derived from and modelled by film rather than philosophy might look like. Brakhage's films illuminate the possibilities of the present when understood as contingent, provisional, to be assembled and potentially disassembled. They cultivate a mode of perceptual thought which lends an ethics of persistent re-examination to the practice of film-philosophy.

Notes

1. Wittgenstein, 2009: cxxvii.
2. See Turvey and Allen 2001: 1–36.
3. Ibid., 8.
4. See Rodowick, 2007.
5. Ibid., 101.
6. See Glendinning, 2004: 155.
7. Klevan, 2011: 49.
8. Ibid., 51.
9. In a lecture titled 'Poetry and Film', to which I shall return at various points in this essay, Brakhage speaks of Gertrude Stein's 'A Rose' poem as well as Pound's *The Cantos* with admiration over their 'infinite amount of meditative possibilities' as he revisits and re-reads them. (See Brakhage, 2001: 190–191.)
10. Turvey and Allen, 2001: 9.
11. Sitney, 2002: 348.
12. Carroll, 2006: 174.
13. Ibid.
14. Mullarkey, 2009: ix.
15. See Carroll, 2006: 181.
16. Rodowick, 2007: 99.
17. Gehr, 2008: not paginated.
18. Ibid.
19. Ibid.
20. See Doane, 2002: 87–89, and 220–223.
21. See Gehr, 2008: not paginated.
22. Brakhage, 2001: 180.
23. Ibid., 181.
24. Brakhage, 1963: not paginated.
25. Stein, 1990: 484.
26. Brakhage, 2001: 185.
27. Perloff, 1996: 87.
28. Wittgenstein, 2009: 52e.
29. Brakhage, 2001: 174.
30. This passage is only present in the first print of the lecture's transcription. See Brakhage, 1978: 101.
31. Brakhage, 1963: not paginated.
32. Wittgenstein, 2009: 218e.
33. Wittgenstein quoted in Brakhage, 1963: not paginated. See Wittgenstein, 1922.
34. See Creeley, 1976.
35. See Wittgenstein, 1922: 2.0131.
36. See Creeley, 1976: 11.
37. Brakhage, 1963: not paginated.
38. Ibid.
39. Creeley, 1993: 83.

40. Ibid.
41. T. S. Eliot, *The Waste Land*, line 63: http://www.bartleby.com/201/1.html (accessed 21 January 2012).
42. Brakhage, 2001: 179.
43. Wittgenstein, 2009: 3e.
44. See Sitney, 2008.
45. See Cavell, 1989 and 1988.
46. Cavell, 1989: 18.
47. Wittgenstein, 2009: xxix.
48. Emerson, 2000: 55.
49. Wittgenstein, 2009: 3e–4e.

6 Perceiving War's Horizon in Stan Brakhage's 23rd Psalm Branch

Christina Chalmers

In Wahrheit singen, ist ein andrer Hauch[1]

'I can't go on!' – to begin in *medias res* with Stan Brakhage's spliced interjection to the 'war film' *23rd Psalm Branch* (1966–67), scratched onto black leader, is to begin with a pivotal moment in his consideration of his own aesthetic.[2] Brakhage later explained the significance of this invasion of filmic space by an authorial voice: 'I found that just as in the world at large, when man as a society screams: "We can't go on. We must have peace", that's when the war is really beginning to take hold'.[3] In *23rd Psalm Branch*, war's ubiquitous death fugue intensifies but never subsides. The thematisation of political guilt throughout the film is double; Brakhage sees himself as collusive with 'thought patterns' structuring war; and he also sees himself as failing to fight against destructive forces within the film's 'war' itself. 'Thought patterns are – as endless as … precise as eye's hell is'.[4] I will investigate this problematic through thinking about collusion and realism as relations to documentary material and formalist strategies: thinking through Adorno's assertion in *Aesthetic Theory* that: 'Art struggles against … collusion by excluding through its language of form that remainder of affirmation maintained by social realism: This is the social element in radical formalism'.[5] Anxiety about formal propriety dramatised within the film indexes the threat of collusion: does the application of Brakhage's radically 'innovative' style efface or emphasise war's horrors? Critics have argued that *23ʳᵈ Psalm Branch* fails to achieve a sufficiently political consciousness of war. David James argues that in *23ʳᵈ Psalm Branch* Brakhage's aesthetic 'confronts its own limitations'; it is in this sense, perhaps, a limit case for that aesthetic.[6] Delving into this problematic of collusion and political commitment, it will be necessary to situate Brakhage in relation to predecessors similarly involved in war's representation. How does he modify their visions and techniques through formal innovation?

Another view of the imperative to innovation – apart from Adorno's idea of its 'negative magnitudes', as he describes in *Aesthetic Theory* – is the demystifying perspective that culture involves recyclage as much as newness.[7] Leon Trotsky's *Literature and Revolution* (1924) attempts to offer criteria for a materialist analysis of innovation. For Trotsky, the culturally novel is inseparable from larger social change. One crux of his argument with the formalist Viktor Shklovsky over the historical particularity of form results in the observation that: 'The fact that ... different classes ... make use of the same themes, merely shows how limited the human imagination is'.[8] This appropriation of 'themes' is not simple emulation, for 'artistic creation is always a complicated turning inside out of old forms, under the influence of new stimuli which originate outside of art'.[9] Unbridled creative fecundity opposes but also invites the process of sculpting material into appropriate form, a process which appropriates and upturns 'old form', perpetually reversing the inversion of art's *camera obscura*, allowing one to see the world more truthfully. The positing by Trotsky of the human imagination's 'limitation' can be seen as antithetical to Brakhage's insistence on the sovereign subject; his argument that the medium of film is 'the visual instantiation of the imperial sovereignty of the Imagination', according to Annette Michelson's rephrasing of his project.[10] However, conceptions of literary influence such as those of Trotsky might lead us to speculate that Brakhage's unease about form is a complex conversation with filmic and literary predecessors manifest in the repetition and transformation of themes and techniques.

Brakhage's relation to political consciousness cannot merely be bracketed away as a case of outmoded romantic idealism, as critics have done. Rather than merely *engagé*, Brakhage could be seen as performing a type of 'autonomy'. In the process of doing so, he exhibits the resistance of material to its own abstraction and becoming autonomous. To understand the relation to innovation and political commitment, one can compare him in theory and practice to his most explicitly political predecessor, whom he discusses in his lectures: Eisenstein, similarly to Trotsky embedded in the Russian revolutionary moment and its aftermath. This juxtaposition derives from *Artforum*'s January 1973 special issue on Eisenstein and Brakhage, which involved different perspectives on the two directors, and which included Annette Michelson's direct comparison in her essay 'Camera Lucida/Camera Obscura'. This contrast requires pursuing more closely by analysing the political situation of influence. In Brakhage's 'turning inside out' of Eisensteinian form and technique it is possible to individuate a complex of attitudes towards society, war and the place of the individual artist in relation to these. Any understanding of Brakhage, further, has been and must be refracted through the lens of Eisenstein as his progenitor; the encounter allows us to 'see thru into' Brakhage as Brakhage 'see(s) thru into' Eisenstein.[11]

In 'Camera Lucida/Camera Obscura', Michelson argues that Eisenstein and Brakhage's 'forms diverge' – they are 'respectively epic and lyrical'.[12] This appraisal must be scrutinised; distinctions between the rational and romantic, the epic and lyric have become critical platitudes in writing about Brakhage, especially after P. Adams Sitney's influential argument that Brakhage oscillates between lyrical and mythopoeic modes.[13] Brakhage indeed claims his work is a kind of 'lyric' art. *23rd Psalm Branch*'s Part II is 'a series of short films that … are rather like sonnets'.[14] The problem of relating an aural, linguistic medium to film is circumvented through Brakhage's emphasis on the visually rhythmic qualities of silent film. He transposes Charles Olson's centring on breath as a rhythmic material in his 'projective verse', onto the visual plane. Olson's ideal is a verse linked to 'possibilities of the breath, of the breathing of the man who writes as well as of his listenings'.[15] The exclusion of certain sensations in silent film is rewritten as heightened awareness; visual cadences intimate deep physiological processes such as the beating of the heart. For example, this occurs when Brakhage mimics Peter Kubelka's flicker effect in *Arnulf Rainer* (1960) on 8mm film (and partly because of 8mm's strictures). Through this effect, like a constant blinking of the eyes, our awareness of how the viewer's 'physiology act(s) in the face of controlled media' is increased.[16] This is a kind of proprioceptive encounter of the paranoid era of new media. Physiology inscribed as rhythm then comes into an interaction with the pounding movements of war in *23rd Psalm Branch*; both acting as part of the same rhythmic field. The bodies of the filmmaker and viewer, whose movements structure the film, overlap with the social body which heaves in its death throes, breathing spasmodically through the fumes of atomic destruction. The body returns to centrality as the locus of creative movement, as in Olson's poetics, but the body politic is problematised as the origin of auto-destructive tendencies.

The eye's exploration of the rhythms of war is tortured in its 'lyricism'. 'Eye's hell' never ends; war permeates the veins of society and one's own veins. In

113

Brakhage's *The Dante Quartet* (1987) the transcendence of 'hell' is a state in which *'Gesang ist Dasein'*.[17] *23rd Psalm Branch*, on the other hand, is a dissonant 'song' in its uneven flickering. Any hopeful and beatific, harmonic accord between natural and social rhythms only exists in rare, *heavenly* states of song such as the *Dante Quartet*. Brakhage's feeling, instead, that he 'must stop!' derives from his difficulty to 'raise grief to music' in a way that documents war's horror truthfully.[18] Brakhage's jerky interjections emphasise a refusal to affirm that society is capable of reaching towards perfection, leaping over into harmony. Yet Brakhage's performance of this faltering *salto mortale* – society's cut – perpetuates a formal strategy of violent, continual disruption which is one with the war itself. An aesthetics of immanence breaks down: he tells Guy Davenport that during the Vietnam War his inspiration only comes in 'desperate bursts' unlike the 'sea-surge, our source of being, in living' that occurs 'when there is no war storm to disconnect' him from it.[19] An unproblematic harmonics of war entails the absorption of discordant energies which threaten an experience of sublimity; an absorption Brakhage can no longer effect.

Metaphors of lyric and song are echoed in Part II's section 'Peter Kubelka's Vienna', where images of Kubelka playing the recorder structure the tempo of the film's cuts. Voltas (to follow the sonnet analogy) structure the whole trajectory of the film, as well as the whole series *Songs* (1964–69) of which *23rd Psalm Branch* is only a thirtieth part. Grief and trauma, memory and forgetting, reach their vectorial confluence in axial moments such as 'I can't go on' or the shift between Part I and II, which moves from a representation of mnemonic processes to a more thorough investigation of historical documents or 'sources'. Micro-levels of formal expectation and surprise within the 'lyrics' comprising the film are related to the macro-level of epic form the *Songs* try to achieve. A collection of 'songs' or lyrics and epic form are not mutually exclusive, something to which Ezra Pound's *The Cantos* (1925–62) attest – the 'most important' book in Brakhage's life.[20]

The interrelationship between epic and song can be brought back to social commitment through the idea of Pound himself that 'An epic is a poem including history'.[21] Brakhage's visual lyre records this history as constant interference rather than melodic strains, something linked to this sense of 'inclusion' as, also, a deliberate intent to be a receptor for historical material. The passive element of receptivity must be stressed here, rather than the form-giving – sovereign – activity of the individual self. For Georg Lukács in *Theory of the Novel* (1920), 'the character created by the epic is the empirical "I"', the 'epic man' intimately connected to 'historical reality' unlike the 'intelligible "I"' of drama with its emphasis on the normative'.[22] Does the authority of the film's lyric 'voice' break down, by playing against other historical voices and becoming one element in an 'empirical' panoply?

One problem of deciding that *23rd Psalm Branch* is a 'poem including history' is that Brakhage has insufficient faith in 'history' to take on this grandiose condition of epic. He rejects teleological history in favour of an encounter with a Steinian continuous present. Among his contemporaries, we see a similar rejection: at a 1963 poetry conference, Olson and other poets discuss 'History' and Vietnam. All participate in rejecting a 'Thucydidean' idea of objective history, labelled by Olson and Robert Duncan 'histology', in favour of a Herodotean emphasis on 'story' – '*istorin or 'find[ing] out for yourself*'.[23] Robert Creeley argues, 'There's only "here", you can only walk in the facts', while Duncan quotes Alfred North Whitehead: 'The congress of saints is a great august body and it had no place to meet except right here'.[24] Olson tempers the at times fully subjectivist opinions of his contemporaries with an emphasis on the way that subjective mediation can be more 'objective' than the historiography of the objectivists. He argues that the rejection of temporal in favour of spatial metaphors (in the use of the word 'here') is a shift away from positivism towards histories predicated on real human agencies registering time's imprint in the present. Moving away from what he argues is an, in fact, solipsist empiricism, he claims, 'you are yourself in the experience of that other purpose', reaching out towards an agency greater than the individual self. In so-called empirical methodologies this self merely experiences and projects outwards the crude materiality of the present.[25] Inflecting these ideas with tones of struggle, Diane di Prima re-writes Olson's phrase in 'Revolutionary Letter #75': 'history is a living weapon in yr hand / & you have imagined it, it is thus that you / "find out for yourself"'.[26] What is Brakhage's approach to this question?

Brakhage is vitally concerned with the types of depth possible in a 'history', but he does not simplistically provide resolution for these questions. *23rd Psalm Branch* scrambles chronology, in juxtaposing diverse scales of reference, locations and directions, his modes ranging from the personal and diaristic to documentary and historical. This is argued as a rethinking of history's relation to the self, allowing Brakhage to treat historical events in the order that their memory affects him in the present. Mixing historical report, memory, and 'visionary' response, he presents evocations of domestic life and references to personal breakdown alongside crowd formations and footage of atomic bombings. Letters to Jane Brakhage write themselves along the same plane that crowds and tanks move across: this movement's axis is the filmmaker/viewer's position of vision.

Midway through Part I, Brakhage links three images metaphorically by cutting rapidly between them; a man digging a grave, a cupboard full of corpses, an open doorway which insinuates darkly the curves of a woman's body. Implications of psychosexual trauma link to greater historical destruction; the film's apocalyptic mood is inseparable from personal convulsion emblematised in the ominous presence of the almost threatening female figure. Eisenstein: 'two film pieces of any kind, placed together, inevitably combine into a new concept, a new quality, arising out of that juxtaposition'.[27] Images synthesise to create a new unity encompassing personal distress and historical tragedy. In Brakhage rather than Eisenstein, is this a centring on the self – a collapsing of the external along the fold of the self, confirming a lyric mode – which projectively accumulates historical material around its gathering personal narrative? Apocalyptic intimations, implied in montages of bombings and Brakhage's correspondence about Vietnam, are a kind of failed teleological possibility, a replacement for historical perspective; Sitney has argued the film is an 'apocalypse of the imagination'.[28] This looping imaginative potentiality closely links to the subjectivism implied in Brakhage's comments on films like *Scenes from Under Childhood* (1967–70), in which Brakhage has it that there is no necessity to differentiate between self and other; infantile blurring of boundaries is a potent 'metaphor on vision' for Brakhage. Such affirmation of a kind of infantile regression, however, while a deconstruction of binaries, implies an aggression that moves beyond the bounds of the family drama, providing the contours and limits for the material used in *Scenes from Under Childhood*. In *23rd Psalm Branch*, Brakhage's formalist aesthetic becomes his own bad object, as society's apocalyptic tendencies become inextricable from Brakhage's surfeit of personal guilt.

Brakhage argues this link between self and historical destiny manifests itself as a positive union in Eisenstein, whose genius is seen as his attempt to exorcise early-life traumas *through* an historic struggle for expression. Discussing *October* (1928), Brakhage writes that, 'the artist-in-him and the revolutionary man were in accord with each other … one of those rare miracles of coincidence of creative person and politics in agreement'.[29] Brakhage does not achieve the same confluence; in the absence of this bind, he cannot achieve a sense of historical transcendence which for Eisenstein is fulfilled in the October revolution. War emerges as an indicator of social contradictions latent in an imagined harmonic existence.

Brakhage's subjectivism does not extricate him from social guilt. It only increases his sense of collusion. Near the beginning, images of a woman's vagina are intercut with naked photographs of his children and aerial views of cities photographed in war. Nakedness suggests defenceless innocence where the eye of the filmmaker merges with the offensive, attacking eye. Not only do 'thought patterns' imported from a war context subject his family to a hostile gaze, his private sensualities are implicated in the visual objectification of cities' topographies. The guilt of sexual memory blends into that of implication in war. Yet, the film also contains a counter-tendency to this imperative to make war familial, drawing war into the family drama. Brakhage later writes to Davenport that he attempts to

> give meaningful form to the newsreel pictures of 1938–'39, treating the 'movements' and 'massings' … as exactly as a scientist would edit the microscopic images of germs to show-forth their germination and, thus, the history of a particular disease.[30]

Olson plays on a similar sense of 'histology' as cell-study in his discussion of history and in 'Place; & Names'. This universalising, retrospective position of scientific historian is at odds with the film's subject-orientation. These can only reach any kind of relation through the figure of Brakhage himself: 'I am editing in the rhythms of remembrance thereof, the most personal (which I believe, as always, to be the most *uni*-versal)'.[31]

The film, thus, stylistically dramatises a condition where splits emerge within a conception of self as universal symbol; there is a type of surface tension in Brakhage's newsreels which is a resistance of these materials against his attempt to deface them into the shape of his own memory. We might use the later essay of another of Brakhage's contemporaries, J. H. Prynne: 'Resistance and Difficulty' (1961), which demonstrates theoretical frameworks borrowed from phenomenology through which we might read this tension and contortion: 'the reality of the external world may be constituted … on the basis of the world's perceived existence, the resistance that it offers to our awareness'.[32] Does Brakhage's historical material function in this way, 'offering' a cognitive difficulty? Images of Hitler, Mussolini and other political leaders are shown in rapid sequence; making parallels between 'liberal' America and fascist dictatorship; Nazi crowd patterns juxtapose representations of shapes moving across the eyelids made by painting on film, showing corresponding patterns in history and optics. At several points, Brakhage draws patterns of circles across the screen over these historical images, such as might be found in a work by Sigmar Polke. These dots attempt to transform the images into plays of shapes comparable to the constantly dematerialising grids of Hollis Frampton's *Snowblind* (1968) or, earlier, László Moholy-Nagy's *Ein Lichtspiel Schwarz Weiss Grau* (1930). The newsreel images, however, resist overwriting or tessellation; they persevere as material produced by *other* people. Brakhage's nets of dots exist on a separate plane which rubs against the plane of the newsreel but does not merge with it; they register a friction. But the image underneath is still visible; making sense of historical material by overlaying patterns on it or juxtaposition more properly intensifies its strangeness and distinctness rather than incorporates it. One of the facts that occasions

Brakhage's guilt is the contradiction of physicality and dematerialisation, as Fred Camper has argued.[33] Brakhage moves between the reflexive possibilities of Gidal's 'materialist film' and 'an idealist negation of physicality'.[34] Trying to dematerialise newsreels into a play of light or instance of 'closed-eye vision' is an attempt to dissolve the resistance of historical material against the attempt to yoke it into subjective presence.

The obliteration of otherness implied in equating the personal with the universal is a violence committed. Brakhage continues as much as he opposes war's aggression. Eisenstein, unlike Brakhage, is capable of fully inhabiting this violence as emblematising an agency for which revolutionary violence has become part of the programme for social change. Eisenstein argues stridently against the more pacifying aesthetics of his contemporary Dziga Vertov: the revolution does 'not need *Kino-glaz* but *Kino-fist*'.[35] Partly because that other he seeks to destroy is fully identified with a social class. Brakhage's sense of universal self appears to achieve only a profound falsity, non-totalising; since he cannot achieve Eisenstein's 'cosmic alignment with a glyph of the people', a larger social body reaching towards a 'universal' condition.[36] This might usefully be compared to the historical proletarian subject, Lukács' 'identical subject-object' of history, with its channelling of violence in the sanctions of the revolutionary party.[37] V. I. Lenin's imperative to 'convert the imperialist war into civil war', provoking revolution, is one Brakhage only attempts aesthetically.[38] In 'Hypnagogically seeing America', Brakhage explains his attempt to combat TV's 'prophetic hypnosis', where the intimation of 'closed-eye vision' in the TV's grainy texture allows images to be easily assimilated to viewers' memory processes. 'HOW to defeat this phony deja-vu? … sharpen the eyes!'[39] *23rd Psalm Branch* is an attempt to 'play the whole trick back in extreme slow motion', making himself and viewers aware of the visual illusion.[40] Feeling he has been 'bugged' with guilt over Vietnam through TV, he launches a counter-attack to its propaganda war, offering a new optical training.[41] His overlapping of social and individual body, in the material body of the breathing film, however, means that an aesthetic 'civil war' also entails war against himself and his own authorial presence.

If Brakhage deconstructs oppositions between objective and subjective historical consciousness, but finds this deconstruction uncomfortable, the question becomes one of the viewpoint from which the universal is confronted. 'Inclusion of history' is not the only element keeping the poles of lyric and epic separate. Prynne's discussion of Olson's *The Maximus Poems* is another interesting light on the way Brakhage negotiates Eisenstein's 'epic' heritage. In order to achieve perspective on the cosmic situation of man one must recognise,

> There is only one place you can see that from and that is from the curvature of the limits … the local trick for seeing it is for doing it by the delicate inversions of the lyric. The larger [approach] … is to go right out to … the burning glass of the whole round … then you find you truly were estranged from that which was most familiar.[42]

The basis for epic/lyric distinctions thus becomes a perspectival relation occurring at this curvature of the limits, which we might compare to the limit case of the film itself. Epic is the condition of viewing from the outside inwards, which gains perspective on the minute particular from the viewpoint of the whole. The lyric conversely centres on a persona projecting their condition outwards, circling the whole back into the partiality of the self through 'inversion'.

Brakhage tries to confound such internal/external distinctions in their reference to directionality. This compares to Olson's ambiguous senses of 'Proprioception' which rely on equivocal neologisms merging senses of outward-moving expression with interiorising self-awareness. Nothing should interrupt the transference of creative energy. Equally, as Prynne argues, Olson's rigid structure in *Maximus*, with its definite arch and direction, is unlike the 'continuous interlocking' movement inwards and outwards of *The Cantos*. For Brakhage, these questions of interior and exterior are always understood as related to cinematographic technology. It is through this technology that Brakhage confronts aesthetic questions of the non-coincidence of truth and harmony. One of his direct interlocutors, Maya Deren, argues that one must acknowledge the truth of the lens' perception, its 'absolute fidelity'.[43] But for Brakhage, the self's projection *onto* the film is indistinct from the recording of external reality. Techniques like painting over and baking film become expressive possibilities rather than untruths or impositions on external material. For Pruitt, the opposition between the 'passively photographic' and 'imaginatively formalistic' increases the intensity of its dialectic in Brakhage.[44] These distinctions may seem to disintegrate but only become more minutely interrelated.

Brakhage pursues his opposition to society's 'war inclination' through a 'destruction of all two- or three-dimensional logic'.[45] How might we understand this link between perspectival logic and war? Paul Virilio has argued that cinematic representation of three-dimensional space and depth has historically acted as 'a training-ground for the dynamic offensive' of war.[46] This relationship penetrates into the essence of cinematic technology: '*cinema is war*'.[47] Brakhage's destruction of perspective is against the '"absolute realism" of the motion picture' for its ideological-technological complicity with this state of affairs.[48] In *23rd Psalm Branch*, he dramatises the process of deconstructing perspective. Images shot in Louis Zukofsky's house show him becoming reflexive about this process. He makes parallels between Leon Battista Alberti's *costruzione legittima* and war photography when he parallels Zukofsky's circle- and square-patterned table-cloth, shot from a variety of different angles in quick succession, with aerial photographs of city grids about to be bombed. The process of achieving correct perspectival composition of a tablecloth's lattice of shapes is a counterpart to shooting photographs (/bullets/bombs) from the sky in war. For Virilio, perspective is linked to 'aerial reconnaissance', which 'became cinematographic' after the First World War.[49]

Brakhage attempts to move forward from this kind of perspective towards cinematic 'impressionism'.[50] Yet, Brakhage's film has also often been compared to Abstract Expressionism. In Abstract Expressionism, rotations of depth and perspective are eradicated – de-rooted – and the visual plane experiences flattening which can be argued as a move into presence. Brakhage desires of the 'camera eye' a 'telephonic compression of [zooming potential] to flatten perspective'.[51] There is a sense that Brakhage's whole project in *23rd Psalm Branch* is to mount his counter-war on the basis of a *disfiguration* of perspective, rather than the confirmation of oppositions (epic/lyric, history/individual, outside/inside) through a sense of visual field and directionality coterminous with 'compositional logic'.[52] The question of perspective is a nodal point where questions of juxtaposition, contradiction and collusion meet.

Disfiguration is anti-figurative, against complicit representationality through the modification of images. Images of roads or bodies are upturned to emphasise the construction of directional bearings. The camera constantly moves towards and away from objects such as bottles and flowers, de-familiarising their perception through fast alternation of close and distant shots. Streetlights flash on the screen as patterns of isolated circles of light against a dark background, superimposed over other images. Their intelligibility as representational of a scene on a road or street becomes strained, since there is no means of making sense of their relation to one another perspectivally. As simply points on an undifferentiated plane, there are no orthogonal or transversal lines that link them together; these axes are obscured by superimposition. Elements of utility are subtracted from the knowledge of territory the image offers, wrenching that visual perception away from optical strategies continuous with military intelligence gathering. The metaphor of disfiguration is particularly apt for the film's use of perspective, especially given the frequent reference to disfigured bodies, as in the footage of corpses scattered from the opening throughout the film. A problematic this might lead to is how to think the metaphor of filmic breath and projective verse without a living, breathing body to which it symbolically refers. Brakhage's war film starts to resemble a kind of undead film.

In Part II the film moves back in time 'to sources', an investigation of the Second World War through Brakhage's impressions of Eastern Europe and his imagining of German histories through montages of newsreel footage. The short sequence prior to the first 'sonnet' shows movement along roads and streets, linking it by association to the opening of the film as a whole with its fast panning along forest roads alternated with images of corpses. The opening interlude literalises the idea of moving 'to sources', representing a journey backwards in time along roads of remembrance to the junctures of historical memory. A sense of perspective and direction, of leaving the 'coast', to use Prynne's phrase, is vital to the functioning of this metaphor. This is also a looking back to Europe. However, a sense of depth is again estranged in the play of shapes that superimposition produces. Instead of being a logical figure which expresses movement along a road, the movement towards a horizon is de-familiarised in the crossing and uncrossing of lines which would otherwise form the parallel lines and vanishing point of linear one-point perspective. The lights running along the roadside are defocused to become abstract lines of light interacting with other, indistinct lines of light and shadow. We see a move away from the representation of a road with a horizon, to a series of lines interposed by lines moving in opposite directions; the stripes of cloud on the sky jar with the projection of perspective in their angular tilt. Car lights are merely a play of red circles. This compares to what Hollis Frampton later does in *Noctiluca* (1974), playing with perspective to make a 'moon' seem like streetlights and *vice versa*. This might recall Merleau-Ponty's discussions of perspective: 'In free perception, objects spread out in depth'.[53] The disfiguration of perspective interrogates the pivots of *temporal* movement too; going backwards into the past is also a move forwards and also a 'continuous present'. The edifice of 'History' seems to be disassembling. The disappearance of the vanishing point is an evaporation of the historical shore, but also a recognition that one cannot escape war's horrors through easy metaphors of spatial demarcation borrowed from war's own repertoire. It does not, however, function as egress, puncturing or a definitive break with the war Brakhage seeks to oppose.

The perception of 'flattening' can, conversely, be seen as a heightened agonistic tension between different perspectives. The visual field gains rather than dissipates vanishing points. Superimposition does not flatten but overlays, makes images deeper rather than merely lacking figurative depth, more textured, more palimpsestic, showing contradictions that exist within a composition, and makes these compositions less univocal. Brakhage blasts through dimensionality to reveal multiplicity. He attempts to render the physiological fact of 'visual-memory's superimposition on any external scene being looked-at'.[54] Superimposition is an attempt at subjectivising the static image as well as objectifying the contradictory character of subjectivity. Juxtapositions of Kubelka's and his own impressions of Vienna show the constant combination of his own and other people's consciousness. Brakhage's multiple perspectives try to incorporate the resistance of material earlier discussed; but in the visual field this is also a *persistence* of, even if an attempt at the overcoming of, 'man-made laws of perspective'.[55] The film militates against perspective even as in doing so it becomes profoundly guilty of its own effacement of historical proportion; disfiguration is also seen as a type of moral violence against bodies real as well as symbolic. This is part of collusion: 'The war *is* as in thoughts'.[56] To end the war, to see its horizon, demands playing by its rules.

Some of Adorno's comments on montage are apposite:

> It is unable to explode the individual elements. It is precisely montage that is to be criticized for … adaptation to material that is delivered ready-made from outside the work.[57]

Adorno goes on to discuss construction's illusions to *Sachlichkeit*, critiquing it as 'plenipotentiary of logic and causality transferred … from the domain of objective knowledge'.[58] Brakhage's techniques of destroying 'compositional logic' also attempt to supersede construction. Can Brakhage's use of superimposition be argued as a kind of writing of subjective agency into film, superseding Eisensteinian montage? As much as turning the old form 'inside out', Brakhage turns it 'outside in', confounding Michelson's senses of epic and lyric by a kind of 'continuous interlocking'.[59]

How does Brakhage finally justify his attempt to 'look upon the horror and then devise some dance with it'?[60] Kenneth Anger remarked that the Brakhages should erect a temple of peace to counteract the 'temple of war' raised during the film's production. It is precisely this aspect of collusion, in fact, which is the film's notional redeemer: 'artists take entirely onto themselves what they are creating out of'.[61] Brakhage tries to self-crucify, confessing *mea culpa* to help his film surmount the point past which his aesthetic cannot go. Ultimately the film dramatises the curvature and disfigurations of these limits: he 'transposes the cycle of guilt into the image, which reflects it and thereby transcends it', voiding his film of self- and social affirmation, making it a negative space of historical representation.[62] It may seem a canny move that allows Brakhage to play the Lord that helps us to walk through the valley of the shadow of death and fear no evil. It is Adorno's conviction, however, that all art is 'contaminated by the untruth of the ruling totality'; Brakhage's is one way of trying to move past this deadlock.[63] Acceptance of failure is implied as an ability to achieve a different, supposedly *truthful* perspective or 'seeing through' (from *perspicere*) – the reflexivity of seeing 'thru into myself seeing thru into you seeing thru into yourself seeing thru into me …'.[64]

Notes

1. III, 'Die Sonette an Orpheus', Rainer Maria Rilke.
2. See Brakhage, 1982: 110.
3. Ibid., 111.
4. Brakhage in Wees, 1988: 46.
5. Adorno, 1997: 64.
6. See James, 1982: 35.
7. See Adorno, 1997: 64.
8. Trotsky, 1957: 174.
9. Ibid., 179.
10. See Michelson, 2005: 38.
11. See Brakhage, 1982: 15.
12. Michelson, 2005: 39.
13. See Sitney, 2002.
14. See Brakhage, 1982: 111.
15. Olson, 1997: 15.
16. See Brakhage, 1982: 112.
17. See Rilke, 2006: 724.
18. See Zukofsky, *A 11*, quoted in *23rd Psalm Branch*.
19. See Brakhage 1982: 79.
20. See Ibid., 224.
21. Pound 1960b: 86.
22. See Lukács, 2006: 47–48.
23. See Olson, 1978: 3.
24. Ibid., 4–5.
25. Ibid., p. 8. This still seems to lack the dynamics of, for example, a Benjaminian historical perspective.
26. Di Prima, 2007: 103.
27. Eisenstein, 1986: 14.
28. Sitney, 2002: 217.
29. Brakhage, 1972: 103.
30. Brakhage, 1982: 82.
31. Ibid., 82.
32. Prynne, 1961: 27.
33. See Camper, 2001/2002: 94.
34. See Gidal, 1989: 16.
35. See Eisenstein, 1978: 21.
36. See Brakhage, 1972: 96.
37. See Lukács, 1971: 149.
38. See Lenin, 1970: 22.
39. Brakhage, 1982: 105.
40. See ibid., 105–106.
41. See ibid., 106.

42. Prynne, 1971: not paginated.

43. See Deren, 1978: 63.

44. See Pruitt, 2001/2002: 123.

45. See Brakhage, 2001: 34.

46. See Virilio, 1989: 35.

47. See ibid., 34.

48. See Brakhage, 2001: 23.

49. See Virilio, 1989: 23.

50. See Brakhage, 2001: 16.

51. See ibid., 23.

52. See ibid., 12.

53. Merleau-Ponty, 1993: 86.

54. See Brakhage, 1982: 105.

55. See Brakhage, 2001: 12.

56. Rendered by Wees, 1988: 45.

57. Adorno, 1997: 73.

58. See ibid., 73–74.

59. Lukács might describe such an interlocking as evidence of 'minor epic form' in his determination that minor forms of epic are not 'empirical' but are moulded through the 'subject's form-giving, structuring, delimiting act, his sovereign dominance over the created object', which 'is the lyricism of those epic forms which are without totality'. However, it remains simplistic to simply equate Brakhage with the lyric. See Lukács, 2006: 51.

60. See Brakhage, 1982: 85.

61. Ibid., 90.

62. See Adorno, 1997: 69.

63. See ibid., 73.

64. Brakhage, 1982: 16.

7 Stan Brakhage's Temporality, Disjunction and Reflexive Process

Stephen Mooney

I've been having (after some ten years of work) an immense difficulty making a splice … I'm speaking aesthetically, not technically, natch – all touched off by John Cage's appearance here, long talks between us, the listening to his music, and subsequent readings of his marvellous book SILENCE. Cage has laid down the greatest aesthetic net of this century. Only those who honesty encounter it (understand it also to the point of being able, while chafing at its bits, to call it 'marvellous') and manage to survive (i.e. go beyond it) will be the artists of our contemporary present. All those pre-tend artists who carry little gifts in their clutching, sweaty hands (the 'cookie-pushers' as Pound calls them) will no more be able to get thru that net than the monkeys who are caught by gourds with small holes in them filled with fruit (monkey grasps fruit, hole too small to withdraw hand, monkey too dumb to let go of fruit, etc.)[1]

Stan Brakhage's body of work stands out as one of the great cinematic encounters with visuality; of the camera eye seeing itself. But Brakhage's significance extends far beyond the world of the screen in this regard, and the methodological encounters with complex reflexive temporality that his cinema engender and interact with is an area of key importance. That his work engaged seriously with developments across avant-garde art forms is clear, as Tyrus Miller points out,[2] but it is in the intersections between Brakhage, poetry and temporality that I find the most vibrant resonances. Much has been written about the artistic and professional, as well as personal, relationships that Brakhage formed with the many poets whose work and methodologies he was interested in, such as the Black Mountain School poets and the Beat poets. R. Bruce Elder's *The Films of Stan Brakhage in the American Tradition of Ezra Pound, Gertrude Stein and Charles Olson* stands as a seminal text in this light, as are Brakhage's own writings.[3] Many of these poets, and the experimental work they developed, can be seen as forerunners to the contemporary (late twentieth century, and, indeed, early twenty-first century) innovative poetics and poetry that I am concerned with in this piece. By *innovative poetry* I specifically mean poetry variously and incompletely collected under terms like 'linguistically innovative', 'parallel tradition', 'avant-gardist', 'British Poetry Revival', 'Cambridge poetry', 'alternative poetry', 'Alt-poetry', 'Language poetry', 'conceptual poetry', and so on; poetry that has stood somewhat, or extremely, in opposition to what one might refer to (again, incompletely) as mainstream canonical poetry.[4] Rather than suggesting that the films of Stan Brakhage, or his cinematic theories, have *directly* influenced specific contemporary innovative poets and poetries, my contention is that through his interaction with some of these poetic precursors, Brakhage's cinema has a tangible and real methodological significance for contemporary work in poetry and poetics, especially those that methodologically engage and complicate the temporal field of the reader. Examples of these personal and artistic interactions abound. He frequently discussed his ideas with poets such as Charles Olson, Robert Creeley, Ronald Johnson, Allen Ginsberg and Michael McClure, for instance, and was profoundly interested in, and influenced by, the ideas being explored in the more experimental poetry of his contemporaries. He sayd, about an 'angry action' of Michael McClure that he related to previous chapters of his own *Metaphors on Vision* book, that it:

> [reminded] me immediately, I only looking-up [Clyfford] Still later, of: "ONE PERCEPTION MUST IMMEDIATELY AND DIRECTLY LEAD TO A FURTHER PERCEPTION". and of that entire section of Charles Olson's STATEMENTS ON POETICS which most perfectly describes for me the working processes which have come increasingly into their own thru each attempt on my part while filming and editing to avoid John's Cage, per chance, these last few years. Per Se: … and then, of principle, from Figure of Outward, Robert Creeley: "FORM IS NEVER MORE THAN AN EXTENSION OF CONTENT".[5]

These interactions were clearly more than simple interests, and extended to methodological influences, as Brett Kashmere notes when he says that:

> Throughout the fifties and sixties Brakhage forged relationships with poets such as Kenneth Patchen, Kenneth Rexroth, Robert Duncan, Michael McClure, Robert Creeley, Charles Olson, Allen Ginsberg and many others. Their ideas, techniques and encouragement had a significant impact on Brakhage's development as a filmmaker[6] [,]

and quotes Bruce Elder, who makes an explicit association between Brakhage and the poetics of Allen Ginsberg:

> Like [William Carlos] Williams, [Charles] Olson, and Brakhage, Ginsberg contends that the intensity proper to a work of art is a matter of dynamics, and like [these three], Ginsberg

contends that the dynamic force that impels creativity is a push that originates within the artist's body and is directed outwards, at the world.[7]

Elder notes the significance of Cézanne's practice to Ginsberg's poetics, and relates this to the practices of Olson, and Brakhage:

> Ginsberg shares with Olson, and Brakhage too, the idea that artmaking should be reactive, not imitative. Thus when speaking of Cézanne's practice of constructing a visual form by simplification, analysis, and recombination, rather than by imitating reality, Ginsberg noted "Cézanne is reconstituting by means of triangles, cubes and colors – I have to reconstitute by means of words, rhythms … phrasings". Conceiving the problem of poetic composition in this way, led Ginsberg to put emphasis on the activities of words and phrases.[8]

From this same *Paris Review* interview that Elder quotes, Ginsberg himself identified his interest in the experience of the equivalent of Brakhage's visual play with rhythm in Cézanne's painting:

> I suddenly got a strange shuddering impression looking at his canvases, partly the effect when someone pulls a Venetian blind, reverses the Venetian – there's a sudden shift, a flashing that you see in Cézanne canvases. Partly it's when the canvas opens up into three dimensions and looks like wooden objects, like solid-space objects, in three dimensions rather than flat.[9]

Elder's assertion that, for Ginsberg, creativity stems from a 'push that originates within the artist's and is directed outwards, at the world' seems somewhat incomplete. Ginsberg himself, in relation to the poetics of *Howl*, was more precise:

> The last part of *Howl* was really an homage to art but also in specific terms an homage to Cézanne's method, in a sense I adapted what I could to writing … just as Cézanne doesn't use perspective lines to create space, but it's a juxtaposition of one color against another color (that's one element of his space), so, I had the idea, perhaps overrefined, that by the unexplainable, unexplained non-perspective line, that is, juxtaposition of one *word* against another, a *gap* between the two words – like the space gap in the canvas – there'd be a gap between the two words which the mind would fill in with the sensation of existence. … The interesting thing would be to know if certain combinations of words and rhythms actually had an electro-chemical reaction on the body, which could catalyze specific states of consciousness. I think that's what probably happened to me with Blake … that there is a hypnotic rhythm there, which when you introduce it into your nervous system, causes all sorts of electronic changes – permanently alters it.[10]

This imbuing of language with the effective capacity that such an alteration implies, relates a focus upon the *interactive* essence of perception that I contend is at the heart of Brakhage's significance to contemporary innovative poetry; perception as a temporally embedded series of processes related to our individual experience of time's passage and of representations of such. Merleau-Ponty described this in *Phenomenology of Perception* as a phenomenological temporality related to the bodily, stating that 'Time is, therefore, not a real process, not an actual succession that I am content to record. It arises from *my* relation to things'.[11] This emphasis strongly suggests the disjunctive temporal visuality of

Brakhage's cinema. The importance of the specific location of the rhythms and tones of his biological self at the heart of his compositional processes in Brakhage's filmmaking has been remarked upon by many. Marilyn Brakhage, for example, states that:

> Going to the biological, rhythmical sources of experience – always returning to biological 'ground' – while continuously and complexly re-envisioning and re-presenting those inner movements, Brakhage worked for fifty years towards the creation of a new, visual form that would not only make manifest our interior lives, but that would give to the eyes something analogous to what music gives to us through hearing – writing, as he did (in 1991), with unwavering conviction, that 'Film is . . . at one with the synapting Human nervous system in evolution'.[12]

Fred Camper phrases it like this: 'Brakhage's films are held together by a unique combination of composition and rhythm, each considered in relationship to the other. Yet his rhythms, particularly in recent decades, avoid predictability.'[13] That these rhythms are held in relation to specific, often bodily, temporalities becomes clear, and as with the poetry Brakhage was interested in, and that which followed, this specific relation becomes a function of the complex temporal operation of specific uses of image, space, or movement, or of specific words and other textual elements in poetry. This in operation locates process, the making of the work, and very specifically temporal considerations in process, within the biological individual. This is an example, I would suggest, of reflexivity, or self-reflexivity, in the work, where there is a foregrounding in the work of the processes involved in its composition. The work examines and displays its own methods of composition as part of its operation and its realisation as a piece of 'art'. Brakhage's own letter to the poet Ronald Johnson (October 1990) was clear:

> I suppose that in this sense I'm an artist a bit like Anton Webern who composed music which seems (at his best) to turn on itself, like a mobile and resist all sense of 'continuity' … I personally came more and more to believe … that a biological evolution of aesthetics (ie: an aesthetic base on the sense organs themselves, their inner processes – rather than just the immediate reception of the external world, the fashioning input into stories, symbols, soforth/mythos) would reveal an outside limit of being human (what Olson called for, again and again, those last years) … the movies permit an exteriorization of moving visual thought process … .[14]

His belief in 'a biological evolution of aesthetics', and his relating of this to Olson's poetics is key. The privileging of temporal rhythm as linked to individuals' biological exteriorisations and brain rhythms removes the temporal authority from traditional structural form and endows the film-maker (or writer or composer) as well as the viewer (or reader or audient) with their own temporal autonomy; a temporal relativity in effect.

Brakhage's hand-painted films, in particular, have provoked much comment from critics in this light. Fred Camper, for example, has stated that 'even the abstract hand painted films have a sense of duplicating, in their flicker, the mix of intentional and chaotic body rhythms imparted by his handheld camera'.[15] Clearly, it is the complex biological perception or experience of temporal movement as it relates to the subject matter of the films, not just that of the camera technology, or the physicality of holding the camera, that Camper is identifying here. Brakhage's cinematic techniques display, in this sense, the temporal awareness of the bodily as compositional, and as receptive; the temporalising that the bodily engenders.

In connecting this temporalising that the bodily engenders to an *interactive* essence of temporal perception in Ginsberg's work and that of other poets, linked to the disjunctive temporal visuality of Brakhage's cinema, it is useful to examine the relationship between process and interaction (or reflexivity) in the concurrent field of experimental music, specifically in the work of John Cage. Michael Nyman, for instance, in his book *Experimental Music* states that:

> Experimental composers are by and large not concerned with prescribing a defined *time-object* whose materials, structuring and relationships are calculated and arranged in advance, but are more excited by the prospect of outlining a *situation* in which sounds may occur, a *process* of generating action (sounding or otherwise), a *field* delineated by certain compositional 'rules' … to bring about acts the outcome of which are unknown' (Cage).[16]

He further explains, taking again as one of his examples Cage:

> In the music of both men [Pierre Boulez and John Cage, representing Avant Garde and Experimental standpoints, respectively], what is heard is indistinguishable from its process. In fact, process itself might be called the Zeitgeist of our age. The duality of precise means creating indeterminate emotions is now associated only with the past.[17]

This emphasis on process, and its relation to a field concept, of an 'open field' rather than a 'closed system', is especially important when locating 'acts the outcome of which is unknown'. These acts signify a conjunction or co-existence of fields in a temporal sense – that of the process's determination and that of the event itself. The intervention of further fields of temporal negotiation relating to specific actors (composer/performer/audient) initiates a complex temporal structuring that is by definition variable and dynamic.

The concept of field that I will focus upon is that emphasised by John Cage, where a multitude (or multiplicity) of simultaneities co-exist alongside, within, overlaying each other, interpenetrating. That is, objects can occur in the same space as other objects within the field, and with the frame upon objects within the field, and of the field itself, conceived of as multiple and variable; a field concept with no fixed points. This concept of field differs somewhat from, for example, Charles Olson's conception of 'projective or OPEN verse' (field composition)[18] in poetics, where there exists an emphasis upon the relation of the objects within the field to the presence of the poet within that field.

This variability that I have referred to in relation to process is highly significant, and releases the notion of 'process' from the notion of strict determination – 'unfixing' it in its anchoring sense, and also in its dynamism – with the temporal field no longer dictated by process in a formalist way, but delivering a dynamic reappraisal of causality, and of temporal determination. As such, the use, and documentation, of chance procedures by John Cage and others in music has a direct significance for the work of Jackson Mac Low, Joan Retallack, and other poets.[19] The unfixity of process these composers and poets propose (in terms of variability and flexibility of compositional, notational, and performative procedurality moving away from fixed or rigidly defined characteristics) achieves a further reflexive procedurality, and what I refer to as an 'awareness of process' within specific works so formulated. I view the temporal aspects so reflexively used as incarnating awareness, or self-awareness, in the poem, in the composition or, indeed, in the film. Not only can it be said that a poem is in some sense structurally 'reading itself', but that this reflexivity is a form of meta-reflection where the action of the reader, and writer, in relation to the processes of the poem brings about an awareness of their role in the composition of the poem's temporality. As Aodhán McCardle puts it in relation to the poetry of Lee Harwood: 'Our experience of the poem is also the poem experiencing itself'.[20]

Multiple examples in Brakhage's filmmaking spring to mind. For instance *The Domain of the Moment* (1977) with its blurrings and melding of motion and shot, where the image seems to spill over itself as the moment is expanded beyond the momentary. Brakhage overlays flashes of the same movement sequences simultaneously and with tiny delays, suggesting not just a splitting of vision, but also splittings and recombinations of time. Combined with the roaring of high speed, rapidly changing, hand painted celluloid, as well as scratchings on the film, that intercut these images, the effect is to foreground a re-versioning of the moment though the foregrounding of the film's own techniques of doing so. The film is temporally re-conceptualising itself as it unfolds in the real time of viewing for the viewer. This reflexivity, or experiencing of itself, suggests an abstracted sense of a degree of independence not only from the writer/composer/film-maker, and from the composition process itself, but also from a deterministic realisation of the piece, that locates unfixedly between the piece and its external interactions and relationships.

The use of variable, especially mathematically derived, bases from which process as a function is developed in musical composition effectively codifies (or attempts to codify) aspects of this unfixity. But the freedom of interpretation attached to the realisation of process, the performance itself, and to other materials used in composition loosens that codifying process itself, once again emphasising the co-existent and contradictory nature of variability (or 'unfixity') in relation to process. In the work of experimental arts practices such as those of Brakhage, Cage and certain innovative poets like Bruce Andrews, Joan Retallack, Jackson Mac Low, etc., the outcome of process can be described as openly parameterised – i.e., described in relation to parameters that have been loosened from a definitive sense of codification to a more variable or indeterminate conception of codification, through the use of unorthodox methodologies and processes in composition, and in thinking about the outcome of these in performance. This is an expanded and complicated notion of parameter, where the code applied to the notation of the work (for example, Cage's pictorial scores) is not rigidly or fixedly enforced or envisaged, compositionally, notationally, or in terms of performance. Codification is subject, therefore, to variability or flexibility. This allows for greater interpretive practice for the reader/listener/viewer in the codification process, as a codifier, and as a decodifier. Cage himself says of his use of process:

> What might have given rise, by reason of the high degree of indeterminacy, to no matter what eventuality (to a process essentially purposeless) becomes productive of a time-object. This object, exceedingly complex due to the absence of a score, a fixed relation of the parts, is analogous to a futurist or cubist painting, perhaps, or to a moving picture where flicker makes seeing the object difficult.[21]

This relation of the time-object to the processual is unequivocal, and is not unrelated to Gilles Deleuze's cinematic conception of the 'time-image'. Deleuze defines the 'movement-image' in relation to cinema as providing an 'intermediate image, to which movement is not appended or added'.[22] It is linked to an indirect representation of time through successions of shots. In the movement-image, time is subordinate to movement, as with the rhythm of an ordered sequence of shots that follow physical movement. In the time-image, on the other hand, this subordination is reversed: movement is subordinate to time;

> The time image does not imply the absence of movement (even though it often includes its increased scarcity) but it implies the reversal of the subordination; it is no longer time which is subordinate to movement; it is movement which subordinates itself to time. It is no longer time which derives from movement, from its norm and its corrected aberrations; it is movement as *false movement*, as aberrant movement which now depends on time.[23]

With the time-image (and here, Cage's time-object) the temporal scape itself is experienced: the soundscapes devolving from the specific temporal scapes negotiated by the process, the composer, the performer and the audient, for example. A specific application of this, in terms of poetry, is the collaborative performance work of Bruce Andrews, such as 'Movement/Writing//Writing/Movement' (from *Ex Why Zee*) where an internalised sense of temporal incidence is specified in explicitly 'language' terms in the textuality of the poem, and related to *'movement possibilities and "modern-dance" limitations and from S.S.'s* [the chore-ographer Sally Silvers'] *composition'.*[24]

> 1. 1st movement, TORSO SLING. *Parallel interest in concealment.* The piece begins by standing off to the side of the performance space but still visible, back to the audience. (Normal, focus = nouns convention, stiff centrality.) (Peripheral vision = off to side.) (Hidden point, or origin – or else, material is constructed right before our eyes, not just referred to.) *Bulletoid. Some progress detoxified inconsequentially decisive putty.* Fling the entire body out into space using only the momentum that can be initiated from the torso.[25]

The text 'draws material' from Andrew's text 'Unit Costs (A Score for Movement)' and is written reciprocally in relation to Sally Silvers' movement and performance piece 'Lack of Entrepreneurial Thrift',[26] presenting the reader with a temporal scape that foregrounds movement as instruction and as action. A presentation of a textual 'direct time', foregrounding movement to such a degree that it forces the reader to likewise foreground their own movements in time as part of the readerly function.

Similarly, Brakhage's films often foreground the movements of the viewer, particularly of the eyes. An example is *The Process* (1972). Camper notes that:

> The rapid-fire flashes of *The Process* creates a very different rhythm from that of *Mothlight*, but the photographed objects that Brakhage juxtaposes with solid colors are similarly denied stability. Brakhage's catalog note for the film refers to memory as the "electrical…firing of nerve connection[s]". While Brakhage's films always undercut any dualities they may set up, his note goes on to suggest that while the photographed images involve "re-constructing 'a scene'", the flicker represents the very process of thinking, and insofar as those associations hold, the film foregrounds the act of perceiving over the thing perceived.[27]

This emphasis on the act of perceiving is crucial; the continual flickering and flashing of solid colour panels and of dark and light over- and under-exposed images both stimulate and replicate the blinking of the viewer in response to the flickering past of the viewer's real time – the effect replicates both the camera's capture of the movie flicker of time and the viewer's awareness of that movement as manufactured. The viewer becomes aware of their eyes' physical interaction with constant visual interruption and simulated blinking.

Many of his films that combine different visual techniques are also of interest here. As an example, *Yggdrasill: Whose Roots Are Stars in the Human Mind* (1997) is made up of a stunning array of cinematic visual modes of representation and the frames with which these are portrayed. Sometimes there is a clear frame, sometimes a frame within a frame, and sometimes there is no sense of frame at all, as images meld visually into each other in different forms, such as painting or scratching on celluloid combining with flarings and blackenings, movement shots, blurrings, landscape shots, and rapid shifts in focus and superimposition. These combine in different velocities, vectors, and constructions of movement –

they take on almost a motility of their own – such as the languid, swaying, liquid movement of light on water or the frantic melee of streams of hand painted, gloriously coloured independently mobile painting blazing in motion in different sections of the frame or the explosions of fireworks across the screen's movement. Genevieve Yue comments that 'Yet *Yggdrasill*, too, is riddled with gaps, moments of black, like small breaths, between flashes of color. For human sight is as much about recognizing its own limits, even as it opens widely'.[28] The disjunctive juxtapositions this film presents as visuality – the constant shifts in visual forms and velocity – foreground an awareness in the viewer of the eyes' and the brain's construction of a complex variable temporality that supplants the blistering barrage of movement, both within frames, and across them. The viewer's real time grappling with temporal encounter in response to the visuality of this film generates the direct time of the image (see plates 30 and 31).

Victor A. Grauer, with his interest in neutralisation of pitch field and screen space, and his focus on what he calls 'negative syntax', in his on-line book, *Montage, Realism and the Act of Vision,* connects Stan Brakhage's film work with the experimental compositional work of Cage and other experimental and avant-garde composers. Grauer defines negative syntax in the following way:

> If perspective space can be regarded as equivalent to conventional pictorial syntax, then its negation, negative space, is, in effect, the negation of that syntax. In this sense, negative space is equivalent to what we may call 'negative syntax'.[29]

His demonstrations of this within the work of Brakhage and others is of particular interest to the examination of the multitudinous nature of temporal interaction in complex experimental work in poetry and poetics from Charles Olson to the present day. His assertion that 'Brakhage's neutralizations of screen-space may be understood in the light of those neutralizations of the pitch-field so characteristic of musical modernism'[30] is important in connecting the drive towards disruption and negation across twentieth century art forms, and illustrates similar developments and experimentation in the contemporary poetry and poetics of the day. In textual terms, negative syntax can be thought of as exhibiting through the neutralisation of closed forms of reading that poetic techniques such as cut-ups, word-splits, splicing, non-semantic juxtapositions, and other disjunctive and interruptive techniques cause in resisting the assured, or unimpeded, narrative formulation of syntax in poetic language that has often traditionally been the proposed form of reading poetry.

Grauer himself makes an explicit connection, in terms of negative syntax, between film and poetics:

> Of all the many influences on Brakhage, none has been more direct than that of the American poet, Charles Olson. Olson's work and his theories regarding his own poetic language relate

strongly both to negative syntax and le sémiotique. The parallels are particularly evident in his key essay, 'Projective Verse', in which he speaks of the opening of 'closed form' and 'composition by field', and links poetry to the body via breath.[31]

These same issues of disruption, alienation, negation and temporal complication, for example, in visuality and cinematics, that Brakhage's film work seeks to address, can be seen to have their textual equivalents in twentieth and twenty-first centuries innovative poetry. For instance in the unusual and/or disorienting ways of organizing the links between language elements in the poem, such as between letters, words, lines, or other semantic, visual, and phonetic, blocks and clusterings. Examples abound in the works of Olson, Mac Low, Ulli Freer, Gilbert Adair, Maggie O'Sullivan, the Language writers, and many others.

Thinking, then, in more detail about process and reflexivity across these art forms, and in relation to Brakhage, Cage is again a good place to start. In his commentary on *Music for Piano 21–52* he located process in this work firmly within a temporal structure that is, at the least, complex in its internal relation of element to whole as a timed event, or rather a series of untimed timed events:

> A performance is characterized by the programmed time length calculated beforehand and adhered to through the use of a stop watch. This is primarily of use in relation to an entire page, secondarily of use in relation, to say, a system; for it is possible that, though the space of the page is here equal to time, the performance being realized by a human being rather than a machine, such space may be interpreted as moving, not only constantly, but faster or slower. Thus, finally, nothing has been determined by the notation as far as performance time is concerned.[32]

Works that acknowledge such a complex temporal makeup, as I have suggested, can be said to obtain a certain procedural reflexivity in their performance, and particularly in their articulation of the interaction of a listener/viewer/reader. This has compositional implications for the notion that temporality and the 'flow' of time are functions of, and a product of, consciousness, that the phenomenologies of Bergson, Husserl, Heidegger, Merleau-Ponty and others explore, linking the experience of time to the perceptions of the experiencing subject. 'Compositional' works, such as these might be called, that acknowledge the reflexivity of their temporal realisation as works, certainly can be viewed as phenomenologically focused in that they effectively engage with a phenomenological awareness of temporal experience and perception. Indeed, they can be said to manifest this across multiple frames of perception (composer/writer/film-maker, musician/performer/projectionist, audient/reader/viewer, etc). We can also say that they appear to encompass a phenomenological focus as part of their procedurality. For example, Joan Retallack's positions in 'A Brief Experiment In Linguistics', from the 'EX POST SCRIPTO' section of *How To Do Things With Words*. The piece is subtitled '(please provide sign interpreter for performance)', immediately

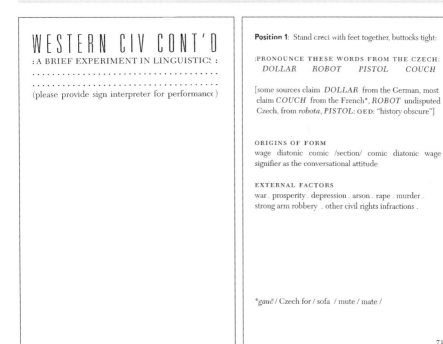

WESTERN CIV CONT'D
: A BRIEF EXPERIMENT IN LINGUISTICS :
....
....
(please provide sign interpreter for performance)

Position 1: Stand erect with feet together, buttocks tight:

:PRONOUNCE THESE WORDS FROM THE CZECH:
DOLLAR   ROBOT   PISTOL   COUCH

[some sources claim *DOLLAR* from the German, most claim *COUCH* from the French*, *ROBOT* undisputed Czech, from *robota*, *PISTOL*: OED: "history obscure"]

ORIGINS OF FORM
wage diatonic comic /section/ comic diatonic wage
signifier as the conversational attitude

EXTERNAL FACTORS
war . prosperity . depression . arson . rape . murder . strong arm robbery . other civil rights infractions .

°gauč / Czech for / sofa / mute / mate /

71

*Figure 1. Joan Retallack, from 'A Brief Experiment In Linguistics' (*How To Do Things With Words*, 1998: 70–71).*

invoking a sense of mediation, of language, and of the performative. What follows are a series of texts called 'positions' which combine physical and vocal instructions with linguistic information, and word operation, as positions incorporate and reincorporate linguistic, word and physical actions and operate upon them. 'Position 1' (see Figure 1) sets the scene, and introduces (one could say invites) external influences to the action, and the continued actioning, of the text and the performance, foregrounding the reflexive action of the poem, and of the reader/listener/viewer: 'Stand erect with feet together, buttocks tight:/ :PRONOUNCE THESE WORDS FROM THE CZECH:'.[33]

Reflexive procedurality can be identified also in Brakhage's film work. Two specific Brakhage examples that Grauer presents in relation to temporal complexity, and, I would maintain, reflexivity, are *Anticipation of The Night* (1958) and *Cat's Cradle* (1959). In *Anticipation of The Night*, one of Brakhage's first major works, we see great play with light and dark, and with the transition between images, and scenes. An intense, perhaps claustrophobic, sense of presence is created as a shadow figure moves across the screen intercut with rapid representations of movement, as of lights filmed from a running vehicle, or of light and shadow interplayed on the camera lens. Road movement scenes of foliage, and the sky, in light and dark, with rapid, and often disorientating shifts in directional motion add to the sense of discontinuous relationships the eyes' action of viewing raise. A visually, and temporally, variant relation of image to movement in intercut fairground scenes are particularly effective in their complex rhythmic use of light, shade, and motion, alternatively increasing and reducing in velocity, direction, intensity, and focus. This discontinuous visuality cannot but invoke and interact with the temporal sense of the viewer attuning to visual and movement-based representations of temporality in a soundless film such as this. The play with light and dark, and with movement between images, and scenes, is connected to proportional relationships between visual elements,[34] and to directionality as the eye is continually led off the edge of the visual frame in opposing and confusing directions, while other images, and frames, are indistinct or out of focus. These durational relationships combine with the discontinuous temporality invoked by Brakhage's visual effects to force an awareness of our own engendering of temporality as our 'real time' as viewers comes to the fore of the visual experience. In Deleuze's terms we are here acutely aware that movement is subordinated to time (see plate 32).

Cat's Cradle presents us with repeating fleeting and confusing glimpses of two male and two female characters, and a cat, along with still shots of objects such as floral wallpaper and embroidered fabric visually jolting against each other, and merging into and suffusing each other's spaces. P. Adams Sitney describes the intent of the film as designed to explore the 'tensions, identifications, and jealousies' that the encounter produced, but notes that:

> the film itself effaces psychology and develops through its lightning montage of flat surfaces and gestures in virtually two-dimensional space an almost cubist suggestion of the three-dimensional arena in which the four characters and one cat might interact, if only the furious pace of editing could be retarded and the synecdochic framing expanded ... *Cat's Cradle* suggests stasis through, and despite, the speed of the colliding shots.[35]

This framing of the actions of the film's performers, where the part represents the whole, and the whole the part, which Sitney notes serves to obscure individual identities and to fuse them into a form of single androgynous entity, is achieved through the speed of the cuts and the 'incompleteness' of the actions the characters repeatedly perform (in sometimes altered forms). Paul Arthur says of *Cat's Cradle* that it:

> does not entirely suppress our recourse to naming but rather floods our typical eye-brain loop with stimuli for which attached language cues are either less than automatic or, in cases of purely sensory appeal, non-existent.[36]

The compositional action of the camera, interrupting and merging character, image and action suggests an 'almost-awareness' in the film of its generation of a disruptive temporal field, one that the viewer is repeatedly made aware of in relation to the temporal emphasis that they themselves bring, and continually re-bring, to the act of viewing the film.

A useful term that Grauer identifies in relation to Brakhage's disruptive temporality in these films is what he calls 'perceptual weight':

> As with the purely ad hoc rhythms of AON [*Anticipation of The Night*] ... the disjunct proportions of CC [*Cat's Cradle*] tend to disrupt the temporal flow, placing a strong perceptual weight on each shot, no matter how brief or apparently inconsequential.[37]

The use of perceptual weight to disrupt the temporal flow of the film is, as such, a reflexive tool of the film-maker bringing temporality to the forefront of the viewing experience, and the realisation of the film. This is of specific relevance to poetic form. In the work of Bruce Andrews, for example, such a perceptual weight can also be found in the collative composition process he employs and records. Andrews' description of his composition method as akin to film editing, taking clusters of words recorded on cards at different times and recombining them in the composition process, 'into works based on a whole series of other decisions that I'll make later',[38] gives a deliberate emphasis to perceptual weight as a poetic compositional tool. Here specific temporal units of composition (cards, or pieces of paper, in this case) are placed in relation to others, which often resonate disparate or even competing temporal realisations, whether conceptually, as in 'treat me like a labor unit',[39] rhythmically, as in:

speech

nomination[40]

Or, indeed, both, as in:

> electrolysis pogrom – compassion for reverse gar. Nomads
> do the dish adversity a union pup – trade daughters for cost-
> overrun all tax beef franks – wipe mud off TV screen. Cancer
> cancer cancer cancer cancer
> cancer cancer cancer cancer cancer cancer cancer.[41]

The compositional process reflexively constitutes the temporality of the resulting clusters and recombinations, and as readers, we pick up on these disjunctive groupings of rhythmic temporality and are tasked with integrating or reformulating these within, or in response to, our own sense of the temporal scape. Again, our 'real time' temporality is foregrounded. Process viewed as significant in Brakhage's work, then, can be related, as in Cage's work, and in Andrews' work, to the foregrounding of the processes employed in the construction of meaning itself on the part of the film-maker (as with the poet or composer), as well as on the part of the projectionist (as with the actor or performer or musician), and the viewer (as with the reader or listener).

Brakhage's complex cinematic visuality, his use of techniques such as montage, plastic cutting,[42] blurring, superimposition, etc., creates a disjunction between image and cognition, as I have discussed in more detail elsewhere.[43] The challenges these produce for the processes, and the representational strategies, of visual and temporal construction of both the film-maker and the viewer are significant. Narrative function is likewise estranged from meaning formulation in much of Brakhage's work. The perception of the generation of meaning as non-narrative, or what Bruce Elder refers to as 'non-narrative means of "narrating"',[44] is closely linked in Brakhage to the disjunction and destruction of narrative connectivity and narrative aspects of the image and of the image sequence.

Of key importance coming from this is Brakhage's significant work in the area of what I shall call *the passage of meaning*, a crucial area of concern in contemporary innovative poetics. *Passage* here refers to transitionary practices that smooth the movement between visual spaces, used to similar effects in music, but with a twist. Grauer says of this practice:

> Passage, closely related to devices such as modelling and *chiaroscuro*, can be regarded as an art of transition, a smooth 'passage' from one area of virtual space to another. ... Both the 'old master' painters and the Realists used passage as a means of smoothing over discrepancies that could not be incorporated within traditional pictorial syntax (e.g., perspective) and, at the same time, creating a kind of 'void' which the viewing subject could be seduced into 'fleshing out' mentally.[45]

What he describes in Brakhage, though, and it is in this sense that I raise it here, is the use of passage as a *disjunctive* method of opening out negative space, similar to that used by cubist painters:

> Cézanne, whose *ad hoc* approach to composition produced many spatial anomalies, used passage in an attempt to smooth them over, often thereby creating an effect of 'warped' space. The Cubists carried Cézanne's approach to an extreme, ultimately using passage disjunctively, to open form out to the 'negative space' of the 'surface', which ends by itself 'opening' to the negative field, where passage and negative space merge ... Brakhage's 'plastic cutting' functions like *Cubist* passage, using such devices [the fade, the dissolve, the match cut - equivalents to traditional passage] against themselves, 'deconstructing' them in a process which I call 'negative montage', the montage of disjunction, disruption, dissociation.[46]

A similar complexity in the disjunctive transition of meaning in lexical texts is identifiable is innovative poetry. For example, Gilbert Adair's latticework of reference and counter-reference to language itself (and to the work's own operation as a language object) in his *Sable Smoke* series, which relates the difficulties of 'meaning' on the level not of simply relating words to other words (or other units of constructing meaning in the poem), but of relating processes of collating meaning with the construction of meaning, a form of hypertextual and meta-textual collage of meaning formulation. Adair's *Sable Smoke* publications[47] are full of ways into, and ways out of, the poems. Not only do the poems reference each other, backwards and forth, but the referential effects include also connections and movements to external thematic references (literary, cultural, cinematic, and political, to name a few), as well as visual, linguistic and multi-lingual referentiality and meaning formation:

charles (here "sharl") & al
some 90 years later (1896)
force (flash) in
(now)
fabry-perot resonant cavity
"semireflective mirrors"
2 end faces of a semiconductor crystal
("parallel processing")
(faces without inverted commas)[48]

or

rare-earth shells
"again"   "fives"   *durchkomponiert* meat needs   that
stubborn   is glorious   goes on rattling
imaginable *present* total viability *superconductivity* prospects   highways
readily? *tatto'd tears*   under eye "tooth is the whole gold,   doctor f[49]

As cris cheek puts it in relation to the 1995 version of 'Sable Smoke (for Jackson Mac Low)':

> it is a poem which irregularly discusses its own processes and strategies as it moves (along isn't exactly how it moves). It jumps. Front to back – back to front. As it literally comes and goes to transform its essay … The poem attempts to map movements accurately.[50]

The sequence work of Bob Cobbing, such as that presented in *Shrieks & Hisses,* suggests a more visual equivalent in poetics to Brakhage's handling of the passage of meaning. Nicholas Johnson says that in this work, which combines and confuses image and lexical textual form:

> Textual form reassembles the images, the words creating patterns & textures. We recognise Word because we recognise a Line, the direction of Mass in an image: we recognise even if we don't understand, but we recognise presence of letters to generate image-flicker, image meter … If image & text get treated in the same way then they exist on the edge of comprehensibility as either image or text or both.[51]

In Cobbing's work of this sort we see that there are species of thresholds between different types of visual textures that operate in the poetics of the poem – rather than lying stagnant or dormant, these visual thresholds reveal rather than overlay or conceal uncertain areas between the two. Cobbing presents single frames laid out as a sequence (see Figure 2) which in form relates to types of cinematic visuality that Brakhage has explored with a similar emphasis on the thresholds between cinematic frames and visuality. In terms of generating meaning in the poem, these single frames laid out as a sequence give us patternings that array beside each other or overlay each other, or both – suggesting different movements and combinations of movement and, therefore, meaning construction. Rather

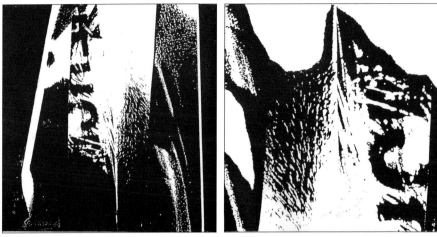

Figure 2. Bob Cobbing, from Shrieks & Hisses *(1999), not paginated.*

than a fixed way of carrying out and conveying these interactions between frames, which would represent a standardised movement from one distinct frame to another, the relationships between them is rendered much less discrete on the one hand, and much less linear (and predictable) on the other.

The non-linear sequencing that Cobbing's and Brakhage's work explore directly challenge the 'accurate' equidistant segmentation that analytical representations of time (world time, clock time, objective time) present. These precise measurements, such as the second, the minute, the hour, supplant, or relegate, other measurements, regarded as 'imprecise', such as weather and seasonal cycles, the length of journeys, a day's work, the duration of a reading, etc. These segments could also refer to the laying out of a *temporal frame* that the lengths of shots, frames, and sequences in cinema relay. Lev Manovich cites Eisenstein's 'methods of montage' as an application of cinematics to time, such as:

> metric montage which uses absolute lengths of shots to establish a 'beat', and rhythmic montage based on pattern of movement within the shots. These methods can be used by themselves to structure a sequence of shots, but they also can be combined within a single sequence.[52]

Gilles Deleuze refers to this idea when he writes, in *Cinema 1*, of the any-instant-whatever (the non-privileging of instants in relation to movement, brought about by the scientific age), where he describes the cinematic as the system that reproduces movement as 'a function of any-instant-whatever that is, as a function of equidistant instants, selected so as to create the impression of continuity'.[53] He goes on to show that the any-instant-whatever refers also to privileged instances in cinematics: 'the any-instant-whatever can be regular *or* singular, ordinary *or* remarkable ... The remarkable or singular instant remains any-instant-whatever amongst the others'.[54] Developed from his examination of Bergson's theses on movement, Deleuze relates shot to movement: 'The shot is the movement-image. In so far as it relates movement to a whole which changes, it is the mobile section of duration'.[55] He defines the 'movement image', then, in relation to cinema as providing an 'intermediate image, to which movement is not added or appended':[56] it is linked to an indirect representation of time through successions of shots, etc.[57]

In his introduction to *Cinema 2*, going 'beyond the movement image' with the 'time image', Deleuze states that temporal structure, or direct time-image, is 'for example, a coexistence of distinct durations, or of levels of duration; a single event can belong to several levels: the sheets of the past coexist in a non-chronological order'.[58] This is very different from a linear beat established by a 'rhythmic montage based on pattern of movement within the shots',[59] and changes the relationship of the frame to the construction of temporality through the image significantly.

Deleuze defines framing, in *Cinema 1*, as limitation, and states later in his argument that 'all framing determines an out of field'.[60] While this is certainly the case in regard to the immediate boundaries of the image, in complex compositional systems such as those examined here in poetry and in Brakhage's cinema, 'fluidity' in relation to the action of framing and movement deregulates these frames, and reinvigorates them as temporal and spatial unfixities, unanchored, interactable and variable, more indeterminate than constant. Deleuze refers to Bonitzer's useful concept of 'deframing', which in this context refers to abnormal views relating to 'another dimension of the image',[61] connected to the concept of the 'beyond the movement image' that he goes on to develop. Therefore, we can view this deregulation and reinvigoration as a form of de-limitation, or un-limiting in this sense. Frame, then, as a basic cinematographic element, can be said to set up a relationship (or relationships) between the components inside it. Its presence modulates the framing effects as *always happening* (as distinct from having happened), as not only can there be different kinds of movement within the framing operation, but the action of framing itself is not fixed in relation to particular components. Framing, thus, sets up a relationship (or relationships) with its own boundaries, and with the action of these boundaries upon the conception of the frame as related to the components inside it, and to other focuses, or concentrations, or scales of frame within a conception of a whole of some sort. Likewise, the outside frame, or 'out-of-field' can be regarded as fluid in its relation to the inside frame, and so operates as an externally delimiting factor in the relationship between frame and elements of frame, frame and frame, and frame and the idea of 'whole'.

The frame then represents an unfixed conception of limitation *and* de-limitation (deterritorialisation, in Deleuze's terms).[62] Brakhage's manipulation of the frame and its action, particularly in his hand painted films suggests this sort of unfixed operation. He wrote himself about 'bending the light and limiting the frame of the image just so ...'.[63] This 'just so' is often productive of an unfixed visuality and temporality. For example, Bruce Elder, discussing the use of pulsating colour frames and the black frames between images in *23rd Psalm Branch* (1966–67) in the context of the *Songs* cycle of films, states that:

> Brakhage was concerned to create films that could stand up to being projected at various speeds, or could run forward or backward. Messiaen also insisted on the importance of using durative values that span the range from very small to very large, and that lack any sense of being created by repeating a module that marks out one unit of duration. The irregular, non-repetitive rhythmic structures that Brakhage uses in the *Songs* show Messiaen's influence, and the pairs of black frames may well represent the minimal unit, the importance of which is stressed in Messiaen's rhythmic theories.[64]

The irregular, non-repetitive rhythmic structure through frame both punctuates and delimits the visual and temporal fields of the films, while the notion of variable speeds of projection built into the make-up of the films' realisation methodologically unfixes the temporal frame even further (see plate 33).

These methodologies of unfixing are also generative of new visuality and newly foregrounded temporality in the abstraction of the frame, as John C. Hanhardt notes, discussing Brakhage's disruptive use of frame:

> In his interplay [in *Anticipation of the Night*] of camera movements from editing, even scratching directly onto the film surface, Brakhage manipulated the tensions between the recognisable photographic image and the abstraction of the film frame ... The disruption of the film frame in *Mothlight* represents the use of the strip of celluloid as a means to make new forms of abstract image.[65]

Cornelis de Bruyn's connection of cinematic 'mistakes' in Brakhage's *Dog Star Man* (1961–64) to the revealing of the technology in and of composition is also pertinent:

> The viewer experiences Brakhage's struggle with nature through his determined scaling of a snow-covered mountain. Brakhage's referential use of cinematic 'mistakes' such as flash frames, splices, flares, frame lines, distortion lenses and the use of a form of Rayogram in gluing material directly into the film strip, revealing the technologies of its making, are all evident in this visually complex multi-layered silent epic.[66]

This technological revealing is also, significantly, the revealing of the complex methodological frames of the film, again foregrounding different presences of frames and of the effects of those frames as the now of the film unfolds to the viewer.

The direct time-image that Deleuze focusses on in *Cinema 2* is clearly, then, of great importance in looking at the work of Brakhage, and is likewise significant when thinking about the presencing of temporality in the work of innovative poets whose work engages with disjunction and unfixity. Deleuze states, through Kant, that 'time is out of joint and presents itself in its pure state', and that movement in the time-image

> is movement which subordinates itself to time. It is no longer time which derives from movement, from its norm and its corrected aberrations; it is movement as *false movement*, as aberrant movement which now depends on time.[67]

What Deleuze refers to as false, or aberrant, movement, relates directly to techniques employed by Brakhage in his cinematographic use of visual language, and those used by innovative poets in the literary medium. Deleuze tells us that 'a movement that avoids centring, in whatever way, is as such abnormal, aberrant', and that 'a direct presentation of time does not imply the halting of movement, but rather the promotion of aberrant movement', and gives as examples alterations in velocities, speedings up and slowings down and reversed sequences, as well as 'the non-distancing of the human body, ... constant changes in scale and proportion ... and false continuities of movement (what Eisenstein called "impossible continuity shots")'.[68] Brakhage's use of abstract techniques such as sideways cutting, linking shots of markedly differing focal velocities, partial images, blurring, disjunctive camera movement, and so on, as well as his use of abstract image in his hand painted and scratched films seems to enter this territory Deleuze is concerned with.

When looking at Brakhage's work through Deleuze's notion of the time image one often finds that in much of the critical material available that examines Brakhage's cinema there is little emphasis on unpicking the notions of temporal unfixity, deterritorialisation and disjunction that are so often of interest in innovative poetry. For example, in the treatment of shot, as a cinematic idea, as momentary – as reflecting individual moments – Elder states that in Brakhage's films '[e]very successive shot appears as new and independent of those that preceded it. Each new shot, moreover, seems a triumph as it marks a new beginning',[69] while Arthur describes 'momentary perceptual transactions' in which the viewer exchanges 'unhindered assimilation of images for intensified contact with pictorial or sensory features that might otherwise go unnoticed'.[70] For Deleuze, in *Cinema 2*, the shot is not viewed as comprising a moment, but rather finds its vitality in its expression of aberrant time, the time image, which as such overflows set momentary boundaries, and disallows the encapsulation, or halting, of movement that moment implies. As such, readings of Brakhage's use of shot like those above, while very sharp in other ways, do not seem to full engage

143

the temporal action Brakhage himself identifies when he says 'much of my life's work constitutes an attempt to subvert the representation photography **IS** by creating a sense of *constant present tense* in each film's every instant of viewing'.[71] Jennifer Reeves gives another example of this emphasis when she relates this 'constant present tense' to Brakhage's hand-painted films, 'in that they demand to be experienced in a succession of immediate visual moments'.[72] The 'succession of immediate visual moments' that Reeves refers to seems to be, in the light of Deleuze's conception of a new sense of time in cinema, an incomplete formulation. What the viewer perceives, I would maintain, is not so much a succession of separate momentary shots that simulate movement or velocity in order to present a constant present tense. Rather, Brakhage's 'every instant of viewing' overruns and out-spills the notion of a momentary frame; the present is not divisible into instants in the way the term 'moment', a term related to analytical time, suggests. Indeed, instant itself is not divisible. As with Henri Bergson's notion of *duration*, or consciousness-time, which cannot be split up or divided into mathematical units,[73] as we do not experience the world in a momentary fashion (i.e., moment by moment), but rather continuously, Brakage's constant present tense is a phenomenological notion. In other words, we get an actual representation of, and engagement with, real time without the intermediary segmentation that 'moment' signifies. The complex interplay of spatial and temporal movements is mediated by an uninterrupted temporal dynamic, which constantly reconstitutes the encounter with cinematic temporality. Deleuze's statement on the validity of aberrant movement, from *Cinema 2*, is worth quoting here:

> Movement is no longer simply aberrant, aberration is now valid in itself and designates time as its direct cause ... The direct time-image is the phantom which has always haunted the cinema, but it took modern cinema to give a body to this phantom.[74]

Deleuze located aberrant movement, and direct time movement, as *present*, not just in the contemporary, but in 'the whole of cinema'.[75] Much of the work of Brakhage and other experimental film-makers can be said to relate to this giving of a body to aberrant movement, and the direct time image, in cinema. In fact, one could say that Brakhage's work truly embodies this new form of movement and direct time that Deleuze describes, particularly in his use of visual techniques to reconstitute the cinematic time of the viewer. Splicings, cuttings, changes of speed and vector, disjunctive camera movements, integration of physical materials with the celluloid, blurrings, superimpositions, submersions, reversals, splurgings, deframing, plastic cutting of images, blankings, etc., are specific examples. Deleuze points to Brakhage in *Cinema 2*, for example, in relation to image, cinematic time, 'punctuation' and absence, noting that:

The absence of image, the black screen or the white screen, have a decisive importance in contemporary cinema. For, as Noel Burch has shown, they no longer have a simple function of punctuation, as if they marked a change, but enter into a dialectical relation the image and its absence, and assume a properly structural value (as in Brakhage's *Reflections on Black* in experimental cinema).[76]

Felicity Colman similarly connects Brakhage, and other experimental film-makers, to Deleuze's conception of direct time:

Experimental films, on the other hand, often tend to push the perceptual boundaries of an image, forcing the viewer to question a number of different planes (and thus forms) of existence: for example, *Meshes of the Afternoon* (dirs Maya Deren and Alexander Hammid, 1943), *Free Radicals* (dir. Len Lye, 1958–79), *Window Water Baby Moving* (dir. Stan Brakhage, 1962) … There are points in these films where perception becomes a time image, not just a motor-image of the material world.[77]

Deleuze's emphasis on aberrant movement, and on the time-image, reflects a break with the idea of time as metrics, and Brakhage's cinema strongly reflects this reconfiguring of time. There has been a similar change evident in poetry in the twentieth and twenty-first centuries. Although 'mainstream' poetry still concerns itself heavily with metrical time, much innovative poetry seeks to expand the role and effect of time in poetic language, coming via developments such as Ezra Pound's 'musical phrase',[78] William Carlos Williams' 'variable foot',[79] Gertrude Stein's 'there is no such thing as repetition',[80] and later, the linguistically innovative poetry of the 1970s, such as that of Bruce Andrews, Charles Bernstein, Tom Raworth, Lee Harwood, Allen Fisher and many, many others.

While many of these specific cinematic techniques that Brakhage used are not directly analogous to textual practices in the experimental and innovative poetries of the late twentieth and early twenty-first centuries, the spirit and operation of their representational and reflexive complexity and experimentation certainly is. This 'giving of a body to aberrant movement, and the direct time image' that Brakhage's cinema so powerfully embodies connects well with, for example, the development of relational temporal operation in the processes of composition and reception, and the value of the performance as a temporal nexus, that much innovative poetry and poetics seek to address.

Notes

1. See Brakhage, 1963: not paginated.
2. See Miller, 2005: 174–195.
3. See Elder, 1998, for a comprehensive situating of Brakhage's work and writing in relation to an American poetics. See also Brakhage's own correspondence with the poets Charles Olson, Robert Duncan, and Ronald Johnson, and his own essay 'Chicago Review Article', all in Brakhage, 2001/2002; as well as McClure, and Anker, 2001/2002. Further writing by Brakhage on poetry, and its relation to his work, can be found in the essays 'Margin Alien', 'Film: Dance', 'Poetry and Film', and 'Gertrude Stein: Meditative Literature and Film' in Brakhage, 2001. Of interest here are also Tyrus Miller, 2005, and Elder, 2005a, as well as James, 1982.

4. See Sheppard and Thurston, 2009: 3, for a more comprehensive analysis of these terms.
5. Brakhage, 1963: not paginated. Author's italics.
6. Kashmere, 2003: not paginated.
7. Elder, 1998: 435.
8. Ibid., 437.
9. Ginsberg, 1956: 25.
10. Ibid., 28–30. Author's italics.
11. Merleau-Ponty, 1995: 412. Author's emphasis.
12. Brakhage, Marilyn, 2008: not paginated.
13. Camper, 2001/2002: 87–88.
14. Brakhage, 2001/2002: 29.
15. Camper, 2001/2002: 93.
16. Nyman, 2002: 4. Author's emphasis.
17. Ibid., 2.
18. Olson, 2005: 39–49
19. It must be here remembered John Cage's own important work in poetry, especially his mesostic work, examples of which can be found in Cage, 1973, 1979, ad 1983.
20. McCardle, 2007: 218.
21. Cage, 1973: 38.
22. Deleuze, 1986: 2.
23. Ibid., 271. Author's italics.
24. Andrews, 1995: 14. Author's italics.
25. Ibid., 14.
26. Andrews and Silvers usefully discuss their collaborative strategies in some detail in an interview: see Andrews and Silvers, 2009.
27. Camper, 2003a: not paginated.
28. Yue, 2011: not paginated.
29. Grauer, 1982: Part 2, Chapter 5, not paginated.
30. Ibid., Part 5, Chapter 10, not paginated.
31. Ibid., Epilogue, Chapter 12, not paginated.
32. Cage, 1973: 61.
33. Retallack, 1998: 71.
34. See Grauer, 1982: Part 5, Chapter 10, not paginated, for a convincing account of the proportional techniques Brakhage uses.
35. Sitney, 2002: 176.
36. Arthur, 2003: not paginated.
37. Grauer, 1982: Part 5, Chapter 10, not paginated.
38. Andrews in *Bruce Andrews*, a LINEbreak radio program, Granolithic Productions (1996): http://writing.upenn.edu/pennsound/x/LINEbreak.php (accessed 19 September 2016).
39. Andrews, 1987: 168.
40. Ibid., 53.
41. Andrews, 1992: 270.
42. Sitney defines Brakhage's term 'plastic cutting' as 'the joining of shots at points of movement, close-up or abstraction to soften the brunt of montage'. See Sitney, 2002: 157.
43. See Mooney, 2009.
44. Elder, 1998: 386.
45. Grauer, 1998: 'Preface' section, not paginated.

46. Ibid., 'Preface' section, not paginated. Author's italics.

47. Published in partial form as *RWC # 3* (1991), *from Sable Smoke RWC # 28* (1995), *PAGES 260–279: from Sable Smoke* (1995) and as *Sable Smoke* (2010).

48. Adair, 1995a: not paginated. Author's italics.

49. Adair, 1991: not paginated. Author's italics.

50. cheek, 1995: not paginated.

51. Johnson, 1999: not paginated.

52. Manovich, 2002. 156–157.

53. Deleuze, 1986: 5.

54. Ibid., 6. Author's italics.

55. Ibid., 22.

56. Ibid., 2.

57. See Deleuze, 1989: 271.

58. Ibid., xii.

59. Manovich, 2002. 156.

60. Deleuze, 1986: 13 and 16.

61. Ibid., 15.

62. '[T]he frame ensures a deterritorialisation of the image', see ibid., 15.

63. Brakhage, 1963: not paginated.

64. Elder, 1998: 112.

65. Hanhardt, 2015: 20–21.

66. de Bruyn, 2014: 22–23.

67. Deleuze, 1989: 271.

68. Ibid., 36.

69. Elder, 1998: 272.

70. Arthur, 2003: not paginated.

71. Brakhage, 2001: 210. My italics.

72. Reeves, 2002: 193.

73. Bergson, 1911: 250.

74. Deleuze, 1989: 41.

75. Ibid., 41.

76. Ibid., 200.

77. Colman, 2011: 77.

78. See Pound, 1960b: 3–4.

79. See Thirlwall, 1962: 183–184.

80. See Stein, 1957: 166.

8 Art as Revelation: The Origins of a Sacred Calling

Marco Lori

So it's revelation, I think, essentially what the art process is for.[1]

D uring his life Stan Brakhage held many controversial, contradictory, or simply odd positions. Among this last category are a set of intertwined peculiar beliefs as regards the spiritual value and function of art, epitomised by his notion that art necessarily entails revelation of a spiritual kind. Despite the apparent vagueness of this concept, I would like here to probe into it more deeply in order to investigate a possible origin for this and other positions that were part of his perspective about spirituality and art, considering how they sometimes contributed to his ideas and stances on other issues. In considering Brakhage's cultural milieu against these specific positions, the figure of poet Ezra Pound, with his occult-derived ideas about spirituality and art, came to impose itself, because of the strong affinities between his positions and those of the film-maker. A line of inquiry about such issues must however remain an hypothesis, since Brakhage's own formulations were generally vague, sometimes contradictory, usually enigmatic, scattered throughout the years, and apparently naive. This is to say that he never came to clear and precise formulations, not only because such matters naturally resist that, as we shall see; but also because of a more general obscurity anyone who is familiar with his jargon is used to. But still, the insistence and fervour with which he came back repeatedly to such points demand the attempt to place them in an historical and cultural perspective.

Brakhage declared that he created in a state of trance, intended as a mystical state. During such a trance, he found himself to be simply an instrument operated by superior forces. He named such forces 'Muses', and described them as manifestations of an ineffable divine. Some of these ideas may sound close to a Romantic heritage, of which he always considered himself part; or to Transcendentalism; or also to the general revival of mysticism in the 1960s counterculture, in some of the most radical expressions of the politics of consciousness. While each of these possibilities could be investigated, I shall here instead focus upon a fourth possibility: that Brakhage derived the majority of his spiritual ideas and stances, directly and/or indirectly, from the influence of Ezra Pound, and in particular from the echoes of a medieval *Weltanschauung*, later to become an occult tradition, from which Pound took inspiration. The function of art that Pound discerned in these remote sources was, indeed, the eliciting of spiritual revelation and a consequent communion with the divine. In investigating this lineage of influence, I shall consider Brakhage's accounts of his creative process and of art in general, as a system which draws its coherence from historical roots.

The artistic presence of Pound was certainly very important in Brakhage's career, through both direct and indirect influences. Pound was not simply one figure among many others, but was a primary inspiration for many of Brakhage's friends and mentors; a constant, living, though often physically distant, presence within his cultural milieu.

The first contact Brakhage had with Pound's work was on the occasion of his sixteenth birthday (1949) when a group of friends gave him Pound's epic poem *The Cantos* as a present.[2] The present was intended as a joke, for the text was extremely complex, but Brakhage actually came to treasure the book 'all his life',[3] defining it 'the single most important book in my life'.[4] His study of Pound became progressively more intense and formed an essential part of his artistic apprenticeship:

> But at every stage of gained knowledge *The Cantos* reveal more and more to me. ... Pound goads me on because at each turn in the reading of him I come to new mysteries which he has set significantly within learned reach.[5]

Among Brakhage's friends and mentors, Pound was held in high esteem as a poet and as a guiding artistic figure.[6] A fellow member of the New American Cinema, Maya Deren completed a master's thesis in 1939 on the influence of French Symbolism on 'Anglo-American modernist poets' such as Pound and Eliot.[7] In 1957, Hollis Frampton visited the poet imprisoned in St. Elizabeths Hospital in Washington 'almost daily' for a year.[8] In a 1962 seminal essay titled 'Notes on the New American Cinema', the movement's staunch advocate Jonas Mekas defined the primacy of the artist over the critic by paraphrasing a famous Pound dictum: 'it is the artist, with all his imperfections, who is the antenna (e. pound) [sic] of his race, not the critic'.[9] Brakhage later quoted the same dictum in a 1996 interview.[10] Similarly, film-maker Willard Maas, during a famous 1953 debate about film and poetry with Maya Deren, Arthur Miller, Dylan Thomas and Parker Tyler, demonstrated his intimate familiarity with Pound's work by quoting by heart Pound's definition of the image.[11]

In addition to fellow film-makers, there were many poets in Pound's lineage who had been close friends with or mentors of Brakhage: Robert Duncan, Charles Olson, Louis Zukofsky, Michael McClure, Ronald Johnson and Guy Davenport. Among their many expressions of appreciation for Pound, I shall only quote from those most significant to this investigation. McClure, for instance, dramatically depicted the situation faced by poets of Brakhage's generation:

> We saw that the art of poetry was essentially dead—killed by war, by academies, by neglect, by lack of love, and by disinterest. We knew we could bring it back to life. We could see what Pound had done … .[12]

The same emphasis on the use of Pound's work as an 'instrument' for subsequent art was also made by Olson:

> He seems to me definitely our Grandpa … . But the mind of Ez, that's the thing, that's the flare to light us back. He seems to me to have put himself in our hands as the cleanest sort of instrument … .[13]

Ronald Johnson, whose poetry became particularly relevant for Brakhage in the 1990s,[14] likewise insisted upon Pound as a bridge:

> There are few enough people who learned what Pound was really getting at. Olson did, and Hugh Kenner and Guy [Davenport]. They became men of great culture and went back into time to find what was live.[15]

It was perhaps Guy Davenport who most succinctly expressed this general point about the whole of Pound's work, with the formula '*to find the best in the past and pass it on*'.[16] This seems to be an idea common to all these artists: finding value in Pound's effort to recover from the past something still useful and alive for the future. Given Brakhage's personal friendships with all of these artists, and his personal study of Pound's texts, it is worth considering the possibility that this was a sort of 'given fact' in Brakhage's mind. Thus I shall try to establish what Brakhage came to treasure as Pound's 'heritage'. It is likely that each of them interpreted this revivified history in a personal way, much as Pound himself did, with different nuances based on personal interests and attitudes. For my specific hypothesis, Robert Duncan seems to have been particularly relevant in 'bridging' or reinforcing some ideas from Pound for Brakhage. It is Duncan who explicitly expressed positions very close to those of Pound, connecting spirituality and art, as well as giving a glimpse into the theoretical and historical content of them. So it is plausible that the young film-maker found confirmations and reinforcements in the older San Francisco poet. Duncan for instance wrote:

> As important for me is Pound's role as the carrier of a tradition or lore in poetry, that flowered in the Renaissance after Gemistos Plethon, in the Provence of the 12th century that gave rise to the Albigensian gnosis, the *trobar clus*, and the Kabbalah, in the Hellenistic world that furnished the ground for orientalizing-Greek mystery cults, Christianity, and neo-Plato-nism.[17]

Duncan clearly refers here to the mix of occult doctrines and figures that, according to the studies of Demetres Tryphonopoulos and Leon Surette,[18] were at the root of Pound's beliefs. Among the artists in Brakhage's milieu, and in particular among those he had the occasion to personally befriend and spend time with, Duncan remained the closest to Pound's mystically-oriented ideas. Given the strong familiarity of the film-maker with the San Francisco poet during the crucial years of Brakhage's artistic apprenticeship, Duncan seems to be a prime candidate for the reinforcement of such ideas in Brakhage's mind. Similarly, I shall consider Duncan only as a reinforcement of Pound's positions for Brakhage.

Brakhage befriended Duncan in the Autumn of 1952, when the nineteen-year-old film-maker moved to San Francisco to live in Duncan's basement, a mere three years after receiving *The Cantos* as a birthday present.[19] In the two years he was there he participated in the evening gatherings hosted at Duncan's house:

> Duncan's house was my school and he was my teacher. Every evening there was a discussion about films, plays, poems, music, and paintings.[20]

During one of these discussions Duncan might have easily pointed out, as he would in essays written shortly after that time, how it was clear to him that Pound, especially in the essays *The Spirit of Romance* and 'Cavalcanti', was not turning to medieval knowledge with 'the antiquarian's concerns', but was rather in search of 'enduring terms'.[21] Alongside the search for such still-timely terms, Pound also expressed the belief that sudden revelation is 'the point of the writing', and likewise that the aim of the writer is 'revelation'.[22] Brakhage went on to expand such potential to all art. Duncan too drew from Pound's writings exactly that conclusion, and regarded the work of art as a 'mystical experience' that changes the work's audience.[23] For this reason, he felt that the main concern of the artist is 'to make real what is only real in a heightened sense':[24] to try to convey through the work that higher state, that eternal state of mind, that experience of the divine, which the artist is specially attuned to enter. Whether Brakhage's conviction that the art process entails spiritual revelation came directly from Pound, through the mediation of Duncan, or from elsewhere, it certainly followed this line of thought, where '[t]he arts traditionally exist in mystery'.[25]

The content of the tradition that Pound reworked was drawn from the occult lore he was exposed to during his formative years in London and Paris. The turn of the twentieth century marked the peak of a revival of occult interests. In Europe the major centres were London and Paris, both cities where Pound resided.[26] Pound's friendship and famous collaboration with W. B. Yeats provided his introduction to occult studies, while the scholarly books and teachings of theosophist G. R. S. Mead nourished and deepened Pound's occult interests.[27] From Mead, Pound would adopt the view that Gnosticism and Neoplatonism were the historical chains of transmission for Hellenic and pagan elements within the Christian world.[28] The origins and the often eccentric content of Pound's positions in relation to such 'spiritual' lineage were first comprehensively traced by Demetres Tryphonopoulos in his 1992 *The Celestial Tradition*, and by Leon Surette in his 1993 *The Birth of Modernism*, and I draw upon their scholarship and vocabulary in my account of Pound's ideas. These two scholars consider the occult knowledge popular at the time, which was further developed by many intellectual figures close to Pound, as central to the formulation of Pound's core ideas about the meaning and function of art, and likewise to the outlining of the theoretical content of Pound's purported historical tradition.

Since Brakhage openly acknowledged the importance and influence of Pound on such issues, I shall here open a small parenthesis about the critical consideration of occult or mystical elements in the assessment of Brakhage's ideas. Among the critical writings on Brakhage, it is only in Bruce Elder's work that occult references or vocabulary surface, though they are considered only tangentially, and not directly in relation to Brakhage's conceptions of art. For instance, when considering Henri Bergson's theories in relation to Brakhage's films,[29] Elder recognises the cultural importance of the 'occult revival' (at least in France, although its epicentre was in London) between the end of the nineteenth and the beginning of the twentieth century as a favourable condition for the reception, though not for the formulation, of Bergson's theories. Elder in fact regards Bergson as a relevant precursor to some of Alfred North Whitehead's ideas, and consequently to Charles Olson's quasi-scientific perspective on art; a perspective that will be wholly embraced by Elder, especially in its jargon, and that would, according to him, constitute a cornerstone influence on Brakhage's ideas.[30] Despite this narrow position, Elder cannot avoid conceding that many of Bergson's ideas possess a strong Gnostic tendency, and he acknowledges that Bergson read Plotinus and eventually became 'increasingly more enthusiastic about the mystical philosopher in his later years'.[31] Furthermore, the 'American Tradition' in the title of Elder's monograph is crucially influenced by Ralph Waldo Emerson, whose Gnosticism he equally recognises[32] as having helped shape that 'American religion' which, according to Harold Bloom, 'is really Gnosticism and not Christianity'.[33] Likewise the 'Gnostic metaphysics' of *The Cantos*[34] or the occultism of Pound[35] do not pass unnoticed. In a note to a 2005 essay about Brakhage and Dante Alighieri, Elder observes that Robert Duncan's ideas were also 'shaped ... by his occultist upbringing':[36]

> Raised in a house of hermetic practitioners, Duncan continued to take an interest in arcana all his life. His work was deeply influenced by the occultism of Ezra Pound, whose coterie believed that Dante's strong interest in the Troubadours and the Templars indicated a covert adherence to their unorthodox mystical traditions.[37]

Despite the presence of all these passing mentions, occultism is not considered in the investigation of Brakhage's ideas, even as Elder regards the influence of occult philosophy as important in the 'shaping' of *all* American art between the 1920s and the 1960s.[38] In the absence of any prior study about occult-derived elements in Brakhage's spirituality, the works of Tryphonopoulos and Surette offer a helpful starting point, given the attention they focus upon Pound's philosophical lineage, and given the influence Pound had on the North American artistic scene. The influence that occultism had on Pound and the influence Pound in turn had on Brakhage, do not entail that Brakhage was an occultist; nonetheless, it is important to outline the content of the poet's occult-derived ideas to determine if they have generated further ideas in the film-maker.

The tradition that Pound wanted to revive was a mystic cult of Amor, a system intended to link humans, nature and the divine, dating back to the Eleusis fertility rites. Pound believed the lineage of this tradition included such figures as Homer, Sextus Propertius, Ovid, Virgil, the Neoplatonics, Johannes Scotus Erigena,[39] Robert Grosseteste, the troubadours, Peire Vidal, Cavalcanti and Dante. Some of these figures, like Erigena, Grosseteste, Vidal, Cavalcanti and Dante, would come to be included in Brakhage's own pantheon (and outside of Pound's perspective it would be certainly puzzling to find them within a film-maker's personal pantheon).[40] According to Pound's view of this tradition, a secret wisdom was passed on from one individual to another within this 'timeless brotherhood of artists who share a sacred mystery or arcanum esoterically expressed in art'.[41] Duncan had an analogous perception of artistic tradition when he drafted a similar list composed of Dante, Shakespeare and Milton as bearers of a 'poet-lore handed down ... from poet to poet' in order to reveal through art 'the nature of the divine world'.[42] According to occult thinking, to which Pound subscribed, this tradition was carried on in secret by its alleged members. Each member interpreted some of its elements in an idiosyncratic way, but the main content of it, a secret content, was preserved against mainstream, institutional, and other external forces, thanks to the members' secrecy.

The term occult, which I here adopt in the specific sense of Tryphonopoulos and Surette's vocabulary, becomes then an umbrella term for a set of different disciplines and doctrines which have been organised by each occultist in an idiosyncratic way (and in this sense it comes close to the common usage of the term mysticism). It pertains to what is beyond ordinary knowledge, involving supernatural forces which seem to require secrecy. The obscure beliefs nourishing the occult tradition are often archaic, unconventional doctrines that had been overwhelmed, opposed or suppressed by mainstream institutional ideas. Tryphonopoulos outlines it as a sort of religious thought outside of religious orthodoxy (including for instance movements such as Gnosticism, Hermeticism, Neoplatonism, Cabalism, and Theosophy) and always involving the possibility of unmediated experience of the divine.[43] Surette further enlarges the term's theoretical reach by including 'any other mystical, illuminated, pneumatic, or visionary tradition whatsoever'.[44] This also because occultism is usually highly personal and 'very thin on dogma and practice'[45] since it postulates the actual possibility of a subject having a *personal* contact with a deity, whomever or whatever it is.

While occultism varies greatly in practice across different places and times, its similarities would necessarily include a heterogeneity of knowledge which flows into its beliefs; the unorthodox nature of such knowledge (often labelled as heresy in the past); and the extreme freedom of the student of occultism in picking through and reworking ideas, due to the refusal of any orthodoxy or dogma. A consequence of these features of occultism is that, when one tries to define common aspects of this knowledge, it is necessary to stick to more or less general formulations. A similar situation is faced by anyone who tries to clarify Brakhage's positions in relation to spirituality and art.

From the perspective of Pound, Duncan, and Brakhage, a work of art becomes the perfect instrument for eliciting revelation, assuming the function, the value, and sometimes the form of a ritual. In a definition very close to that of Brakhage, Tryphonopoulos describes *The Cantos* as a text

> specifically designed to bring about, in those readers who are open, pure of heart and willing to hear, the … true and complete seeing and knowing. The text can be the bridge … through which the initiate can attain revelation, the unmediated vision of the deity.[46]

Apart from pointing out the core property of a work of art for this line of thought, one which applies for Brakhage as well, such a perspective offers more historical substance and theoretical consistency to Brakhage's otherwise obscure belief that every time he read *The Cantos* he came 'to new mysteries which he [Pound] has set significantly within learned reach'.[47] Perhaps Duncan reinforced this impression, as he notably considered Pound's poetry as a ritual.[48] Pound himself confirmed that interpretation when he explained the unique value of troubadour and Tuscan love poetry for its having made a distinction between a simpler song and a *canzone* as a 'ritual' with 'its purpose and its effect', 'subtler' in its nature and designed to elicit its 'revelations to those who are already expert'.[49] Similarly Brakhage wished that his own art could be 'of some use to someone',[50] and that this use could indeed be of a spiritual kind:

> That would be one of my most fervent, hoped-for intentions, that humans could use my work in some spiritual way, in some meditative way. Because then you're making it your own in a way that is freeing. One of my problems with a lot of religions is the tendency of people to get hung up on them.[51]

It is instructive to observe how his vocabulary and his sense of his own films remain richly suggestive of occult spirituality, particularly in light of the history of the ideas he professed about art. Brakhage was not an occultist in the same sense as, for instance, his film-maker friends Kenneth Anger or Harry Smith; but in retracing the history of Brakhage's ideas about art, and mainly through Pound and Duncan, it becomes difficult to avoid the conclusion that they were influenced by and derived from some typically occult themes.

As previously mentioned, Brakhage often stated that his work was made under a sort of trance. As he described it in one of the most significant of such statements,

> I work in a trance state. ... [I]f I were called to the phone for something urgent, it took me up to thirty seconds to answer a question. The brain was coming up out of deep working concentration. Sometimes I hesitate to use the word "trance". The Western way to put it would be "concentration", except that we have diluted the meaning of concentration and shifted it away from a spiritual accent, because *this* kind of trance is certainly one where you could hope to, expect to, meet angels and hear voices ... .[52]

Thus the meaning of trance is charged with a 'spiritual accent', while in non-spiritual terms one might speak of a very deep concentration. During this state the artist seems to be connected with another plane of existence, one so alien to quotidian matters as to seem a part of another world in which there is an actual danger of losing oneself and literally going crazy. At the same time this state seems to produce a different mode of awareness, with a sensibility and receptivity conducive to artistic creation. In that sense, the difference between a normal state and an artistic trance would be a difference of modality or sensibility and not necessarily another place magically visited by the mind, as in a dream. It is possible to frame Brakhage's trance state as his personal version of that heightened state of perception from which, according to Pound and Duncan, art is born. This trance state would then also represent, in the occultist perspective, the access granted to some particular individuals, in this case artists, to that mystical experience that they try to share and elicit through the work of art.

What Brakhage was talking about is clearly shown in a short film made by his wife, Marilyn Brakhage, during her husband's shooting of the *Visions in Meditation* series (1989–1990) in Mesa Verde and in the deserts of Colorado and New Mexico in 1988. In this short piece entitled *For Stan* (2009),[53] we can see the kind of spasmodic movements he was forced to make in attempting to convey with the camera what he was experiencing in his mind. While he runs around, closing his eyes between shots, panning the camera and changing the focus, it is possible to perceive the tension and focus of his mind and body during these acts. In the associated activities of filming, such as changing rolls or changing lenses, the same concentration is visible, though coupled with an extreme efficiency. Another interesting aspect is that even when he walks around in search of his next shot, he never seems to wander randomly; everything he does seems previously studied or prepared. Thus, the two most striking aspects of his process of filming that emerge from this piece are his idiosyncratic movements and his visibly deep concentration. The creation of hand-painted films, while obviously requiring a different creative process than the photographed example above, also induced in Brakhage a trance-like state.

In describing his trance state, Brakhage claimed that he was possessed by the Muses. These forces supposedly drove the artist in the creation of his work, taking control of the whole process while he lacked rational awareness during the trance. The Muses differed in names, forms and kinds, perhaps depending on the artist's particular attitude or sensibility in the moment of 'possession'. Brakhage described the Muses in interviews:

> For me the Muse is a persuasion. It often feels like a force in Nature that moves through certain people, but it should never be appropriated by human beings.[54]

> In my work process it is no surprise that there are over a hundred dimensions, and that "creatures" move through these dimensions … .[55]

According to Brakhage, the Muses are forces that are part of nature and thus of this world. They can neither be controlled by the will of the artist nor humanised, as they are in popular depictions, since they are inclinations operating from within. In fact, in trying to give an idea of them, Brakhage also defined them as 'manifestations of the unconscious' in order to stress the fact that they are ineffable to the human mind while still present and real, rather than connected to some sort of psychological fantasy.[56] The different manifestations of these forces constituted for Brakhage the shared content of dreams, fantasies and myths. Thus, the ineffable and mysterious dimension from which the Muses arise could also generate 'fairies, elves' or 'demons'.[57] This apparently quite idiosyncratic view is close to Pound's definition of myths as 'explications of mood' intended as a 'psychic experience', where one 'understands Persephone and Demeter' or 'the

Laurel', or where one may have 'met Artemis', experientially.[58] What Brakhage defined as Muses, then, was a version of Pound's core idea about Greek myths.

Because of the 'possession' experienced during the trance state and the consequent manifestation of unknown forces that took over the creative process, Brakhage was insistent that the artist becomes a mere instrument.[59] The Muses allegedly manifested themselves and gave the work to him in his trance state, using the artist as a mere instrument:

> … something beyond me is shaping the kinds of film I make and how I make them, and I am merely the instrument for this process.[60]

It seems that Brakhage did lose control over his actions, and yet this loss of authorial control was quite dissimilar to, for instance, chance operations because of the directed, if ineffable, drive of these mysterious forces. Even if the question of control and authorship within such mystical terms cannot be definitively answered, the idea of the artist as instrument may be critically understood not only in terms of the deflection of authorship, but rather (especially for his later years) as a particular way for the artist to come to terms with his inability to explain what he was experiencing: the ineffable source of his creative urges.

The Muses manifesting themselves during the trance state seemed to come to Brakhage from an ineffable dimension that when accessed coincided with an illuminated or heightened state, and with the idea of the divine. Even if comprehending or defining this state in rational terms is impossible, various definitions have been attempted. Brakhage, for instance, highlighted the mysterious quality of such a state by employing terms such as 'ineffable', 'unknown', 'unconscious' or 'Unnameable', to define both the Muses as well as god.[61] What Brakhage meant by 'unconscious' was not something primarily or exclusively psychoanalytic, as the term would suggest, but more simply something unknown. In fact, he equated the unconscious with both the unknown and the ineffable.[62] The unconscious, the unknown and the ineffable are three interchangeable terms in Brakhage's vocabulary and they define the fundamental trait of his idea of the divine. The other primary features of his understanding of the divine included manifestations such as the Muses, which would account for imagination and myths, and the heightened state through which an artist creates his work, defined as trance.

Pound was more specific about these concepts, but his ideas once again bear a striking resemblance to Brakhage's. For the poet, the very nature of the ineffable was something that could only be experienced for brief moments and never rationally comprehended. Pound warned that 'trying to rationalize the prerational is poor fishing'.[63] He also asserted that 'the Gods exist',[64] and that, for him, a god was 'an eternal state of mind'.[65] As a state of mind, a god is therefore something actually attainable. He further explained:

> When is a god manifest? When the states of mind take form. When does a man become a god? When he enters one of these states of mind.[66]

States of mind are dependent upon a range of emotions, and for this reason Pound was referring to the gods as a plural category. The 'insistence on the ineffability of genuine revelation'[67], typical of occult thought remained constant in Pound, as it was also significantly always present for Brakhage: the Muses that propelled Brakhage's work were defined as 'manifestations of the unconscious', or more precisely 'genetic manifestations that people shouldn't presume upon'.[68] For both the poet and the film-maker, the fact that the divine state of mind could be reached through emotions, which are typically subjective and difficult to precisely define or even rationalise, broke down any traditional dogmatic borders between the human and the divine. Indeed, when Brakhage used the term 'genetic' to describe the Muses, he implied a material connection with and access to the divine. The ineffability, multiplicity/multiformity and personal and subjective accessibility seem to be the three main traits of this idea of the divine for both Pound and Brakhage.

Being convinced of 'the ineffability of genuine revelation', another important point established by both Pound and Brakhage was the inescapable veracity of such experiences. For both the poet and the film-maker, experiential knowledge was paramount to their spirituality, and direct experience overruled any considerations of whether their revelations were real or fantasy: if they experienced them, the revelations therefore must be true. Whereas fantasy, imagination and personal dispositions were understood as elements that influenced the access to the divine state of mind, the veracity of the existence of the divine state was for both artists beyond question. Due to their direct experiences, they regarded revelation as empirical, but the awareness of the divine could never be rationally expressed. For this reason it was still necessary for them to speak of beliefs:

> I mean or imply that certain truth exists. ... Truth is not untrue'd by reason of our failing to fix it on paper. Certain objects are communicable to a man or woman only "with proper lighting", they are perceptible in our own minds only with proper "lighting", fitfully and by instants.[69]

For Pound, the point was not whether or not these truths exist, as for him they certainly did, but how to reach the right disposition in order to access them. With such a set of beliefs, art could be understood as a privileged way of reaching such a disposition. For his part, Brakhage had a lifelong quarrel with P. Adams Sitney about the veracity of such revelatory experiences. This quarrel, and the position held by Brakhage, demonstrate how for him, just as with Pound, the existence of certain truths was unquestionable and could not be confined to mere fantasy. The visual phenomena that Brakhage tried to translate into films with his extremely heterogeneous and inventive techniques were an attempt to convey what was going on in his perceptual apparatus, the act of seeing in general, but also that spiritual drive that urged him to create which manifests itself in the mind of those with the right sensibility. All of this, he felt, would have no meaning whatsoever (neither his attempts nor the states he was trying to represent) if his imagery could be confined to the category of mere fantasy. In a conversation published in 1973 Brakhage lamented,

> the minute P. Adams refused to search for his own hypnagogic vision, we had our next quarrel, which sprang up when I said I am the most thorough documentary film maker in the world because I document the act of seeing as well as everything that the light brings me. ... He and many others are still trying to view me as an imaginative film maker, as an inventor of fantasies or metaphors.[70]

The 'act of seeing' was then a sort of 'bridge' towards *everything else* that light brought to him. In line with his tendency to consider himself as an instrument of mysterious forces, he thought of his artistic efforts as an act of documentation. The explicit statement quoted above precedes the publication of the first edition of *Visionary Film*, where Sitney proposed the canonisation of Brakhage as the foremost visionary film-maker. Sitney, in discussing Brakhage, famously employed the term 'mythopoeia', intended as the creation of myths based on classical, literary ones, and intended as visionary fantasies, imagination's *extravaganzas*. Sitney argued that since *Reflections on Black* (1955) Brakhage had begun 'to transcend the distinction between fantasy and actuality, moving into the cinema of triumphant imagination',[71] and thus rejecting any kind of empirical truth about what the film-maker was physically or spiritually experiencing or tried to convey in his films. Brakhage was sill arguing this point in January 2002, a year before his death, when he stated:

> I always had a documentary streak in me, and in fact, my biggest argument with P. Adams [Sitney] was about this issue. ... He always argued with that. He needed to keep the outside and the inside separate, I guess.[72]

Here he neatly caught the essence of Sitney's position of wanting 'to keep the outside and the inside separate', thus rebutting the critic's idea that he transcended 'the distinction between fantasy and actuality' only to exclusively privilege the former and establishing the indisputable primacy of 'triumphant imagination'. William Wees, who brilliantly established a parallel between Brakhage's imagery and actual peripheral visual phenomena – thus focussing on one of the material facts that Brakhage attempted to document – stressed how 'viewers of his films, including many critics, seem to have great difficulty equating the imagery of the films with the phenomena of actual visual perception'.[73] That

Wees had in mind precisely Sitney is demonstrated by a similar remark made in the same book just a few pages later, where 'Sitney's refusal to close his eyes to find equivalents of Brakhage's painting on film' is taken as a paramount example demonstrating the general 'prejudice against the body as the source of art'.[74] The body is the starting point and instrument, as well as place, of the whole process of revelation, since the Muses are 'genetic manifestations'. To rebut this point results in impairing the whole spirituality Brakhage's intended for his art. Whatever Sitney's reasons are for his positions, his refusals and his consequent confinement of Brakhage's films to a mere celebration of fantasy *de facto* greatly limit the possible implications and resonances of Brakhage's art.

Brakhage's idea of myth was influenced by Pound, and, in its peculiar role within their spiritual tradition, it was not only a device used to bring art closer to the multiplicity and dynamism of reality, but also and especially intended to draw viewers closer to ineffable mysteries. It was intended as a sort of spiritual device. For Pound, myth played a very important role in art, but not in a simple, traditional, motivic way. Rather, the mythic image, or situation for Pound represented the transmission of an internal crisis leading to a spiritual metamorphosis, which would be the real function of the myth. As previously mentioned, myths for Pound were 'explications of mood', wherein a god is a 'state of mind'. The states experienced by the subject – trance states in the case of Brakhage – are those which put the human into contact with the divine, through a form of possession by mysterious forces. The mythic explications of such ineffable matters were for Pound not only necessary due to the ineffability of the experience itself, but also were necessitated by the persecution of enlightened subjects (mainly artists) throughout history. Thus, within his occult-influenced view of history, myths were also cloaking devices.

Because of its clandestinity, 'the secret mind of Europe'[75] had to devise from the beginning a subterfuge in order to hand on the mystery and to secure its continuation. This device was, for Pound, myth. In line with the occult understanding of myths 'as records of contacts between the human and the divine',[76] Pound stressed the concealing function of the myth, and in a famous passage he explained the process of mythopoeia in quite precise terms:

> I believe in a sort of permanent basis in humanity, that is to say, I believe that Greek myth arose when someone having passed through delightful psychic experience tried to communicate it to others and found it necessary to screen himself from persecution. Speaking aesthetically, the myths are explications of mood: you may stop there, or you may probe deeper. Certain it is that these myths are only intelligible in a vivid and glittering sense to those people to whom they occur. I know, I mean, one man who understands Persephone and Demeter, and one who understands the Laurel, and another who has, I should say, met Artemis. These things are for them real.[77]

The translation of revelatory experiences into myths is no longer necessary because of the danger of persecution, but rather because of the experiences' ineffable nature. So, since 'the whole greek [sic] time had been a mythopoeic sense, and concern with the un-named',[78] the myth remained for Pound the primary form in which a revelation was communicated, as it 'cannot be translated, paraphrased, or otherwise made explicit or manifest'.[79] The 'mythological exposition' is a device through which one is permitted 'an expression of intuition without denting the edges or shaving off the nose and ears of a verity'.[80] Robert Duncan defined the myth in similar terms.[81]

Surette pointed out that in studies of Modernism the importance of mythopoeia is usually considered in 'an explicatory rather than investigative spirit'.[82] But if its relevance can be (partly) traced to major contributions in anthropology flourishing during Pound's apprenticeship[83] or as a purely 'stylistic resource', a myth's occult aspect and its function as 'a source of inspiration and thematic enrichment' should also rightly be stressed.[84] In the same spirit, an occult-inspired perspective can suggest that Brakhage created his own myths because it was the only way in which he could hope to communicate the experiences he underwent.

The last part of Pound's statement on myth, in which he explained how someone can experience and thus understand Demeter or Persephone because they are real states, can offer a means of understanding some of the cryptic descriptions Brakhage gave of his trance state and of the Muses. These entities that enter the subject, a subject who can 'hope to, expect to, meet angels and hear voices',[85] in order to stimulate possibly the same state of mind Pound was referring to, were described by Brakhage as different for each individual sensibility:

> I do bar certain entities from moving through me because they are not of my kind. I cannot dance with them. I bar just exactly some of those that—and I am not making a value judgement here – Kenneth Anger or Harry Smith can use very well and make a great, magnificent, powerful beauty from. *These* I don't work with, so I do have my prohibitions in the trance state.[86]

Brakhage's Muses seem to be at the very least forces of persuasion which inform the nature of the work of art as the final outcome of the creative process. The form of the artwork can indeed be a myth in Pound's sense, a form necessary to transmit the experience the artist undergoes in meeting and being possessed by the Muses. As a consequence, the work of art can then be an aid to the receiver in accessing the divine. In such a view, art becomes a tool or guide to revelation, and it may be regarded as a spiritual activity. This idea derives from the traditional 'hermeneutic of Hellenistic Neoplatonism', for which a myth, when intended in a particular and concealed way, can reveal 'the nature of the divine'.[87]

The function of the myth can thus be considered from an investigative angle, as what was passed down from the Hellenic world to the Middle Ages was not only and not primarily 'a specific reading, a specific interpretation' of the myths, but 'an idea of the scope of their meaning'.[88] Pound, for instance, listed different figures within his 'conspiracy of intelligence'[89], without worrying too much about historical accuracy or evidence 'because they all wrote about the same thing'.[90] And, while Brakhage was even less precise than Pound, he inherited the same idea about art as the expression by special individuals of something ineffable that happened to them, in order to drive the receiver of the work of art to a similar ineffable state or plane of existence. What remained constant throughout Brakhage's career was his intention that the work of art serves to both express and induce a spiritual process, an occasion for spiritual revelation.

An historical parenthesis: Agamben's account of a medieval *Weltanschauung*

Pound's so-called 'tradition' is not completely the result of his imagination; on the contrary, it reworks some Gnostic and Neoplatonic themes that had survived and were later recovered by the troubadours and the Italian *Dolce Stil Novo*. Consequently, those who attached themselves to, or were influenced by, such tradition (and this includes Brakhage) absorbed ideas that have their historical roots in a remote past. Many elements of Pound's heterogeneous philosophy are in fact part of genuine historical traditions, and it is here useful to briefly recapitulate Giorgio Agamben's account of such a medieval synthesis of different doctrines, as this will historically anchor Brakhage's spiritual ideas about art to a cultural frame much more consistent than naive and mystical gibberish. Through this historical perspective, a good deal of Brakhage's vocabulary and views can appear less idiosyncratic, and new meaning can be found in Brakhage's claim to be part of a tradition of 'artists of all kinds'.[91]

What in the mind of Pound was a secret tradition, an esoteric brotherhood of artists and philosophers, was, for the love poets of medieval Provence and Tuscany, an ancient and elaborate agglomeration of diverse disciplines pointing towards an understanding of the relationship between visible and invisible forces. In 'The Word and the Phantasm: The Theory of the Phantasm in the Love Poetry of the Duecento', Giorgio Agamben retraces this medieval *Weltanschauung* as an encounter between Aristotelian phantasmology and Stoic-Neoplatonic pneumatology.[92] The result was an harmonious synthesis of intersecting fields of knowledge he terms pneumophantasmology. In some medieval poems, for instance, one can easily find notions of medicine, cosmogony, religion and physics, all sitting side by side. Agamben's essay will here be summarised and simplified in accordance with the needs of this investigation.

In medieval psychology and physiology, the theory of sensation established that 'sensible objects impress their forms on the senses', and thereafter this impression (phantasm) is 'received by the phantasy, or imaginative virtue, which conserves it even in the absence of the object'.[93] This idea was first attested by Aristotle, who intended this impression as 'movement' or 'passion produced by the sensation'.[94] After entering the phantasy/imagination, the impression assumes a status different from sensation, and 'it is not possible to identify it with operations that are always true, like science and intellection'.[95] The name 'phantasm' comes from *phantasia* (imagination), which, as Aristotle observed, is etymologically connected with light (*phaos*), because for the Greeks sight was the most important sense and light was its necessary element.[96] The phantasm, this sensual impression re-elaborated by the imagination, would also be fundamental for memory, which is 'the possession of a phantasm as icon of what it is a phantasm of';[97] for cognitive processes (so far as being considered a 'necessary condition of intellection'),[98] in dreams; and in language.

To the circulation (reception, re-elaboration and re-transmission, in the case of art) of these impressions was coupled the very ancient doctrine of the 'pneuma', which provided a sort of physiological ground for it. The pneuma, often identified in air-like elements such as breath, wind and spirit, was for Aristotle the cause of male fertility, a necessary element of life which is of an 'astral nature'.[99] According to this theory, the pneuma circulates into the body, transforming itself through a particular circulatory system separated from the blood's circulation. For the pneuma, as in the case of blood, problems with the circulation were said to cause illness.[100]

From this medical theory, the Stoics created a cosmology and psychology centred around the pneuma. For them it was a fire, a vital principle, of which the stars are made and living beings are vivified in a 'single pneumatic circulation [that] animates the intelligence, the voice, the sperm, and the five senses'.[101] The Neoplatonics interpreted the pneuma as a 'vehicle (*ochema*) or subtle body that accompanies the soul during the course of its soteriological romance from the stars to the earth'.[102] Furthermore, for the Neoplatonics the pneuma assumed some features which were later echoed by Pound as well as Brakhage's ideas of trance, Muses and of art as spiritual revelation:

> During earthly life, the pneuma is the instrument of the imagination and, as such, it is the subject of dreams, of astral influences, and of the divine illuminations (in divination, when according to Iamblichus, "the ethereal and luminous vehicle circumfusing the soul is illuminated by divine light" and "the divine phantasms, moved by the will of the gods, seize our imagination"; and in ecstasy, which is explained by Iamblichus as the descent of a divine pneuma into the body).[103]

The Neoplatonics extended the notion of pneuma and prepared the ground for its medieval reception. For this reception, a decisive role was played by medicine, for which the spirit was the medium between soul and body, 'participating in the nature of both' (and present in the body in three different forms in the liver, the heart and the brain), and in the three chambers of the brain producing imagination, memory and reason.[104] Thus, a 'single pneumatic current'[105] would enact not only life in the body but in every one of the faculties, including the mental ones. This scientific explanation sealed all potential philosophical speculations into a coherent system which was supposed to find its verification in reality.

Agamben's conclusion about this medieval *Weltanschauung* is useful in giving an overview of this system's various consequences, which, when considered altogether, he terms pneumophantasmology:

> The synthesis that results is so characteristic that European culture in this period might justly be defined as a pneumophantasmology, within whose compass – which circumscribes at once a cosmology, a physiology, a psychology, and a soteriology – the breath that animates the universe, circulates in the arteries, and fertilizes the sperm is the same one that, in the brain and in the heart, receives and forms the phantasms of the things we see, imagine, dream, and love. Insofar as it is the subtle body of the soul, it is in addition the intermediary between the soul and matter, the divine and the human, and, as such, allows the explanations of all the influxes between corporeal and incorporeal, from magical fascination to astrological inclinations.[106]

Eventually this whole tradition that was retraced by Agamben fell 'into the half-light of esoteric circles'.[107] This was because of the antagonism from scholastic theology, which recognised only the medical value of the pneuma and thus confined the whole doctrine to the domain of medicine, separate from all the soteriological and cosmological elements that granted to the pneuma the role of 'concrete and real mediator of the 'ineffable union' between soul and body'.[108] This is why Pound recovered these concepts not only through the reading of the poems, but also through the help of occult lore. And it is also the reason for Pound's insistence that the followers of this tradition had suffered persecution, which he then felt had, in turn, necessitated the esoteric function of myths.

Given the influence of Pound, and Duncan, on Brakhage's ideas, Agamben's pneumophantasmology stands as a valid reference for an hypothesis about their remote origins. This view of reality characterised by the interconnection of all its aspects (visible and invisible ones) corresponds to Brakhage's core understanding of things and phenomena. It can constitute an indirect origin to his ideas about how the invisible world is connected to the visible one, stressing the role of the body and bodily experiences; and how one can, through specific means, elicit in others the experience of such spiritual dimensions.

165

Dante according to Brakhage

At a certain point of his career, Brakhage produced a work which explicitly draws from Pound's tradition and pneumophantasmology, more than other titles in his oeuvre. The film illustrates Brakhage's view about spirituality and art and was the result of both a decisive moment in his life and career, and of many years of studying one of the major figures of his and Pound's pantheons. The film is the 1987 *The Dante Quartet*. While critical work on the film has been abundant, especially from two of the world's most renowned Brakhage scholars, Sitney and Elder, the film has never been considered as indebted to occult and mystical elements. This work marks a divide within Brakhage's life and artistic career: the long, belated end of his first marriage and the beginning of the relationship with his second wife. As is often the case with Brakhage, profound changes in his personal life also intensely affected his artistic production and ideas. Particularly at the end of the 1980s, fresh energies poured into his art, driving the films of his last decade towards an increasing abstraction[109] and a profound spirituality. The biographical occurrences that sparked the film do not exhaust its meaning(s), but they add a personal layer to the palingenetic meaning of the work, as was the case for the original source of inspiration, Dante's *Commedia*.

The Dante Quartet was completed in 1987, and it was directly inspired by the *Divina Commedia*. The film took seven years for its four parts to be completed, or 37 years if one includes Brakhage's study of the *Commedia*.[110] This work, alongside few others, such as the *Faust* series (1987–89) and the *Visions in Meditation* series, is one of the most representative of the major changes Brakhage's life and art underwent between the end of the 1980s and the beginning of the 1990s. His marriage to Marilyn Jull in 1989 finally brought peace to his personal life after the long period of crisis at the end of his first marriage culminated in divorce in 1987. *The Dante Quartet* embodies this whole path from despair to renewal undergone by Brakhage during that period, with its *journey* from one pole to another. The year 1987, when he divorced his first wife Jane, completed *The Dante Quartet* and met Marilyn, becomes then a sort of divide in Brakhage's life and career which opened his final period as an artist. After his second marriage in 1989, he drastically reduced photographing with the camera, increasingly devoting his artistic energies to directly hand-painting on film strips. In particular from 1993 to 1996 he produced exclusively hand-painted films.[111]

The Dante Quartet is an explicitly spiritual work, and it is deeply connected with the artist's personal life. What is particularly interesting about *The Dante Quartet*, apart from its date of completion, is Brakhage's direct assessment of it as stemming from the tradition reworked by Pound. Brakhage in fact saw the *Divina Comme-*

dia as part of a tradition that assesses art as spiritual and ineffable revelation in a mystical sense. About the poem he praised

> the essential ingredient, which is a celebration of mystery! That doesn't mean a lack of mystery. Celebration of mystery allows the maker to acknowledge, by the way he or she has done something, that he or she knows something. But this knowledge also acknowledges mysteries. And the work reverberates.[112]

Apart from the similarity of this description with the vocabulary of Pound and Duncan, in light of pneumophantasmology, we can see how this was not a simply idiosyncratic judgement. The specific literary reference of the film's title and its sections' titles, as well as its peculiar and precise structure, the techniques employed, or the specific personal occurrences from which the work sprout, also help in identifying the cultural origins of Brakhage's ideas about spirituality. In this sense, apart being one of the cornerstone works of Brakhage's filmography, *The Dante Quartet* is the perfect example to attest the echoes of the positions described above. In fact the film takes the *Commedia* as a basic inspiration for re-staging a personal crisis and subsequently overcoming it (namely, the collapse of Brakhage's first marriage), conveying to the viewer a journey towards final illumination; in perfect concert with a tradition in which artists hand down one to another the 'essential ingredient' of their art: the 'mystery'. The film expresses the will to conquer the crisis by concluding with a vision of an ultimate heaven.

The film has a four-part structure. The first part, *Hell Itself*, is a hypnagogic or closed-eye vision of the optic feedback from Brakhage's nerves as he experienced pain from the 'collapse' of his 'whole life'.[113] It is important to point out that before the awareness of a way out, represented by the second part *Hell Spit Flexion*, which would eventually force the subject to pass through the metamorphosis of the third part *Purgation*, in order to become attuned to the divine; the first, hellish part is brighter than the heavenly one. But this is a false brightness, a dangerous and distracting one. In the film, in fact, the values of brightness and darkness are partially modified: *Hell Itself* is very bright, while *Hell Spit Flexion* and *Purgation* are darker with a heavier impasto. Elder rightly points out that this is because the brightness of the first part 'threatens to distract the soul from the quest for wisdom',[114] while the darkness is associated with 'meditative concentration and spiritual focus'[115] in search of the final illumination. This positive view of purgatorial darkness is connected by Elder to Pseudo-Dionysius the Areopagite,[116] corroborating the possibility that in this inversion there are Neoplatonic echoes. But even more in line with Pound's occult tradition, would be to read this purgatorial darkness as the *dromena* of the Eleusis rites. It is possible to retrace this reversal directly to Pound's and Duncan's remarks about the *Commedia*. Pound in fact commented that 'hell is the state of man dominated by his passions', while Duncan described how Dante was 'tempted to linger' in the 'alluring and side-tracking beauty ... of sound and image', defining the artistic result as 'art for art's sake'.[117]

Hell Spit Flexion envisions the possibility of a 'way out'.[118] In fact, this part is framed inside a screen upon a black background, giving the idea of a distant passage out from the dark place where the viewer dwells. *Hell Spit Flexion* was defined by Brakhage as 'the most rhythmically exact of all my work ... inspired by memories of an old man coughing in the night of a thin-walled ancient hotel',[119] underlining the connection between the rhythm and the act of coughing up, getting rid of the pain of that moment.[120] The hotel memory he refers to may have been a reminiscence of the hotel rooms he lived in during the separation from his first wife. Elder relates *Hell Spit Flexion* to 'the transitional zone of Ante-Purgatory'[121] corresponding to cantos I-IX of Dante's *Purgatorio*, following Duncan's discussion of this 'sub-section' in a 1965 lecture on the *Commedia*.[122] The Ante-Purgatory section takes place at the base of the Purgatory mountain where souls are waiting to access the gate Dante reaches in canto IX, beyond which lies real purgation.

The third part of the film, *Purgation*, represents the transformation prior to heaven, or the metamorphosis before reaching the heavenly state of mind. The central theme of this part, according to Sitney, is the 'suggestion of the passage of light'[123] as a sign of new beginning, formally echoed by the 'recycling' of film strips (some passages are painted and scratched over Billy Wilder's *Irma la Douce*).[124] *Purgation* suggests also the passage of time, with its 'nearly twenty fades to blackness'[125] and its moments of 'holding a frame still'.[126] After this comes the fourth part's celebration of a heavenly state of mind: *existence is song*. The title is taken from a sonnet by Rainer Maria Rilke that posits song as the primal element underlying all existence. The concept of song at this point stands very close to what Brakhage defined in the 1970s as 'light',[127] and a connection between Dante and Rilke was in his mind at least since 1963.[128]

The scheme of *The Dante Quartet*, a descent through crisis and out into illumination, echoes the rites of Eleusis, which Tryphonopoulos identifies as a general structuring principle behind *The Cantos*, or at least the principle that Pound kept in mind while initially building the poem (prior to 1945). While this scheme does not completely account for the whole of *The Cantos*, it nevertheless 'remains the only embracing structural principle possessed by this enormous poem',[129] The scheme that Tryphonopoulos identifies in the poem is the tripartite ritual of palingenesis employed in the Eleusis mysteries. Palingenesis is an ancient Greek term defined as the 'motif of transformation' and renewal in occult thought, meaning 'literally "backward birth" or rebirth; a death to the old life and rebirth to a new, higher one'.[130] The occult circle in Kensington, where Pound carried out most of his occult apprenticeship, believed that wisdom is achieved 'through a palingenetic experience'.[131]

The Eleusis ritual was an initiation for presenting the candidate (*mystes*) with the mystery. The mystery celebrated was that of Persephone, consisting of 'a ritual descent to the underworld and a subsequent return to the world of the living'.[132] The first stage was the *katabasis*, the descent, followed by the *dromena*, a moment of confusion in the darkness preceding the final stage, the *epopteia* or illumination.[133] During the illumination the divine was revealed to the candidate who entered into contact with it, becoming a god himself or discovering his latent god-like nature.[134] In the case of *The Dante Quartet*, then, *Hell Itself* would stand as the *katabasis*, *Hell Spit Flexion* and *Purgation* as the *dromena*, and *existence is song* as the *epopteia*.[135] The meaning of this structure is also the one of Dante's *Commedia*, according to an occult interpretation. The different moments of the original procession are not necessarily literally mimicked, but they are intended as movements in the awareness of the subject, as moods or states of mind. In the description of *The Dante Quartet*'s abstraction one has to resort to a parallel with states of mind in order to give an idea of the film's effects on the viewer; this being often the case with Brakhage's hand-painted films. The emotional suggestiveness of the imagery was sought for by Brakhage and it is a further point derived from Pound. Pound in fact pointed out that Dante intended Hell, Purgatory, and Paradise as states of mind and not places, and this opinion was further sustained by his comment that such a view is 'part of the esoteric and mystic dogma'.[136]

The idea of song in *existence is song* expresses an all-encompassing spiritual principle. About song, Brakhage stated:

> … I believe in song. … I believe in the beauty of the singing whale; I am moved deeply at the whole range of song that wolf makes when the moon appears, or neighborhood dogs make – that they make their song, and this is the wonder of life on earth, an I in great humility wish to join this.[137]

The heavenly state finally achieved at the end of *The Dante Quartet* is intended as one of communion with the rest of existence, of the overcoming of personal pains and of awakening of the self to the wonders of creation. This celebratory spirituality is the one that will indelibly mark Brakhage's final years. Also in this case Brakhage's ideas seem to overlap with those of the figures sharing Pound's occult tradition: singing as a principle common to all creation seems in fact to have been influenced by Duncan's *Dante Études*, wherein Duncan, seeking 'intentions in Dante's intentions',[138] mentioned the 'choral soundings' of 'whales and wolves'.[139] Everything spoke to him,[140] providing an answer for the poet's 'ultimate need'.[141]

As a unifying principle and as the specific activity of the heavenly, illuminated state, song overcomes the arbitrary limits of rationality. For instance, such a state resolves, in mystical terms, what Brakhage defined as 'Dualities' by overcoming the 'complex nature of Being'.[142] Such a nature remains complex but at the same time allows a glimpse of being at one with the cosmos. Thus, in *existence is song*, the oppositional forces are at peace – they sing together, so to speak. This can be intuited by the presence of the only two clearly recognisable images in *The Dante Quartet*: the brief shots of an erupting volcano and of the moon's craters. Even if in other moments of the film it is possible to glimpse transparent images beneath the layers of paint, due to the fact that Brakhage often painted over used film, it is only in these two cases that referential images are meant to be recognised. For this reason, they often appear to the viewer as quite puzzling. Sitney, for instance, explains them by speculating that the artist accesses and conveys with this work the 'oceanic undifferentiated structure of the unconscious in which multiple perspectives and contradictory values coexist timelessly'.[143] This could be partly in line with the beliefs that Brakhage discussed, except that Sitney then pushes further towards a Freudian interpretation by evoking the psychoanalytic theory of artistic creativity of Anton Ehrenzweig.[144] The abstraction reached by Brakhage through hand-painting would, according to Sitney, 'recontact both the oral and anal levels of ... fantasy formation',[145] with the oral represented by the inspiration and the anal represented by the projection/production in the artistic process.[146] This would explain the brief images of the erupting volcano (anal phase) and of the moon's craters (oral phase), which could work as a perhaps unconscious explanation of such a process.

But it is possible to frame the coexistence of opposites within a different context: namely, in the tradition of Pound's 'undivided light' or Duncan's 'variety of the one'. While the coexistence of opposites in the work seems clear to all of its critics, about psychological speculations one can only be sure of Brakhage's desire for a renewal in his life, as Sitney himself points out.[147] An harmonious coexistence may only be possible on an intuitive and mystical level, because from the rational point of view there is no way to avoid the existence of conflicting forces in nature. But the work of art can harmonise what the rational mind separates.

In Gnostic terms, the final aim of revelation is not only a spiritual renewal or rebirth of the soul (palingenesis), but also communion with the divine, becoming one with divinity. The revelation is a mystery, and the celebration and contemplation of the 'unity of the mystery'[148] becomes a funtion of spiritual art. As with

Pound's intentions for *The Cantos*, the audience of such work is meant to be driven towards the 'great healing', intended 'to make whole', 'to join the solar and lunar parts of mankind'.[149] This would overcome the opposites that the mind creates, revealing 'the kinship of all things'.[150] The ecstatic joy of such a revelation is the one carried on by Pound's mystical tradition, 'the tradition of the undivided light'.[151]

Robert Duncan seems to have not only inspired Brakhage's metaphor of singing along with creation, but also followed Pound in his task of reaching unity through multiplicity and fragmentation, revealing unity within the multiplicity. According to Duncan, in the interplay of opposite, contrasting or complementary elements, dualities can be overcome, and the work of art (in Duncan's particular case, the poem) is the privileged place for such a process:

> Poems then are immediate presentations of the intention of the whole … the great poem of all poems, a unity, and in any two of its elements or parts appearing as a duality or a mating, each part in every other having, if we could see it, its condition – its opposite or contender and its satisfaction or twin. Yet in the composite of all members we see no duality but the variety of the one.[152]

This passage is used by Elder to explain how opposites are synthesised in Dante's *Purgatorio* and in Brakhage's *purgation* (though this may perhaps have been better expressed in *existence is song*), and how both Dante and Brakhage believed that 'all the momentous dualities and minute conflicts in life are really only passages in a vast cosmopoetic process tending towards unity'.[153] Elder, then, like Sitney, does not fail to recognise in *The Dante Quartet* the urge to shape a unity out of contrasting elements. But again, as with Sitney, the occult, mystical content of the artistic traditions to which Brakhage was part is not considered when investigating the origins or the meaning of Brakhage's ideas or of Brakhage's spiritual endeavour. Even if Brakhage, for instance, once declared that 'Freud's Unconscious … joins opposites as ONE, at once, in Timeless fusion',[154] it is still puzzling to interpret a volcano and the moon's craters as anal and oral manifestations. Brakhage intended the term 'unconscious' mainly literally, as something that cannot be known.

In the following example, interpretations that eschew the occult genealogy of Brakhage's artistic ideas can lead to wilful and rather odd conclusions as regards, again, the ineffable nature of the divine. In *The Dante Quartet*, according to Elder, the hellish part of the film represents the fear of loneliness, of being distracted by the delusory light of a solipsistic art, while the heavenly part represents a state of joyous communion. Elder notes that the fear of loneliness is opposed to the identification of the self with a 'larger matrix'.[155] One may see this matrix as creation itself, with its immanent revelation. But Elder concludes that the

171

mystical journey out of the 'false (solipsistic) imagining',[156] instead of providing a passage towards communion with creation and a tension in order to goad the spiritual revelation, uncovers a 'sense of reality as ephemeral', a desire for identification with a 'transcendent Nothing'.[157] For Elder, '[t]rue singing results … from allowing the self to dissolve in a greater nothingness'.[158] In order to support such a conclusion, he quotes part of Brakhage's definition of the experience of 'God-as-stillness' in the 1995 article 'Having Declared a Belief in God':

> [there is] the ultimate sense of deity as all-pervasive and encompassing peace and protective-ness; but this, too, is a feeling of movement, of being so much at-one with an intricacy of cosmic rhythms, with felt radiant particle/waves (as Niels Bohr would have it) in cancellation of chaos and stasis at one once forever.[159]

In this statement, Brakhage defined the sense of the divine as both stillness and movement, and at no point does he state a desire to 'dissolve in a greater nothingness'. Furthermore, the mention of the Danish physicist is used by Elder to support his theory, because his name would stand 'for the idea that reality is coreless'.[160] In the context of Pound's 'great healing' and Duncan's 'variety of the one', this passage appears as a fairly straightforward remark on the fragmented, antithetical, but harmonious hidden nature of reality. In fact, Niels Bohr's coat-of-arms carried the inscription 'Contraria Sum Complementa' (opposites are complementary),[161] the essence of the principle of complementarity which he introduced in Physics.

In 2005 Elder published an extended essay on *The Dante Quartet* and the relationship between Brakhage and Dante.[162] This essay explicitly discusses Brakhage's ideas in relation to medieval thought and contains many interesting examples of overlapping concerns with the present essay. But what is interesting and singular about Elder's essay is that none of the occult and spiritual elements at the root of Brakhage's cultural heritage are considered. For this reason, Elder comes close to many relevant points regarding Brakhage's spirituality, but without ever reaching conclusions that seem justified in the context of Brakhage's own actual statements and beliefs. In light of Elder's work, the occult philosophical beliefs subscribed to by Pound, and later highlighted by Tryphonopoulos and Surette, as well as the medieval doctrines present in Dante, and later retraced by Agamben, appear all the more crucial to the understanding of Brakhage's personal belief in art as a primarily spiritual activity.

Elder concludes that the main affinity between Brakhage and Dante is in their belief that the ultimate function of a work of art is 'to impart energeia';[163] or, in Duncan's words, either 'directly through philosophical discussion or indirectly through poetic example', to consider the poem, and by extension the work of art, 'as both a transformer and a transmitter of energy'.[164] This conclusion is remarkably similar to Charles Olson's technical definition of a poem as 'energy transferred from where the poet got it … all the way over to, the reader'.[165] Elder, in fact, quotes this crucial statement in his essay,[166] and recognises the philosophical origin of Olson's statement to be Whitehead, who, according to Elder, 'has instructed us' to recognise change as reality and thus not to privilege 'the permanent over the impermanent'.[167]

What seems clear from Brakhage's statements and the allusions in the titles of his films is that the transfer of energy was not his primary concern in the creation of his films. Likewise, to reduce Dante's own intention in writing the *Divina Commedia* to the transfer of energy is to oversimplify the poet to the point of misreading. As we have seen, given Brakhage's statements about his trance states and the Muses, as well as the inspiration he explicitly drew in the past from the works of Pound and Duncan, it would not be much of a stretch to speculate that Dante was relevant to Brakhage as a central figure of Pound's and Duncan's occult tradition. What this tradition offered to Brakhage was not so much, or not only, a series of operative prescriptions, but an outline of the belief in art as the place for spiritual revelation and the ineffable communion with the divine. To reduce Brakhage's aesthetic to what Elder calls Olson's 'methodological' poetics[168] would be to completely overlook the historical origins of Brakhage's spiritual beliefs, as well as his understanding of the mystical and occult functions of art, an understanding shared with Pound and Duncan and absent in Olson. Given Brakhage's constant insistence on the importance of spirituality, rather than any methodological prescriptions, in his art, it is fair to assume that for Brakhage the meaning of the art practice, its *why*, was of greater concern than the technical methodology of the practice, its *how*.

The key to Elder's conclusion is the same concept of energy that Olson employed. Elder gives a more sophisticated background to the concept by considering it in relation to Aristotle's definitions of *dynamis*, *energeia*, and *entelecheia*.[169] Although the concept of *energeia*, which Elder seems to employ as an umbrella term, resembles the idea of the pneuma, it is used in a more scientific and modern sense, even when Elder, in one passage, recognises its hybrid status as a 'spiritual principle' not 'separable from the body'.[170] The umbrella concept of *energeia* is used to move the discourse towards a scientific/philosophical doctrine of change typical of Olson and Whitehead's process philosophy, previously also featured in Elder's 1998 monograph on Brakhage. At the same time, the concept of *energeia* becomes more literal in Elder's attempt to define exactly what the work of art *actually* transmits from one subject to the other. This overlooks the mystery within which the arts exist, according to Brakhage, as well as the ineffable content of the revelation. Furthermore, the substitution of the pneuma by the functions of energy discards not only a necessary cultural background, as outlined by Agamben, but also its connections with the movements of the phantasm, and thus the possibility of the creative force providing a spiritual explanation of the relationship between human and divine, or at least an echo of such a synthesis. *Energeia* for Elder is, in fact, confined to only providing fuel for the soul.[171] In contrast, the final aim of the synthesis present in medieval love poetry was to elevate the subject in the direction of the divine as well as to reveal how the subject has something of the divine in its own nature.

Under the light of Pound's ideas and pneumophantasmology, it is precisely in the celebration of subjectivity, that Elder qualifies as a primal difference, an 'anomaly',[172] that Brakhage's attempts come close to the core intent of Dante's art. In this celebration the phantasm which produces the imagination through the sensible impression of the love process is the 'copula' of 'the *individual* and the unique possible intellect',[173] and through it the phantasm is also the connection at the 'vertex of the individual soul' between 'individual and universal, corporeal and incorporeal',[174] making the subject 'suddenly conscious of the reality of the nous, of mind, apart from any man's individual mind'.[175] That is to say, according to the philosophical tradition that Pound revivified, through subjectivity the active intellect, the divine, the eternal state of mind can be revealed. And it is possible to interpret in this new light Brakhage's paradoxical statement that the truer he was to his 'own particularities of being' (in these terms, his individual mind and how it 'copulates' with the active intellect), the more he became 'clear to everyone else' (through the experience of the active intellect).[176]

The Dante Quartet was created in a state of trance, with the consequences we have already seen: possession by the Muses, the artist as instrument of the creative process, and the possibility of eliciting in the audience a spiritual revelation. The Eleusis mysteries' scheme, present also in the *Commedia* and in *The Cantos*, is the myth behind Brakhage's expression of his palingenetic journey. The general palingenetic tendency of the work is evident in the structure, in the 'recycling' of used film, and in the re-interpretation of Dante's main work. Following his own words, Brakhage 'used' the *Commedia* in a 'spiritual way' by making it 'his own',[177] and through his personal experience, making that work reverberates by 'acknowledging' its 'mysteries'.[178] Furthermore, in the work other occult-derived elements are prominent, like the relevance of the body for the spiritual process (an aspect common to both Pound and Duncan, but already present in pneumo phantasmology), and the tendency to mystically harmonising the contradictions and multiplicity of reality, and thus trying to achieve a communion with creation. To understand all these interconnected aspects of the work, and how they amount to a view of art as spiritual revelation within a sacred call, it is necessary to frame Brakhage's spirituality in the perspective of Pound's 'tradition' and its historical roots.

Coda

I have tried to give the coherence of a quasi-system to some apparently odd spiritual beliefs held by Brakhage in relation to art. This has been attempted by proposing a possible historical origin of such ideas and outlining the more theoretical and general points sustaining this system. There are many other aspects that can reveal echoes of Pound's occult-inspired tradition, deriving especially from the convergence of spirituality with the corporeality of the world, establishing an identity between spirit and matter. Issues such as the stance towards the physical world, science, the body, sex, love, and rhythm bear further similarities between Brakhage and Pound. These constitute viable topics for further investigations about Brakhage's spiritual quest.

Brakhage's spiritual view of reality relied heavily upon the materiality of the world. Similarly, in pneumophantasmology the body was not only the instrument of spiritual revelation, but it became also its place, and an integral part of the process. Also in Brakhage's spiritual quest the physical world becomes not only a functional part of spirituality, but is also necessary for it. It serves as the origin and vessel of spiritual manifestations. As poetry was considered in pneumophantasmology as 'dictated by inspiring love',[179] Brakhage identified 'creativity' with breathing, 'as the name 'inspiration' implies'.[180] Elder frames this point alongside the primary importance that Olson granted to the body, and he remarks that the poet went 'as far as to relate breath … to the phallus'.[181] But we can now trace the origin of such an idea much farther than Olson.

Pound tried to simplify, for the sake of explanation, the whole pneumophantasmology with the admittedly reductive definition 'the aesthetic or interactive vasomotor magnetism in relation to the consciousness'.[182] The body, and a sort of 'scientific' view of it, was central, but Pound strongly opposed any position that conceived of the physical world in merely mechanical, needs-based ways. This was consistent with the occult revival of the late nineteenth and early twentieth century, which was opposed to a materialistic and techno-quantitative world (as a consequence of the industrial revolution), but was not at all hostile to the field of science. Occultists hailed scientific discoveries, such as the discovery of radium, as confirmations of their theories of a universe composed of radiant forces that influenced and intersected with one another and moved through all the planes of reality.

Brakhage had a very similar understanding of, and interest in, science.[183] As was already evident in *Dog Star Man* (1961–64), he never isolated scientific facts from spiritual ideas. So, for instance, in describing the Muses as external and mysterious forces possessing him and thus making him an instrument while under a trance, Brakhage attempted to explain them according to what 'the people' he knew 'in the sciences' had told him: 'that there are well over a hundred dimensions'.[184] Similarly, as we have seen, in trying to define the essence of the divine he mentioned physicist Niels Bohr.[185] For Brakhage, science and spirituality were complementary knowledges, much as Pound and the occult movements had theorised. And, much like them, Brakhage used scientific notions to explain rather than to reject spiritual issues.

Both Brakhage and Pound regarded sex as one of the most positive and intense physical experiences, for the possibility that this activity, when practised in a 'noble' way, so to speak, can involve sensations that go well beyond the material realm, even while deeply rooted in such a dimension. Seemingly contiguous with their emphasis upon revelatory experience, sex for them was an activity in which the union of spiritual with scientific facts, the convergence of matter and spirit, could become immediately clear in everyday perception.[186] Consequently, Brakhage saw the male and female categories primarily in mythical and mystical terms, as embodiments of complementary cosmic forces.[187] More than socially-determined roles, Brakhage regarded genders as forces that everyone has within him/her-self in different proportions. The dichotomy between male and female was considered not simply physical (mechanical) but also cosmic. What Brakhage was looking for with this polarisation was a biological underpinning of mystical categories.

As the necessary condition for sex, love for Brakhage and Pound was 'not a desire but a divine attraction that helps stimulate our spiritual development'.[188] Also Elder recognises that Brakhage was 'committed to the modern proposition that ardent sexual desire is among the highest forms of love'.[189] The kind of refined love they advocated could become 'interpretive of the divine order' by stimulating an 'interpretation of the cosmos by feeling'.[190] Similarly, Duncan believed that '[s]exuality is your boundary with the universe and with the person you touch'.[191] Such beliefs go hand-in-hand with Brakhage's 'sense of the body that identifies … with the cosmos',[192] with a direct correspondence between the *micro* with the *macro*, so to speak. Ronald Johnson held a similar position since, in a 1997 conversation with Brakhage, he stated that he believed brains 'were made to communicate with the universe'.[193] Brakhage, Duncan and Johnson were all echoing Pound in recovering the 'ancient hypothesis that the little cosmos 'corresponds' to the greater',[194] which indeed likewise constituted 'the central theme of the troubadours'.[195]

The theme of the correspondence of earthly, everyday life (the *micro*) with spiritual and cosmic realities (the *macro*) was present in many Brakhage's films in different ways. A concise list could for instance include: *Dog Star Man, Star Garden* (1974), *I ... Dreaming* (1988), *Stellar* (1993), and *Yggdrasill: Whose Roots Are Stars in the Human Mind* (1997). For instance in *Dog Star Man* many of these points were already present. In the film in fact an identity is established between micro and macro realms; materialist scientific knowledge is employed in the service of spiritual theories; the body is featured as the primary form of identity for human beings, and at the same time it is used to correspond to, or commune with, the cosmos; male and female genders are depicted as complementary mystical poles rather than as socially-constructed categories; the sexual interaction of bodies represents a spiritually elevating activity that can possibly bring them closer to a sense of cosmic unity; and the superimposition of visual phenomena, combined with hand-painted abstraction, reflects internal nervous activity through which the external world is perceived, embodying further proof of the inextricable relationship between internal and external, self and other, visible and invisible, subjective and objective, spiritual and material.

Brakhage's spiritual and scientific understanding of a reality composed of emotions, experiences, inputs and outputs, excitations, energies, invisible forces, complementary polarities, lights, dances, and songs, manifests itself (also aesthetically) in waves, vibrations, radiations, pulses, surges, ripples, beats, and flows. What all these features have in common materially is the ability to manifesting themselves through different kinds of rhythm. Rhythm, as a common attribute of every type of movement in the cosmos, became for Brakhage a crucial element linking bodily, astronomical, emotional, natural, spiritual, and artistic phenomena. It becomes, in a sense, a sort of secret, 'untutored' language through which all the elements of creation influence, communicate, or differ from one another, and through which their similarities and congruence become recognisable. The various elements that Brakhage periodically saw as all-encompassing cosmic forces tending towards an ultimate unity, such as light, song, and dance, all manifest themselves through rhythmic vibrations, waves, or movements. Brakhage's rhythms are clearly perceivable, often pleasurable, and match the emotional tone of each specific film, but at the same time they can be hardly labelled or fitted

177

within the common rhythmic categories of music, poetry, or even cinema itself, except in an extremely generalised way.

The Dante Quartet can serve as a useful example of Brakhage's use of rhythm, specifically in the film's second part, *Hell Spit Flexion*. As I have already discussed, *Hell Spit Flexion* was inspired by Brakhage's memory of hearing a man coughing through the walls of a hotel, a situation that, due to the period in which it occurred and the overall stated meaning of *The Dante Quartet*, came to epitomise for Brakhage his growing distance from his first wife. Brakhage stressed that the rhythmic qualities of *Hell Spit Flexion* mimic the act of coughing, and that the film reflects the physical act of trying to get rid of pain and torment. *Hell Spit Flexion* is the shortest part of *The Dante Quartet*, roughly 40 seconds, as well as being its darkest part. Its hand-painted moments were almost entirely created atop a print of *The Garden of Earthly Delights* (1981). The imagery's space of *Hell Spit Flexion* is re-framed inside a smaller frame within which images are contained: the window has the same shape and proportions of the frame (4:3), but with an area one-fourth of that of the frame.

The detritus-like bits of hand-painting dominating the film might suggest the idea of mucus traces over an internal, dark tissue like the walls of the throat. And the rhythm of the film comes to serve as a kind of protagonist, since the irregular but quick successions of images that come as a 'disturbance' of the blackness, give an almost annoying, insistent sense of coughing in the attempt to get rid of such sediments. In this sense, the value of the hand-painted images in the film is the reverse of their usual function, since they appear here as something the subject wishes to go away and not to contemplate. Their insistent return in this highly somatic piece creates a disturbing sensation of anxiety, like sudden spasms of coughing. The apparently short duration of *Hell Spit Flexion* might likewise correspond to the duration of a long attack of intense coughing, when, for instance, there may be something stuck in the throat.

The rhythm of *Hell Spit Flexion* becomes, then, the expression of a bodily act, inspired by a specific episode in the life of Brakhage and related to his personal situation during that period. The act of spasmodically getting rid of something through repeated attempts is not only indicative of the act of coughing, but it assumes other resonances in light of his personal life and, more importantly, it assumes a potentially universal meaning when considered as part of *The Dante Quartet*. In the context of the complete film, it represents part of the process of struggling towards elevation and spiritual illumination, where, in the moment right after the hellish state of mind, the possibility of a still-distant way out is recognised, and purgation is required to achieve that end. The rhythm is therefore primarily somatic, and clearly perceivable as such by the audience, but it becomes also a fundamental step within a spiritual process that necessarily passes through the corporeality of the world and expresses itself in rhythmical shifts.

It is not easy to discuss in an objective way spiritual matters and beliefs, especially when they are not organised into precise formulations or when their source is not clear. Stan Brakhage's spirituality appears as profoundly personal and acutely idiosyncratic, apart from being rarely and enigmatically discussed. It was certainly unorthodox, undogmatic and dynamic. While he was sensitive to a sort of empathetic human warmth, a sense of communion occasioned by church services,[196] he nevertheless admitted that he never found 'a church or community' properly 'attuned' to his 'own sensibilities'.[197] Even if Brakhage's naturally rebellious mind-set was sometimes in contrast with Pound's extreme syncretism, and even more so with Pound's consequent deviant political ideology, he nonetheless cherry-picked from the poet's barely defined but potent sense of the sacred. This frame, against which I have discussed some of his apparently odd statements and practices, gives back a coherence otherwise unlikely.

The general sense one may draw from the trajectory I have outlined is that of a sort of sacred call for art felt by Brakhage and others attached to the same tradition. Brakhage, in fact, employed the expression 'sacred calling' and characterised it as going 'back to the dawn of time', stating his awareness of being somehow part of an ancient tradition.[198] This is also corroborated by a paraphrase that Brakhage drew from a very interesting and scarcely known letter by Pound. Such a transmission of ideas not only points out once more the profound familiarity that the film-maker had with the poet's work, but it also addresses a central point of their shared beliefs in a quite straightforward way. During a 1997 interview, Brakhage quoted by heart a definition of religion as 'the popularization of the arts'.[199] Pound's original expression was: 'Religion, oh, just another of those numerous failures resulting from attempting to popularize art'.[200] Regardless of Brakhage's liberties with textual accuracy, the two quotes share the sense that art can be not only superior to religion, the sphere within which spirituality most often tends to be articulated, but art could also be a more complete and arcane version of religion.

Charles Boer, writing about Robert Duncan, stresses how Pound and Hilda Doolittle, as Duncan's primary forebears, even when they were not writing about the gods, felt that the gods were always 'there guiding the mind, focussing the eye, limning the voice'.[201] This seems to have also been the case for Brakhage, who credited his own creativity to Muses and gods and a host of mythical creatures, even when the subjects of his work had ostensibly nothing to do with divinity. Boer points to what was crucial for Pound and Doolittle, just as it was for Duncan, Johnson, and, in the final analysis, for Brakhage as well:

> Their generation must now begin to seem puzzling, if not altogether archaic, to younger readers, who are, shall we say, more flattened-out? I mean, Duncan and company *really* took the Gods seriously, not just as mythological decoration, not just as classical nostalgia, and least of all as symbols or poetic bric-a-brac. They *believed.*[202]

Brakhage's spiritual sense of art originated from a personal tendency towards the sacred, and it was further articulated, structured and nurtured by the artists he chose as guiding figures. Beyond discussions about the specific origins of such sense, one thing is certain: he, like Pound, Duncan, or Dante, *believed.*

> I would think every work should have something of God in it, whatever one means by "God", so that you can say you have a sense of the presence of the divine. And I think I share that just very normally with artists of all kinds.[203]

In Brakhage's intentions, art exceeds its commonly perceived boundaries, becoming a sort of cosmic activity connecting the human with the divine, and expressing a precise view of reality as a whole. A work of art such as a film is then designed to move the viewer towards spiritual meditation, and eventually towards a spiritual revelation, without defining such a phenomenon or experience; it is intended to point the viewer towards what is outside and beyond the rational, which is not simply irrational but rationally ineffable. For Brakhage, his meditative films exist within the interstices between spiritual and physical, inner and outer, meaning and meaninglessness, real and artificial, the visible and the invisible. They stand on the verge of such opposing tensions, obeying a restless harmonising force intended to effectively open the viewer to a profound and momentous overcoming of reality's contradictions. All the aspects that Brakhage discussed, whether directly or indirectly inspired by his predecessors and mentors, whether simply confirming the film-maker's prior intuitions or whether discussed or explained in divergent ways in the critical literature devoted to Brakhage, indicate what was for Brakhage a continuous and underlying spiritual quest.

Notes

1. Brakhage in a 1990 video interview conducted by Marilynne Mason, now in Stan Brakhage, *By Brakhage: An Anthology Volumes One and Two*, Blu-Ray (Criterion Collection, 2010): Disc One.
2. Brakhage, 1982: 224; and James, 2005: 2. 3.
3. Ibid.
4. Brakhage, 1982: 224.
5. Ibid., 229.
6. The notorious positions of Pound, namely the political ones, seem to have been simply discarded or overlooked by many of these authors. Robert Duncan perhaps summarises the general stance held by many American poets of his generation by explicitly stating, '… I overlooked the nitty-gritty

Pound of unsettling attitudes. I wasn't going to argue with him any more than I'd argue with my mother about the nature of society.' (Duncan in Peters and Trachtenberg, 1998: 104.)

7. Bruce McPherson in Deren, 2005: 8.

8. Bruce Jenkins in Frampton, 2009: 189 note 1.

9. Mekas in Sitney, ed., 1970: 88. The original article was published in *Film Culture*, Number 24 (1962): 6–16. The phrase Mekas was referring to is: 'Artists are the antennae of the race'. (Pound, 1960a: 73.)

10. Brakhage in MacDonald, 2005: 55.

11. Maas in Sitney, ed., 1970: 183. The debate was originally published as 'Poetry and Film: A Symposium', *Film Culture*, Number 29 (1963): 55–63.

12. McClure, 1982: 13.

13. Olson quoted by Allen and Friedlander in Olson, 1997: 406.

14. See Brakhage, 2001/2002.

15. Johnson quoted in Hair, 2010: 53.

16. Davenport, 1984: 167. Italic in the original.

17. Duncan, 1995: 90

18. See particularly Tryphonopoulos, 1992; and Surette, 1993.

19. Barrett and Brabner, 1983: 10–11. In Duncan's biography, Lisa Jarnot reports the date as 1953, following a 2000 conversation with Jess Collins: see Jarnot, 2012: 125 and 458 note 2.

20. Brakhage quoted in Barrett and Brabner, 1983: 11. See also Brakhage in MacDonald, 2005: 108.

21. Duncan, 1995: 135. For Pound's texts see respectively Pound, 1968; and Pound, 1960b: 149–200.

22. Pound, 1970: 51.

23. Duncan in Peters and Trachtenberg, 1997: 104.

24. Duncan, 1995: 136.

25. Brakhage in Higgins, Lopes, and Connick, 1992: 60. It is interesting that Brakhage did not state something like 'within *this* tradition', or 'within *my* tradition', but used the term 'traditionally'. This might be regarded as evidence of how this specific vision was assimilated by Brakhage as the standard and *true* one, repeatedly reinforced by his friends and mentors, and more generally by the cultural milieu within which he operated.

26. In London from 1908 to 1920, and in Paris from 1920 to 1925.

27. For the influence of Mead in relation to Hellenic and especially Neoplatonic elements of Pound's thought, see Tryphonopoulos, 1992. For a scrupulous philology of occult and occult-related influences throughout the early Modern period, see Surette, 1993.

28. Surette, 1993: 105.

29. Elder, 1998: 76–77.

30. Ibid.

31. Ibid., 477 note 84.

32. Ibid., 158.

33. Ibid., 232. Elder is referring to Harold Bloom's *The American Religion: The Emergence of the Post-Christian Nation* (New York: Simon & Schuster, 1992), which Elder calls an 'extraordinary book'.

34. Elder, 1998: 138.

35. Ibid., 161.

36. Elder, 2005b: 445 note 81.

37. Ibid., 437 note 10.

38. Elder, 1998: 439.

39. Sometimes also written as 'Eriugena'.

40. See Brakhage, 1982: 206–207; Brakhage, 2001: 158; and Brakhage, 2003: 56–57.

41. Surette, 2005: 331.

42. Duncan, 1985: 28.

43. See Tryphonopoulos, 1992: xii.

44. Surette, 1993: 11.

45. Ibid., 15.

46. Ibid., 7. Also, further to this point: 'I suggest that *The Cantos* constitute a text designed to produce initiates as much as it is for initiates; the text's purpose is to occasion a palingenesis achieved through participation in the 'mystery' contained in the text'. (Ibid., 8.)

47. Brakhage, 1982: 229.

48. See Duncan in Peters and Trachtenberg, 1997: 85.

49. Ezra Pound, 1968; 89,

50. Brakhage in MacDonald, 2005: 109.

51. Ibid., 111.

52. Ibid., 114. And earlier, in the same interview: '… there is so much magic in the creative process that I can only touch on it as we talk about these things. These works were made in a kind of trance state where I used various tactics just to keep from sliding completely into insanity, which is always a fear when you get into a really complicated, deep, lengthy work". (Ibid., 84.) For another similar statement see Brakhage in Ganguly, 2002: 144.

53. Included in Stan Brakhage, *By Brakhage: An Anthology, Volume Two*, DVD (Criterion Collection, 2010): Disc Two.

54. Brakhage in Ganguly, 2002: 144.

55. Brakhage in MacDonald, 2005: 114.

56. Brakhage in Ganguly, 2002: 144.

57. Brakhage in MacDonald, 2005: 113.

58. Pound, 1960a: 92.

59. The point becomes a particularly controversial one if discussed in relation to Brakhage's whole career. Since I do not have the space to go into details, I shall just mention the most relevant coordinates concerning what David James effectively termed Brakhage's 'deflection of authority' (see James, 1989: 38). In 1963 Brakhage stated that the signature 'by Brakhage' indicated something produced by his whole family, shifting the authorship of the work away from him (but not yet in the mystical terms considered here) and towards his family (see Brakhage, 1963: not paginated). Such attempt to deflect authorship and create a family cinema failed from the beginning, since he has always been considered 'by detractors and afficionados alike as an unreconsructed egotist, Romantic or otherwise' (James, 1989: 49.). During the first half of the 1990s, and in particular from 1993 to 1996, Brakhage pursued the utopia of making films 'about nothing', trying again to suppress the figure of the author (see Brakhage in Ganguly, 2002: 150). But even during this period the films 'about nothing' carried his indelibly hand-carved signature, apart from titles often referring to biographical occurrences. In 1997 he again corrected his position stating that the signature was just a way of saying 'here's what this creature did', as well as taking responsibility for it, and protect such creations (see Brakhage in Taaffe, 1998: 108). Here the expression 'by way of me' is similar to that employed 34 years earlier, but the source of inspiration is not the family nor the film-maker. What persisted was the idea of the artist as instrument. It is also worth remembering that the signature was for a period the only proof of ownership since his films were 'for many years in the public domain, uncopyrighted' (see James, 1989: 49). This detail constitutes yet a further contradiction in Brakhage's position on authorship. The absence of copyright, at least in the past, contradicts the signature, which in turn openly contradicts Brakhage's 'rhetoric of disengagement' (ibid.). The signature 'by Brakhage' contradicts the meaning of the family creation, which could in turn contradict a Romantic solipsism. Furthermore, Brakhage's notes on his abstract hand-painted films of the early 1990s contradict by their very existence the idea that the films are about nothing. Within this conundrum of facts and intents, later in his life, Brakhage found a resolution in a spiritual perspective, which holds together such disparate tendencies: 'You're absolutely unique and individual, but you're working within a sacred calling that goes back to the dawn of time, so

who can stake a claim and say 'This is mine?'' (Brakhage in Taaffe, 1998: 146.) The spiritual jargon of 'a sacred calling' and of 'the dawn of time', as well as the typical paradoxical language of mystical formulations, supplied Brakhage with a suggestive and effective way of holding together positions that otherwise could only be deemed contradictory.

60. Brakhage in MacDonald, 2005: 84. And later, in the same interview: 'I don't feel like I *make* the films, but that they are made *through* me. … What's good about your work is *given*' (Ibid., 114).

61. Ibid., 113; and Brakhage in Ganguly, 2002: 144.

62. See Brakhage in MacDonald, 2005: 106.

63. Pound, 1970: 45.

64. Ibid., 299; also quoted in Tryphonopoulos, 1992: 3. This is also restated in the same text: 'For the gods exist' (Pound, 1970: 125).

65. 'What is a god? A god is an eternal state of mind' (Pound, 1973: 47).

66. Ibid.

67. Surette, 1993: 15.

68. Brakhage in Ganguly, 2002: 144.

69. Pound, 1970: 295.

70. Brakhage, 1982: 188.

71. Sitney, 2002: 157.

72. Brakhage in MacDonald, 2005: 93.

73. Wees, 1992: 78.

74. Ibid., 91.

75. Pound, 1960a: 104.

76. Surette, 1993: 7.

77. Pound, 1960a: 92.

78. Pound, 1970: 121.

79. Surette, 1993: 31.

80. Pound, 1970: 127.

81. 'Myth is the story told of what cannot be told, as mystery is the scene revealed of what cannot be revealed, and the mystic gnosis the thing known that cannot be known' (Duncan, 1985: 1).

82. Surette, 1993: 18.

83. Ibid.

84. Ibid.

85. Brakhage in MacDonald, 2005: 114.

86. Ibid.

87. Surette, 1993: 27.

88. Robert Lamberton quoted in Tryphonopoulos, 1992: 112.

89. Pound, 1970: 263.

90. Robert Lamberton quoted in Tryphonopoulos, 1992: 112.

91. Brakhage in MacDonald, 2005: 117.

92. See Agamben, 1993. Thanks to Prof. Riccardo Vaia for bringing to my attention this essay.

93. Ibid., 71.

94. Ibid., 75.

95. Ibid., 76.

96. Ibid.

97. Aristotle quoted in ibid.

98. Ibid.

99. Ibid., 91.

100. Ibid., 91–92.

101. Ibid., 92.

102. Ibid.

103. Ibid., 93.

104. Ibid., 94–95.

105. Ibid., 96.

106. Ibid., 94.

107. Ibid., 99.

108. Ibid.

109. Brakhage did not like this term. I am employing it in relation to Abstract Expressionism because of his use of painting on the film-strip. It should be taken here as 'non-referential'. The aim of this essay is not to debate its meaning for Brakhage's art, although such a debate would be crucial to clarify the status of representation within his artistic endeavour.

110. Elder, 2005b: 394.

111. The 'ban' on photographing ended in 1996, just prior to an operation to remove his bladder, when he suddenly started filming above and beneath the surface of the Boulder Creek (see Brakhage in MacDonald, 2005: 43 and 114–115). His mental state was an intense influence upon the artistic outcome, since he did not think that he would survive the surgery (see ibid., 121). The resulting film, *Commingled Containers* (1996), is a profoundly spiritual meditation about human finitude, focussed around the juxtaposition of the stream's surface as the 'fussiness of our daily life' (ibid., 119), and the inner, underground dimension of the stream, where 'something spiritual' lies (ibid., 121). This spirituality was conveyed mainly through photographed or hand-painted abstraction. Brakhage, after *Commingled Containers*, came to frequently express such spirituality through sensations and moods, as through the peaceful acceptance of the finitude of the human condition, or the dynamic and spiritual nature of reality revealed through it: 'I don't know quite what *Commingled Containers* means. It *is* moving. I would think every work should have something of God in it, whatever one means by "God", so that you can say you have a sense of the presence of the divine.' (Ibid., 117.) This quite straightforward explanation can also be validly applied to many films made during his final years, attesting to the increasingly explicit spirituality in his art (in content, form, title and tone) during that period. *Christ Mass Sex Dance* (1991), *Agnus Dei Kinder Synapse* (1991), *Untitled (For Marilyn)* (1992), *Chartres Series* (1994), *Cannot Exist* (1994), *Cannot Not Exist* (1994), *Yggdrasill: Whose Roots Are Stars in the Human Mind* (1997), *The Cat of the Worm's Green Realm* (1997), *The Birds of Paradise* (1999), *The Lion and the Zebra Make God's Raw Jewels* (1999), *The Jesus Trilogy and Coda* (2001), *Panels for the Walls of Heaven* (2002), *Resurrectus Est* (2002), *Dark Night of the Soul* (2002) and *Ascension* (2002) all fit within this category (Sitney makes a similar remark with a more limited list of films: see Sitney, 2008: 321–322). This increased spirituality was lately also marked by the state of constant fear that Brakhage lived in since 1996, a fear for the possible return of cancer (see Brakhage in MacDonald, 2005: 94), which, indeed, would eventually occur. But the spiritual element that clearly blossomed during those years, and imposed itself as the main theme on many of his later films, had already been an underlying trend within his oeuvre.

112. Brakhage, 1982: 229.

113. Brakhage in Ganguly, 2002: 149.

114. Elder, 2005b: 429.

115. Ibid.

116. Ibid.

117. See Pound, 1968: 129; and Duncan, 1985: 150–151 and 159.

118. Brakhage in Ganguly, 2002: 149.

119. Brakhage quoted in Sitney, 2008: 252.

120. Rhythm employed as a means by which the ineffable manifests itself in the physical world, and especially in the body, and through which, conversely, a spiritual revelation can be elicited in others,

is another important point of Brakhage's spiritual art, as I shall mention in the final part of this essay.

121. Elder, 2005b: 395.

122. Ibid., 437 note 3. Elder is referring to Duncan, 1965.

123. Sitney, 2008: 253.

124. Ibid., 251.

125. Ibid., 253.

126. Elder, 2005b: 429.

127. 'All things that are, are light' (Brakhage, 1982: 184). This quotation of Scotus Erigena, is one of the central mottoes of *The Cantos*, and was also the inspiration for Brakhage's *The Text of Light* (1974).

128. See Brakhage, 1963: not paginated.

129. Surette, 1993: 125.

130. Ibid., 15.

131. Ibid., 124.

132. Ibid., 16.

133. Tryphonopoulos, 1992: 104–105.

134. '*Epopteia* means the state of "having seen" and is a general term for revelation. It is exoterically represented by *metamorphosis* or theophany. Metamorphosis exoterically expresses the moment of sudden change, the moment of revelation, the *epopteia*" (Ibid., 104).

135. Peter Mudie, in his contribution to this volume, points out how a tripartite scheme (in that case exposition of a theme, set of developments, and recapitulation) is common to many of Brakhage's hand-painted films. He identifies its origin in the musical form of fugue. I believe that the fugue and the occult-derived theoretical apparatus of Pound, could have worked as reciprocal confirmations of an organising principle for the film-maker. Also, the musical fugue famously constituted one of the formal principles employed by Pound to structure his poem.

136. Pound, 1968: 128.

137. Brakhage quoted in Elder 2005a: 93. The example of whales and wolves was already employed by Brakhage at least since 1982, but this time with the concept of song substituted by art in general as a privileged form of communication with creation: see Brakhage, *The Test of Time*, not paginated; a series of radio programs Brakhage hosted in 1982, now transcribed by Brett Kashmere and available at http://www.fredcamper.com/Brakhage/TestofTime.html (accessed 16 May 2015).

138. Duncan, 2014: 534.

139. Ibid., 539.

140. Ibid., 541.

141. Ibid., 542.

142. Brakhage, 2001: 194.

143. Sitney, 2008: 255.

144. The two studies Sitney employs for this interpretation are Anton Ehrenzweig, *The Psycho-analysis of Artistic Vision and Hearing: An Introduction to a Theory of Unconscious Perception* (London: Routledge & Kegan Paul, 1953); and Anton Ehrenzweig, *The Hidden Order of Art: A Study in the Psychology of Artistic Imagination* (Berkeley/Los Angeles: University of California Press, 1967).

145. Sitney, 2008: 255–256.

146. Ibid., 255.

147. He makes this point about the formal basis of *The Dante Quartet* (the painting over frames of Billy Wilder's *Irma la Douce*, see ibid., 253–254), and on a more general level for all the four films of the *Visions in Meditation* series (see ibid., 347).

148. Pound quoted in Tryphonopoulos, 1992: 2.

149. McDowell and Materer, 1985: 358. See also Tryphonopoulos, 1992: 178 and 187 note 27.

150. Pound, 1970: 124.

151. Pound, 1973: 277.

152. Duncan, 2012: 11.

153. Elder, 2005b: 430.

154. Brakhage, 2001: 202; also quoted in Sitney, 2008: 331.

155. Elder, 2005a: 88–89.

156. Ibid., 92. Elder infers this because he believes the first part is the only part of the film in which no imagery can be seen behind the layer of painting: 'Hell Itself is the only section that lacks photographic imagery'. (Ibid.) This is not actually true: at the very beginning of Hell Itself one can glimpse quite clearly the line of trees of a landscape, and on the right, a standing human figure. What is curious is that Sitney makes the same declaration, using the same expression: 'Only Hell Itself lacks photographic imagery'. (Sitney, 2008: 251.) Nonetheless, this detail does not change the correctness of Elder's comment on the fear of solipsism, since it may also be inferred from the Brakhage's contemporaneous personal crisis as well as from his statements about Hell Itself.

157. Elder, 2005a: 95.

158. Ibid., 93.

159. Brakhage, 2003: 138. Partly quoted in Elder, 2005a: 95.

160. Elder, 2005a: 96.

161. See its reproduction in Fritjof Capra, The Tao of Physics: An Exploration of the Parallels Between Modern Physics and Eastern Mysticism, 3rd edition (London: Flamingo, 1982): 174.

162. Elder, 2005b.

163. Ibid., 419.

164. Ibid., 398.

165. Olson, 1997: 240.

166. Elder, 2005b: 420–421.

167. Ibid., 420.

168. Ibid., 421.

169. Ibid., 408.

170. Ibid., 409.

171. Ibid., 410.

172. Ibid., 435.

173. Agamben, 1993: 83. Emphasis mine.

174. Ibid., 84.

175. Pound, 1970: 44; quoted also in Bush, 2010: 671.

176. Brakhage in MacDonald, 2005: 47.

177. See ibid., 111.

178. See Brakhage, 1982: 229.

179. Agamben, 1993: 103.

180. See Brakhage, 1982: 79.

181. See Elder, 1998: 370.

182. Pound, 1960b: 152. Also in Pound then the physical world was reassessed as functional and often even necessary for the achievement of spiritual revelation. Pound expressed this position in various occasions, e.g. 'it is always this world that matters most' (Pound quoted in Tryphonopoulos, 1992: 163); 'the fall into matter it is not necessarily a bad thing' (ibid., 157 note 42); the body is the 'perfect instrument of the increasing intelligence' (Pound, 1960b: 152); there is wisdom in opposing an 'idiotic asceticism and a belief that the body is evil' (ibid., 150).

183. Already by the end of the 1950s, many science texts started to become deeply important to him, and he also subscribed to Scientific American for 'several years'. (See Brakhage in MacDonald, 2005:

70.) He also became a friend to and did some work for George Gamow, a physicist at the University of Colorado, and through him met with 'a number of scientists' (Ibid., 74–75).

184. See Brakhage in MacDonald, 2005: 114.

185. See Brakhage, 2003: 138.

186. It is important to point out here that the general 'erotic interpretation' Pound attributed 'to the esoteric tradition [… was] very much his own', and 'plainly contrary' to the ideas of the mainstream Kensington occult circles (see Surette, 1993: 142–143). Like Pound, also Duncan maintained, perhaps as a result of the older poet's influence, that in the Eleusis rite an actual 'carnal knowledge', a real 'sexual union', was performed in order to experience the union of 'visible and invisible' (see Duncan, 1995: 107). In fact he, just like Pound and Brakhage, believed that sex is 'a connection, a relation, with the universe' (Duncan in Peters and Trachtenberg, 1998: 112).

187. The personification of a creative force, corresponding also to the state of mind (trance) in which Brakhage works, follows Pound's theory that a god is a state of mind and that myths are metaphors (personifications) of psychic experiences.

188. Bush, 2010: 680.

189. Elder, 2005b: 433.

190. See Pound, 1968: 94.

191. Duncan in Peters and Trachtenberg, 1998: 111.

192. Elder, 1998: 79.

193. See Brakhage and Johnson, 2001/2001: 31.

194. Pound, 1968: 94.

195. See Pound, 1960b: 151.

196. Brakhage in MacDonald, 2005: 112.

197. Brakhage in Higgins, Lopes, and Connick, 1992: 57.

198. Brakhage in Taaffe, 1998: 146.

199. Brakhage in MacDonald, 2005: 112.

200. Pound in a 1907 letter to Mary Moore, quoted in Carpenter, 1988: 77. Mary Moore is not to be confused with the Modernist poet Marianne Moore; Pound heard of the latter for the first time in 1918, while the former had been the dedicatee of the 1909 edition of his book *Personae* (see Carpenter, 1988: 311 and 108). It is not certain where or when Brakhage read this quote from Pound; most likely it was from Carpenter's 1988 biography, though one might be tempted to speculate that it was relayed by his friend (and former student of Pound), Hollis Frampton, who quoted a somewhat similar statement in 1977 (see Frampton, 2009: 261). The latter possibility, however, is unlikely, since the phrase Frampton quoted in his book, while on a similar topic, does not correspond to either Pound's original letter to Mary Moore or Pound's reiteration of the phrase in a letter addressed to William Carlos Williams later the same year (see Surette, 1993: 130). Even though Brakhage simply paraphrased the core idea of Pound's statement, it is clear that he had read Pound's original letter, as he introduced the paraphrase with details absent from Frampton's text, such the time of the letter's composition, Pound's age when he wrote it, and the relationship between Pound and Mary Moore (see Brakhage in MacDonald, 2005: 112). Brakhage's version of the letter's history was slightly imprecise – he erroneously stated that Pound's statement about religion had been the cause of the split between the young Pound and his then girlfriend – but the otherwise correct details would suggest that Carpenter's biography had been Brakhage's source.

201. Boer, 1996: 95. Quoted also in Hair, 2010: 13.

202. Boer, 1996: 97. Quoted also in Hair, 2010: 13–14.

203. Brakhage in MacDonald, 2005: 117.

General Bibliography and References

Abrams, Mark, *The Mirror and the Lamp: Romantic Theory and the Critical Tradition* (New York: Oxford University Press, 1972).

Adair, Gilbert, *for Sub Voicive Poetry* (London: Writers Forum, 2003).

– – –*from Sable Smoke: RWC # 28*, in *Read Write Create*, Number 28 (1995a).

– – –*PAGES 260–279: from Sable Smoke, PAGES, 260–279* (1995b).

– – –*Gilbert Adair: RWC # 3*, in *Read Write Create*, Number 3 (1991).

– – –*Sable Smoke* (London: Veer Books, 2010).

Adorno, Theodor, *Aesthetic Theory*, trans. by Robert Hullot-Kentor (London: Continuum, 1997).

Agamben, Giorgio, *Stanzas: Word and Phantasm in Western Culture* (Minneapolis: University of Minnesota Press, 1993).

Andrews, Bruce, *Ex Why Zee* (New York: Roof Books, 1995).

– – –*Give Em Enough Rope* (Los Angeles: Sun & Moon Press, 1987).

– – –*I Don't Have Any Paper, So Shut Up* (Los Angeles: Sun & Moon Press, 1992).

Andrews, Bruce and Sally Silvers, 'More from: Ten Questions for Bruce Andrews & Sally Silvers', *The Poetry Project*, (2009): https://www.poetryproject.org/more-from-ten-questions-for-bruce-andrews-sally-silvers/ (accessed 19 September 2016).

Arthur, Paul, 'Before The Beginning Was The Word: Stan Brakhage's', *Criterion Collection* (2003): https://www.criterion.com/current/posts/273-before-the-beginning-was-the-word-stan-brakhage-s (accessed 19 September 2016).

Barrett, Gerald R., and Wendy Brabner, *Stan Brakhage: A Guide to References and Resources* (Boston: G.K. Hall & Co., 1983).

Bergson, Henri, *Matter and Memory*, (London: Allen & Unwin, 1911).

Blom, Jan Dirk, *A Dictionary of Hallucinations* (New York: Springer, 2010).

Boaden, James, 'Revisiting Brakhage 5: Vision and its Metaphors', in *LUX Artists' Moving Image* (October 2013): http://www.lux.org.uk/blog/revisiting-brakhage-5-vision-and-its-metaphors (accessed 15 May 2016).

Boer, Charles, 'Watch Your Step', in *Spring: A Journal of Archetype and Culture*, Number 59 (Spring 1996): 95–123.

Bordwell, David, *Narration in the Fiction Film* (London: Routledge, 1985).

Bradley, Richard, 'Deaths and Entrances: A Contextual Analysis of Megalithic Art', in *Current Anthropology*, Volume 30, Number 1 (February 1989): 68–75.

Brakhage, Marilyn, 'On Stan Brakhage and Visual Music', in *Vantage Point*, (2008): https://vantagepointmagazine.wordpress.com/2008/01/31/on-stan-brakhage-and-visual-music/ (accessed 19 September 2016).

– – – 'Some Notes on the Selection of Titles for By Brakhage: An Anthology, Volume Two', *Criterion Collection* (2010): https://www.criterion.com/current/posts/1471-some-notes-on-the-selection-of-titles-for-by-brakhage-an-anthology-volume-two (accessed 13 March 2013).

Brakhage, Stan, *The Brakhage Lectures* (Chicago: The GoodLion, 1972).

– – – *Brakhage at the Millennium: The Words of Stan Brakhage*, *Millennium Film Journal*, Number 47/48/49 (Fall/Winter 2007/2008).

– – – *Brakhage Scrapbook: Collected Writings*, ed. and with an introduction by Robert A. Haller (New York: Documentext, 1982).

– – – 'Chicago Review Article', in *Stan Brakhage: Correspondences*, *Chicago Review*, Volume 47/48 (Volume 47, Number 4, Winter 2001; Volume 48, Number 1, Spring 2002): 38–41.

– – – *Essential Brakhage: Selected Writings on Filmmaking*, ed. and with a foreword by Bruce R. McPherson (New York: Documentext, 2001).

– – – *Film at Wit's End: Eight Avant-Garde Filmmakers* (New York: Documentext, 1989).

– – – *London Filmmaker's Co-op Distribution Catalogue Notes* (London: London Filmmakers' Co-op., 1993).

– – – *Metaphors on Vision*, ed. and with an introduction by P. Adams Sitney, *Film Culture*, Number 30 (1963).

– – – *A Moving Picture Giving and Taking Book* (West Newbury: Frontier Press, 1971).

– – – 'Poetry and Film', in *Credences*, Number 5/6 (March 1978): 99–114.

– – – 'Stan Brakhage to Ronald Johnson', in *Stan Brakhage: Correspondences*, *Chicago Review*, Volume 47/48 (Volume 47, Number 4, Winter 2001; Volume 48, Number 1, Spring 2002): 28–30.

– – – *Telling Time: Essays of a Visionary Filmmaker* (New York: Documentext, 2003).

Brakhage, Stan, and Ronald Johnson, 'Another Way of Looking at the Universe', in *Stan Brakhage: Correspondences*, *Chicago Review*, Volume 47/48 (Volume 47, Number 4, Winter 2001; Volume 48, Number 1, Spring 2002): 31–37.

Branigan, Edward, *Narrative Comprehension and Film* (London: Routledge, 1992).

Bush, Ronald, '*La Filosofica Famiglia*: Cavalcanti, Avicenna, and the "Form" of Ezra Pound's *Pisan Cantos*', in *Textual Practice*, Volume 24, Issue 4 (2010): 669–705.

Cage, John, *Empty Words: Writings '73–'78*, (Hanover, NH: Wesleyan University Press, 1979).

– – – *M: Writings '67–'72*, (London: Marion Boyars, 1976).

– – – *Silence: Lectures and Writings* (Middletown: Wesleyan University Press, 1961).

– – – *Silence: Lectures and Writings* (London: Marion Boyers, 1973).

– – – *X: Writings '79–'82* (Hanover, NH: Wesleyan University Press, 1983).

Camper, Fred, 'Brakhage's Contradictions', in *Stan Brakhage: Correspondences*, *Chicago Review*, Volume 47/48 (Volume 47, Number 4, Winter 2001; Volume 48, Number 1, Spring 2002): 69–96.

– – – 'Program Notes on Brakhage', for the screening *Acts of Seeing: Stan Brakhage, 1933–2003* (2003a): http://www.fredcamper.com/Brakhage/FC.html (accessed 19 September 2016).

– – – 'A Review of Stan Brakhage's Last Films' (2003): http://www.fredcamper.com/Film/Brakhage3.html (accessed 9 March 2016).

– – – 'Three Myths About Brakhage', in *Logos: A Journal of Modern Society & Culture*, Volume 2, Number 2 (Spring 2003b): http://www.logosjournal.com/camper.htm (accessed 13 September 2016).

Carpenter, Humphrey, *A Serious Character: The Life of Ezra Pound* (Boston: Houghton Mifflin Company, 1988).

Carroll, Noël, 'Philosophizing through Film: the Case of *Serene Velocity*', in *The Journal of Aesthetics and Art Criticism*, Volume 64, Number 1 (Winter 2006): 173–185.

Cavell, Stanley, *In Quest of the Ordinary: Lines of Skepticism and Romanticism* (Chicago: Chicago University Press, 1988).

– – – *This New Yet Unapproachable America* (Albuquerque, N.M.: Living Batch Press, 1989)

cheek, cris, untitled piece, in Gilbert Adair, *PAGES 260–279: from Sable Smoke, 260–79* (1995).

Cobbing, Bob, *Shrieks & Hisses* (Buckfastleigh: etruscan books, 1999).

Colman, Felicity, *Deleuze and Cinema: The Film Concepts* (Oxford: Berg Publishers, 2011).

Copland, Aaron, *What To Listen For In Music* (New York: New American Library, [1939] 2009).

Creeley, Robert, *Away* (Santa Barbara, CA: Black Sparrow Press, 1976).

– – – 'Some Sense of the Commonplace', in Tom Clark, *Robert Creeley and the Genius of the American Common Place* (New York: New Directions, 1993): 83–120.

Cubitt, Sean, *The Practice of Light: A Genealogy of Visual Technologies from Print to Pixels* (Cambridge, MA: MIT Press, 2014).

Curtis, David, *Experimental Cinema: A Fifty Year Evolution* (New York: Dell Publishing, 1971).

– – – *A History of Artists' Film and Video in Britain* (London: BFI Publishing, 2007).

Davenport, Guy, *The Geography of the Imagination: Forty Essays by Guy Davenport* (London: Picador, 1984).

de Bruyn, Dirk Cornelis, *The Performance of Trauma in Moving Image Art* (Newcastle-upon-Tyne: Cambridge Scholars Publishing, 2014).

Deleuze, Gilles, *Cinema 1: The Movement-Image* (London: The Athlone Press, 1986).

– – – *Cinema 1: The Movement-Image* (Minneapolis: University of Minnesota Press, 1997).

– – – *Cinema 2: The Time-Image* (London: The Athlone Press, 1989).

– – – *Cinema 2: The Time-Image* (London: Continuum, 2005a).

– – – *Francis Bacon: The Logic of Sensation* (London: Continuum, 2005b).

Deren, Maya, *An Anagram of Ideas on Art, Form and Film* (New York: Alicat Book Shop Press, 1946).

– – – 'Cinematography: the Creative use of Reality', in P. Adams Sitney, ed., *The Avant-Garde Film* (New York: New York University Press, 1978): 60–73.

– – – *Essential Deren: Collected Writings on Film by Maya Deren*, ed. and with a preface by Bruce R. McPherson (Kingston, New York: Documentext, 2005).

Di Prima, Diane, *Revolutionary Letters* (San Francisco: Last Gasp Press, 2007).

Doane, Mary Ann, *The Emergence of Cinematic Time* (Cambridge, MA: Harvard University Press, 2002).

Duncan, Robert, *The Collected Early Poems and Plays*, ed. and with an introduction by Peter Quartermain (Berkeley/Los Angeles/London: University of California Press, 2012).

– – – *The Collected Later Poems and Plays*, ed. and with an introduction by Peter Quartermain (Berkeley/Los Angeles/London: University of California Press, 2014).

– – – *Fictive Certainties* (New York: New Directions, 1985).

– – – *A Selected Prose*, ed. Robert J. Bertholf (New York: New Directions, 1995).

– – – 'The Sweetness and Greatness of Dante's *Divine Comedy*: Lecture given October 27, 1965, at the Dominican College of San Raphael' (San Francisco: Open Space, 1965).

Durgnat, Raymond, *A Long Hard Look at Psycho* (London: British Film Institute, 2002).

Dworkin, Craig, 'Stan Brakhage, Agrimoniac', in David E. James, ed., *Stan Brakhage: Filmmaker* (Philadelphia: Temple University Press, 2005): 132–149.

Eisenstein, Sergei, *The Film Sense*, trans. by Jay Leyda (London: Faber and Faber, 1986).

– – – 'On the Question of a Materialist Approach to Form', in P. Adams Sitney, ed., *The Avant-Garde Film* (New York: New York University Press, 1978): 15–21.

Elder, R. Bruce, *The Body in Film* (Toronto: The Art Gallery of Ontario, 1989).

– – – 'Brakhage: Poesis', in David E. James, ed., *Stan Brakhage: Filmmaker* (Philadelphia: Temple University Press, 2005a): 88–106.

– – – *The Films of Stan Brakhage in the American Tradition of Ezra Pound, Gertrude Stein, and Charles Olson* (Waterloo, CA: Wilfrid Laurier University Press, 1998).

– – – '"Moving Visual Thinking": Dante, Brakhage, and the Works of *Energeia*', in James Miller, ed., *Dante & The Unorthodox: The Aesthetics of Transgression* (Waterloo, CA: Wilfrid Laurier University Press, 2005b): 394–449.

Emerson, Waldo Ralph, *The Essential Writings of Ralph Waldo Emerson* (New York: The Modern Library, 2000).

Gehr, Ernie, conversation with Charles Bernstein, *Close Listening* series, *PennSound* (WPS1, New York: 21 January 2008): http://writing.upenn.edu/pennsound/x/Gehr.php (accessed 12 December 2016).

Eysenck, Michael W., and Mark T. Keane, *Cognitive Psychology: A Student's Handbook*, 4th edn (East Sussex: Psychology Press, 2000).

Frampton, Hollis, *On the Camera Arts and Consecutive Matters: The Writings of Hollis Frampton*, ed. and with an introduction by Bruce Jenkins (Cambridge, MA/London: The MIT Press, 2009).

Ganguly, Suranjan, 'All That is Light: Brakhage at 60', in *Sight and Sound*, Volume 3, Number 10 (1993): 20–23.

– – – 'Stan Brakhage: The 60th Birthday Interview', in *Film Culture*, Number 78 (Summer 1994): 18–38.

– – – 'Stan Brakhage: The 60th Birthday Interview', in Winston Wheeler Dixon and Gwendolyn Audrey Foster, eds., *Experimental Cinema: The Film Reader* (London/New York: Routledge, 2002): 139–162.

Gidal, Peter, *Materialist Film* (London: Routledge, 1989).

Ginsberg, Allen, 'Interview (The Art of Poetry no. 8)', in *Paris Review*, Number 37 (1966): 13–56.

Glendinning, Simon, 'Philosophy as Nomadism', in *What Philosophy Is: Contemporary Philosophy in Action*, ed. by Havi Carel and David Gamez (London/New York: Continuum, 2004): 155–167.

Gombrich, Ernst, *Art and Illusion* (London: Phaidon Press, [1960] 2002).

Grauer, Victor A., 'Brakhage and the Theory of Montage', in *Millennium Film Journal*, Number 32/33 (Fall, 1998): http://mfj-online.org/journalPages/MFJ32,33/grauer.html (accessed 19 September 2016).

– – – *Montage, Realism and the Act of Vision* (1982): http://doktorgee.worldzonepro.com/MontageBook/MontageBook-Contents.htm (accessed 19 September 2016).

Greenberg, Clement, *The Collected Essays and Criticism, Volume 4: Modernism with a Vengeance, 1957–1969,* ed. John O'Brian (Chicago/London: Chicago University Press, 1993).

Gregory, Richard, *Eye and Brain: The Psychology of Seeing* (New York: McGraw-Hill, 2004).

Hair, Ross, *Ronald Johnson's Modernist Collage Poetry* (New York: Palgrave Macmillan, 2010).

Hamlyn, Nicky, *Film Art Phenomena* (London: BFI Publishing, 2003).

– – – 'The *Roman Numeral* Series', in David E. James, ed., *Stan Brakhage: Filmmaker* (Philadelphia: Temple University Press, 2005): 113–128.

Hanhardt, John C., 'Film Image / Electronic Image: The Construction of Abstraction 1960–1990', in Gabrielle Jennings, ed., *Abstract Video: The Moving Image in Contemporary Art* (Oakland: University of California Press, 2015).

Helmholtz, Hermann, *Treatise on Physiological Optics: Volume 1* (London: Dover Publications, 2005).

Higgins, Gary, Rodrigo Garcia Lopes, and Thomas Connick, 'Grisled Roots: An Interview with Stan Brakhage', in *Millennium Film Journal*, Number 26 (Fall 1992): 56–66.

Hoffman, Donald, *Visual Intelligence: How We Create What We See* (New York: W.W. Norton, 2000).

Huble, David, and Margaret Livingstone, *Vision and Art: The Biology of Seeing* (London: Harry N. Abrams, 2008).

Huxley, Aldous, *The Doors of Perception and Heaven and Hell* (New York: HarperPerennial Modern Classics, [1954] 2009).

James, David E., *Allegories of Cinema: American Film in the Sixties* (Princeton: Princeton University Press, 1989).

– – – 'The Film-Maker as Romantic Poet: Brakhage and Olson', in *Film Quarterly*, Volume 35, Number 3 (Spring, 1982): 35–43.

– – – 'Introduction: Stan Brakhage, The Activity of His Nature', in David E. James, ed., *Stan Brakhage: Filmmaker* (Philadelphia: Temple University Press, 2005): 1–19.

– – – ed., *Stan Brakhage: Fimmaker* (Philadelphia: Temple University Press, 2005).

Jarnot, Lisa, *Robert Duncan, the Ambassador From Venus: A Biography* (Berkeley/Los Angeles/London: University of California Press, 2012).

Jay, Martin, *Downcast Eyes: The Denigration of Vision in Twentieth-Century French Thought* (Berkeley/Los Angeles/London: University of California Press, 1993).

Johnson, Nicholas, 'AN ENLIGHTENMENT TO GIVE YOU SOME JUSTIFICATION', in Bob Cobbing, *Shrieks & Hisses* (Buckfastleigh: etruscan books, 1999).

Judd, Deane B., 'Introduction', in Johann Wolfgang von Goethe, *Theory of Colours* (Cambridge, MA: MIT Press, 1970): v–xxvi.

Kashmere, Brett, 'Notes from Underground: Coltrane, Brakhage and the American Avant-Garde', in *Offscreen*, Volume 7, Number 2 (February 2003): http://offscreen.com/view/brakhage1 (accessed 19 September 2016).

Kelly, Robert, 'On The Art of Vision', in David E. James, ed., *Stan Brakhage: Filmmaker* (Philadelphia: Temple University Press, 2005): 32–33.

Klevan, Andrew, 'Notes on Stanley Cavell and Philosophical Film Criticism', in *New Takes in Film-Philosophy*, ed. by Havi Carel and Greg Tuck (London: Palgrave Macmillan, 2011): 48–64.

Le Grice, Malcolm, *Experimental Cinema in the Digital Age* (London: BFI Publishing, 2001).

Lenin, Vladimir I., *On War and Peace* (Peking: Foreign Languages Press, 1970).

Lewis-Williams, J. D., and T. A. Dowson, 'The signs of all times: entoptic phenomena in Upper Palaeolithic Art', *Current Anthropology*, Volume 29, Number 2 (April 1988): 201–245.

Lukács, Georg, *History and Class Consciousness*, trans. by Rodney Livingstone (London: Merlin Press, 1971).

– – – *Theory of the Novel*, trans. by Anna Bostock (London: Merlin Press, 2006).

MacDonald, Scott, *A Critical Cinema* (Berkeley/Los Angeles/London: University of California Press, 1988).

– – – *A Critical Cinema 4: Interviews with Independent Filmmakers* (Berkeley/Los Angeles/London: University of California Press, 2005).

– – – *A Critical Cinema 5: Interviews with Independent Filmmakers* (Berkeley/Los Angeles/London: University of California Press, 2006).

MacDonald, Scott and Stan Brakhage, 'The Filmmaker as Visionary: Excerpts from an Interview with Stan Brakhage', in *Film Quarterly*, Volume 56, Number 3 (Spring 2003): 2–11.

Manovich, Lev, *The Language of New Media* (Cambridge, MA: MIT Press, 2002).

Marks, Laura U., *Touch: Sensuous Theory and Multisensory Media* (Minneapolis: University of Minnesota Press, 2002).

McCardle, Aodhán, 'Visuality: The Visual Condition; an Other Articulacy of Knowing; trying to speech the unsayable, the inlanguagable', in Robert Sheppard, ed., *The Salt Companion to Lee Harwood* (Cambridge: Salt, 2007): 207–25.

McClure, Michael, *Scratching the Beat Surface: Essays on New Vision From Blake to Kerouac* (New York/London: Penguin Books, 1982).

McClure, Michael, and Steve Anker, 'Realm Buster: Stan Brakhage', in *Stan Brakhage:*

Correspondences, *Chicago Review*, Volume 47/48 (Volume 47, Number 4, Winter 2001; Volume 48, Number 1, Spring 2002): 171–180.

McDowell, Colin, and Timothy Materer, 'Gyre and Vortex: W. B. Yeats and Ezra Pound', in *Twentieth Century Literature*, Volume 31, Number 4 (Winter 1985): 343–367.

McMahon, Laura, *Cinema and Contact: The Withdrawal of Touch in Nancy, Bresson, Duras and Denis* (London: Legenda, 2012).

Mekas, Jonas, 'Brakhage. Breer. Menken. The Pure Poets of Cinema', in David E. James, ed., *Stan Brakhage: Filmmaker* (Philadelphia: Temple University Press, 2005): 27–28.

Merleau-Ponty, Maurice, 'Indirect Language and the Voices of Silence', in Galen A. Johnson and Michael Smith, eds., *The Merleau-Ponty Aesthetics Reader* (Evanston: Northwestern University Press, 1993): 76–120.

– – – *Phenomenology of Perception* (London: Routledge, 1995).

Michelson, Annette, 'Camera Lucida/Camera Obscura', in David E. James, ed., *Stan Brakhage: Filmmaker* (Philadelphia: Temple University Press, 2005): 36–56.

Miller, Tyrus, 'Brakhage's Occasions: Figure, Subjectivity, and Avant-Garde Politics', in David E. James, ed., *Stan Brakhage: Filmmaker* (Philadelphia: Temple University Press, 2005): 174–195.

Mooney, Stephen, 'Discontinuous Visuality – Brakhage's 'just seeing', and background temporality in contemporary poetics', in *Jacket*, Number 37 (2009): http://jacketmagazine.com/37/mooney-brakhage.shtml (accessed 19 September 2016).

Mullarkey, John, *Refractions of Reality: Philosophy and the Moving Image* (London: Palgrave Macmillan, 2009).

Nesthus, Marie, 'The Influence of Olivier Messiaen on the Visual Art of Stan Brakhage in "Scenes From Under Childhood", Part One', in *Film Culture*, Number 63–64 (1976): 39–51.

Nyman, Michael, *Experimental Music* (Cambridge: Cambridge University Press, 2002).

Olson, Charles, *Collected Prose*, eds. Donald Allen and Benjamin Friedlander, with an introduction by Robert Creeley (Berkeley/Los Angeles/London: University of California Press, 1997).

– – – *The Maximus Poems*, ed. George F. Butterick (Berkeley/Los Angeles/London: University of California Press, 1983).

– – – *Muthologos*, ed. George F. Butterick (Bolinas: Four Seasons Foundation, 1978).

– – – 'Projective Verse', in *A Charles Olson Reader* (Manchester: Carcanet, 2005): 39–49.

Osterweil, Ara, *Flesh Cinema: The Corporeal Turn in Avant-Garde Film* (Manchester/New York: Manchester University Press, 2014).

Pearce, Joseph, *Tolkien: Man and Myth* (New York: HarperCollins, 2001).

Perloff, Marjorie, *Wittgenstein's Ladder: Poetic Language and the Strangeness of the Ordinary* (Chicago: Chicago University Press, 1996).

Peters, Robert, and Paul Trachtenberg, 'A Conversation with Robert Duncan (1976)', in *Chicago Review*, Volume 43, Number 4 (1997): 83–105.

– – – 'A Conversation with Robert Duncan (1976)', in *Chicago Review*, Volume 44, Number 1 (1998): 92–116.

Pound, Ezra, *ABC of Reading* (New York: New Directions, 1960a).

– – – *The Cantos of Ezra Pound* (London: Faber and Faber, 1975).

– – – *Guide to Kulchur* (New York: New Directions, 1970).

– – – *Literary Essays of Ezra Pound*, ed. and with an introduction by T.S. Eliot (London: Faber and Faber, 1960b).

– – – *Selected Prose: 1909–1965*, ed. and with an introduction by William Cookson (London: Faber and Faber, 1973).

– – – *The Spirit of Romance* (New York: New Directions, 1968).

Pruitt, John, '*Meshes of the Afternoon*: A Model of Visual Thinking', in Ted Perry, ed., *Masterpieces of Modernist Cinema* (Bloomington: Indiana University Press, 2006): 138–58.

– – – 'Stan Brakhage and the Long Reach of Maya Deren's Poetics of Film', in *Stan Brakhage: Correspondences*, *Chicago Review*, Volume 47/48 (Volume 47, Number 4, Winter 2001; Volume 48, Number 1, Spring 2002): 116–132.

Prynne, J. H., 'On Maximus IV, V, & VI', lecture at Simon Fraser University (July 1971), transcribed by McGauley: http://www.scribd.com/doc/8670354/jeremy-prynne-lectures-on-maximus (accessed 12/12/12).

– – – 'Resistance and Difficulty', *Prospect*, Issue 5 (1961): 26–30.

Reeves, Jennifer, 'Argument for the Immediate Sensuous: notes on *Stately Mansions Did Decree* and *Coupling*', in *Stan Brakhage: Correspondences*, *Chicago Review*, Volume 47/48 (Volume 47, Number 4, Winter 2001; Volume 48, Number 1, Spring 2002): 193–198.

Reidl, Clare C., 'Introduction', in Robert Grosseteste, *De Luce (On Light)* (Wisconsin: Marquette University Press, 1942).

Retallack, Joan, *How To Do Things With Words* (Los Angeles, California: Sun & Moon Press, 1998).

Rilke, Rainer Maria, *Die Gedichte* (Leipzig: Suhrkamp, 2006).

Rodowick, David, 'An Elegy for Theory', in *October*, Number 122 (Fall 2007): 91–109.

Ruskin, John, *The Elements of Drawing* (New York: CreateSpace Independent Publishing Platform, [1865] 2013).

– – – *A Joy For Ever, and Its Price in the Market (New York: Cosimo, [1857] 2007)*.

Salinger, Jerome, *Nine Stories* (New York: Little, Brown, [1953] 1970).

Sharits, Paul, 'Hearing:Seeing', in P. Adams Sitney, ed., *The Avant-Garde Film* (New York: New York University Press, 1978): 255: 60.

– – – 'from "Words Per Page"', in P. Adams Sitney, ed., *The Avant-Garde Film* (New York: New York University Press, 1978): 261–263.

Sheehan, Rebecca A., 'Stan Brakhage, Ludwig Wittgenstein and the Renewed Encounter with the Everyday', in *Screen*, Volume 53, Issue 2 (2012): 118–135.

Sheppard, Robert and Scott Thurston, 'Editorial', in *Journal of British and Irish Innovative Poetry*, Volume 1, Number 1 (2009): 1.

Sitney, P. Adams, 'Brakhage and Modernism', in Ted Perry, ed., *Masterpieces of Modernist Cinema* (Bloomington: Indiana University Press, 2006): 159–178.

– – – *The Cinema of Poetry* (Oxford/New York: Oxford University Press, 2015).

– – – *Eyes Upside Down: Visionary Filmmakers and the Heritage of Emerson* (Oxford/New York: Oxford University Press, 2008).

– – – ed., *Film Culture Reader* (Oxford/New York: Praeger Publishers, 1970).

– – – *Modernist Montage* (New York: Columbia University Press, 1990).

– – – 'The Orphic Vision of Brakhage's Cinema', ICI Berlin Institute for Cultural Inquiry: http://www.ici-berlin.org/index.php?id=742&L=1 (accessed 13 December 2012).

– – – *Visionary Film: The American Avant-Garde, 1943–2000*, 3rd edn (Oxford: Oxford University Press, 2002).

Smigel, Eric, 'Metaphors on Vision: James Tenney and Stan Brakhage, 1951–1964', in *American Music*, Volume 30, Number 1 (2012): 61–100.

Sorensen, Roy A., *Seeing Dark Things: The Philosophy of Shadows* (New York/Oxford: Oxford University Press, 2008).

Stein, Gertrude, *Lectures in America* (Boston, Beacon Press: 1957).

– – – *Selected Writings of Gertrude Stein* (New York: Vintage Books, 1990).

Steinhoff, Eirik, ed., *Stan Brakhage: Correspondences*, *Chicago Review*, Volume 47/48 (Volume 47, Number 4, Winter 2001; Volume 48, Number 1, Spring 2002).

Surette, Leon, *The Birth of Modernism: Ezra Pound, T.S. Eliot, W.B. Yeats, and the occult* (Montreal: McGill-Queen's University Press, 1993).

– – – '"Dantescan Light": Ezra Pound and Eccentric Dante Scholars', in James Miller, ed.,

Dante & The Unorthodox: The Aesthetics of Transgression (Waterloo, CA: Wilfrid Laurier University Press, 2005): 327–345.

Taaffe, Philip, *Composite Nature: A Conversation with Stan Brakhage* (New York: Peter Blum Edition, 1998).

Taberham, Paul, 'Bottom-Up Processing, Entoptic Vision and the Innocent Eye in Stan Brakhage's Work', in *Projections: The Journal of Movies and Mind*, Voume 8, Issue 1 (Spring 2014): 1–22.

Taylor, Gregory T., '"The Cognitive Instrument in the Service of Revolutionary Change": Sergei Eisenstein, Annette Michelson, and the Avant-Garde's Scholarly Aspiration', in *Cinema Journal*, Volume 31, Number 4 (1992): 42–59.

Tenney, James, 'Brakhage Memoir', in David E. James, ed., *Stan Brakhage: Filmmaker* (Philadelphia: Temple University Press, 2005): 57–60.

Thirlwall, John C., 'Ten Years of a New Rhythm' in William Carlos Williams, *Pictures from Brueghel and Other Poems* (New York: New Directions, 1962): 183–184.

Trotsky, Leon, *Literature and Revolution* (New York: Russell & Russell, 1957).

Tryphonopoulos, Demetres P., *The Celestial Tradition: A Study of Ezra Pound's The Cantos* (Waterloo, CA: Wilfrid Laurier University Press, 1992).

Turvey, Malcolm, *Doubting Vision: Film and the Revelationist Tradition* (New York: Oxford University Press, 2008).

Turvey, Malcolm, and Richard Allen, *Wittgenstein, Theory, and the Arts* (New York: Routledge, 2001).

Tyler, Parker, 'Stan Brakhage', in David E. James, ed., *Stan Brakhage: Filmmaker* (Philadelphia: Temple University Press, 2005): 20–26.

Virilio, Paul, *Art as Far as the Eye Can See*, trans. by Julie Rose (Oxford: Bloomsbury Academic, 2010).

– – – *Pure War*, trans. by Mark Polizzotti (London: MIT Press, 2008).

– – – *War and Cinema*, trans. by Patrick Camiller (London: Verso, 1989).

Walley, Jonathan, 'The Material of Film and the Idea of Cinema: Contrasting Practices in Sixties and Seventies Avant-Garde Film', in *October*, Number 103 (Winter 2003): 15–30.

Wees, William, *Light Moving in Time: Studies in the Visual Aesthetics of Avant-Garde Film* (Berkeley/Los Angeles/Oxford: University of California Press, 1992).

– – – 'Words and Images in Stan Brakhage's 23rd Psalm Branch', in *Cinema Journal*, Volume 27, Issue 2 (Winter 1988): 40–49.

Wittgenstein, Ludwig, *Philosophical Investigations*, trans. G. E. M. Anscombe, P. M. S. Hacker, and Joachim Schulte (Malden, MA: Wiley-Blackwell, 2009).

– – – *Tractatus Logico-Philosophicus*, translated by C. K. Ogden (London: Kegan Paul, Trench, Trubner & Co., 1922).

Youngblood, Gene, *Expanded Cinema* (New York: E. P. Dutton, 1970).

Yue, Genevieve, 'The Tree of Life: Garden of the World', in *Reverse Shot*, Museum of the Moving Image (2011): http://reverseshot.org/reviews/entry/281/tree_life_garden_world (accessed 19 September 2016).

Videography

Brakhage, Stan, *By Brakhage: An Anthology*, DVD, Two Discs (Criterion Collection, 2003).

– – – *By Brakhage: An Anthology Volume Two*, DVD, Three Discs (Criterion Collection, 2010).

– – – *By Brakhage: An Anthology Volumes One and Two*, Blu-Ray, Three Discs (Criterion Collection, 2010).

– – – *Stan Brakhage: Hand-Painted Films*, VHS (Paris: Re Voir, 2007).

Shedden, Jim, *Brakhage*, DVD (Zeitgeist Films, 2004).

Notes on the Contributors

Christina Chalmers has completed her MPhil in English Literature, Culture and Criticism at King's College, Cambridge, in 2013. She is now working on her Ph.D. at the Department of English, New York University. Her areas of interest are Marxism, Critical Theory, materialist feminism, experimental writing & poetics, avant-garde film, and expressionism. She is a poet, assistant editor, and copyeditor.

Gareth Evans has recently completed his Ph.D. through the Department of Film & Television at the University of Bristol. His thesis focuses on the relationships between a politics of aesthetics and phenomenology in the films of Stan Brakhage.

Nicky Hamlyn is professor of Experimental Film at University for the Creative Arts, Canterbury, Kent, UK, and a lecturer at the Royal College of Art, London. His film and video work has been exhibited at venues and festivals worldwide and three DVD compilations are available from LUX, RGB and the Film Gallery, Paris. He has published numerous essays and reviews and his book *Film Art Phenomena* (2003) is published by the BFI.

Dr. Marco Lori has completed his Ph.D. at Birkbeck, University of London, with a thesis focussed on the spirituality of Stan Brakhage.

Stephen Mooney is a lecturer in Creative Writing at the University of Surrey, where he was also the Poet in Residence in 2012/13. He is an associate member of the Contemporary Poetics Research Centre at Birkbeck, and co-runs the small poetry press, Veer Books. His poetry has appeared in various places and web-places, including as part of the performative poetry grouping 'London Under Construction'. The poetry collections, *DCLP* and *Shuddered*, the latter co-authored with Aodan McCardle and Piers Hugill, were published by Veer Books in 2008 and 2010 respectively, while the trilogy *The Cursory Epic* (2014), *663 Reasons Why* (2016) and *Ratzinger Solo* (2016) has recently been published by Contraband Books.

Dr. Peter Mudie is a Canadian born academic who has lectured on the film avant-garde for over twenty years, authored a number of books/monographs and articles and curated a number of international touring exhibitions from Australia. As a filmmaker and artist he has worked under a range of pseudonyms and has contributed to filmmaker co-operatives in North America and Europe. He currently lives and works in Perth, Western Australia.

Rebecca A. Sheehan is Associate Professor of Cinema and Television Arts at California State University, Fullerton. Her current book manuscript, *In-Between America: Avant-Garde Cinema and the Poetics of Contingency*, argues that philosophical thinking is immanent to American avant-garde cinema and traces the ways in which experimental cinema in America has advanced the field of film-philosophy through developing several strains of philosophical thinking (transcendentalism, pragmatism, skepticism, philosophy of language, and theories articulated by Henri Bergson, Friedrich Nietzsche, and Gilles Deleuze). She is also at work on *Cinema's Laocoön: Film, Sculpture, and the Virtual*, a book manuscript which examines the historical interfaces between sculpture and cinema. Her work has appeared in *Screening the Past, Screen, Journal of Modern Literature, Discourse, Interdisciplinary 19*, and in various edited collections.

Dr. Paul Taberham is Senior Lecturer in animation theory and history at the Arts University Bournemouth. He has appeared on radio, spoken nationally and internationally at conferences, and has been published in *Projections: Journal for Movies and Mind, Animation Journal* and several anthology articles. He is also the co-editor of *Cognitive Media Theory* (2014), and the forthcoming *Experimental Animation: From Analogue to Digital* (2018). In addition, Paul is the author of the forthcoming *The Avant-Garde Filmmaker as Practical Psychologist*, due to be published in 2018 by Berghahn.

Index